P9-BYB-328

Other Books by Karen Pryor

Nursing Your Baby

Lads Before the Wind, Diary of a Dolphin Trainer

Don't Shoot the Dog! The New Art of Teaching and Training

How to Teach Your Dog to Play Frisbee

On Behavior: Essays and Research

Clicker Training for Dogs

Clicker Training for Cats

Click to Win: Clicker Training for the Show Ring

Nursing Your Baby, 3rd edition, with Gale Pryor

Nursing Your Baby, 4th edition, with Gale Pryor

Dolphin Societies: Discoveries and Puzzles,
editor, with Kenneth S. Norris

Reaching the Animal Mind

Clicker Training and What It Teaches Us about All Animals

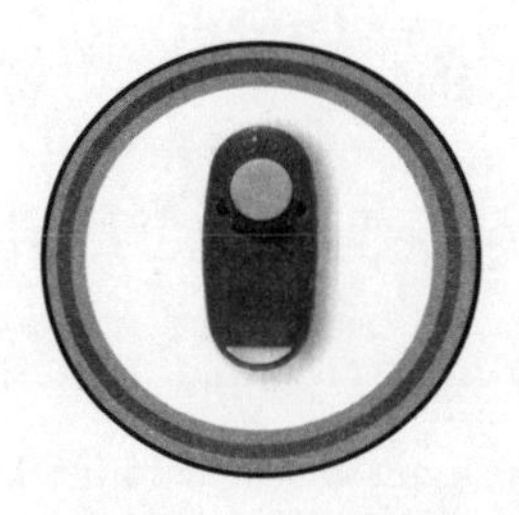

Karen Pryor

To Rene from Pat with love.
Happy Clicking!
Karen Pryor

Scribner

New York London Toronto Sydney

SCRIBNER
A Division of Simon & Schuster, Inc.
1230 Avenue of the Americas
New York, NY 10020

First Scribner hardcover edition June 2009

Manufactured in the United States of America

1 3 5 7 9 10 8 6 4 2

Library of Congress Control Number: 2009002287

ISBN: 978-0-7432-9776-9
ISBN: 978-1-4165-4625-2 (ebook)

To Max, Gwen, Wylie, Ellie, Micaela, Nat, and Maile

With much love

Grandma Karen

Contents

Reaching the Animal Mind

Chapter 1

Reaching Minds

People and Their Animals

I'm standing at the edge of a dusty road in a little town in South America. A barefoot, grimy boy walks past, a very little boy, maybe between three and four years old. He's eating a bun. Behind him trails a skinny puppy, itself very young.

The boy turns around, sees the dog, and raises a threatening fist. The dog cowers dramatically, cringing to the ground. The boy looks up with a huge, triumphant grin: "I scared the heck out of him, didn't I!" He walks on down the road. The puppy gets up and slinks after him—and guess what: the boy has forgotten about the bun. He lets it fall, and the puppy grabs it and runs away.

That's how we've dealt with domestic animals ever since we and they evolved together. We treat them like subordinate, stupid human beings. We dominate them. We punish them. We make them do what we want. And they figure out how to get us to do what they want, anyway. Both sides get some benefit out of the system: in this case, food for the skinny puppy, and a rare moment of superiority for a small boy.

Traditionally the person who actually *trains* animals, beyond these ordinary practices of threatening them one minute and feeding them the next, has always been a special individual. Often it's someone with a "way with animals," a "natural gift." Usually that gift consists of two things: a personal interest in some particular kind of animals (dog trainers train dogs; horse trainers train horses) and a better understanding than the rest of us of the subtle uses of fear and force.

Traditional animal training, the way it's been practiced for millennia, relies largely on force, intimidation, and pain. While traditional trainers may also use praise and rewards, dominating the animal and obtaining control over its behavior are the main goals, and the main tools are fear and pain.

Traditional trainers are abundant among us. Nowadays of course they justify their practices with pseudoscientific explanations about pack leadership and the importance of dominance and of being the alpha animal; but the basic method, in spite of the overlay, is punishment; and people generally accept that approach. Most horse owners still keep whips and spurs in the barn. The walls in pet stores are plastered with choke chains and the aisles lined with shock collars, and people buy them. Maybe you use them yourself. I won't argue with you. Force and intimidation have been working for people since the first dogs hung around the first campfires (or, more likely, around the first garbage dumps).

But that's all obsolete now. Now we have a new way of dealing with animals. Out of real science we've developed a training technology. Like any good technology it's a system that anyone can use. The basics are easy to learn. It works with *all* animals (and that includes people). It's fast. What used to take months, the traditional way, can now happen in minutes. It's completely benign; punishment and force are never part of the learning system. And it produces real communication between two species.

D'Artagnan the Wolf

Erich Klinghammer, a professor at Purdue University, is a well-known ethologist. He is the founder of a research facility in Indiana called Wolf Park. Dr. Klinghammer came across my book *Lads Before the Wind,* which describes the years in which I worked as head dolphin trainer at a pioneering oceanarium, Sea Life Park, in Hawaii. Klinghammer saw that the technology we used for training dolphins would be useful for managing wolves. He invited me to Wolf Park to show his team how to do it.

We modern trainers love the chance to work with a new species. Not just one more dog or horse or dolphin, but something we have never trained before. We begin, always, with curiosity: "Who are you? What can you do? Show me." I had never worked with wolves, so of course I said yes.

A few weeks later I fly to Indiana. At Wolf Park, Erich Klinghammer is eager to have me go into the pens and meet some wolves personally, to "experience their boisterousness." This I am not willing to do. Klinghammer is six feet four with a big Germanic bass voice. He walks through the gate into the main pack's enclosure and booms, "Good morning, wolves!" The wolves gather around him, waving their tails and jumping up to greet him: "Good morning, Dr. Klinghammer!" For me, I think it would be "Good morning, breakfast."

Besides, I don't need to be close to a wolf to work the training magic; in fact, both of us are safer and will feel better with a fence between us. This wonderful technology does not depend on my being able to impress or dominate the wolf. Nor does it depend on making friends first, or on having a "good relationship." That's often a happy outcome, but it's not a requirement: the laws of reinforcement will get the job done.

Klinghammer has selected a large male, D'Artagnan, as my learner. That's a typical wolf name; no one calls wolves Pete or Blackie or Pal. D'Artagnan was raised by humans, so he does not know how to get along with other wolves and has to live alone in a pen on the far side of the park. Klinghammer and I jump into a truck with a couple of students and a large can of dry dog food and drive to D'Artagnan's pen. I get out my dolphin trainer's whistle, pick up the can of kibble, and go over to the chain-link fence. Wolves look a lot like dogs in paintings and even in photographs, but in real life they're quite different. For one thing they don't have pointed ears like a German shepherd, but small, round ears, like a bear; for another, they don't smell like dogs, they smell like fur rugs.

D'Artagnan meets me with a spectacular threat display, snarling, snapping, and lunging at the chain-link fence between us. He is about the size of a St. Bernard but with much wider jaws and bigger teeth, especially the bone-crunching carnassials in back, at which I am getting a really good look.

I'm sure this show of aggression is learned behavior. His hackles are not up, his eye whites are not showing; he's not really that upset. However, he has probably discovered he can sometimes make people flinch, or even run away, by being scary; and that must be fun to do.

The first step toward change is to explain to the wolf that when he hears the whistle, food will arrive. I blow the whistle and throw in some kibble. D'Artagnan just goes on snarling and leaping and snapping at my face. The chain-link fence between us suddenly seems flimsy. I don't want to reinforce his behavior by moving away, but it is indeed difficult to just stand there.

A Jeep full of volunteers and students pulls up. The wolf is quiet for an instant, studying the Jeep. I whistle and toss more kibble through the fence right under his nose. "Oh," he says, and vacuums up the food. I whistle and toss kibble again. Again he eats the kibble. Then he looks at me. I do nothing. He turns away. Good! It's a relief to see the back of that wolf.

So far, I've just paired the whistle with the food, to make it a "conditioned reinforcer," a sound that means "food is coming." I'm now going to start using the whistle to identify for the wolf what action he's getting paid for. This will turn the sound into an event marker (usually just called a marker). So I whistle as he moves away, and toss in more treats. He returns and eats again.

Now that the wolf is listening to the whistle, coming back for more food when he hears it, and has been reinforced for moving away, I can begin "shaping" his behavior. *Shaping* is the technical term for shifting a behavior by reinforcing any moves that happen to occur in the direction you have in mind and ignoring everything else.

In the middle of D'Artagnan's big enclosure, about thirty feet off, stands a small evergreen tree. I tell the watchers, "I'm going to train him to go out and around that tree and come back." Bravado, of course.

I'm going to try would be a wiser promise; but even if it only works for part of the way, it's a useful demonstration. Using a marker signal to shape the behavior of going away from the food, in order to earn the food, helps to shut up the skeptics.

I mark each time the wolf turns away from me, timing my whistle to the stepping of his right front paw. Every time he hears the whistle, I toss in a lump or two of kibble. He snatches them up and then, with increasing confidence, turns and starts moving directly away from me again.

I wait for three strides before I give the whistle, then five, then ten. Now D'Artagnan is so confident he grabs up the kibble and actually trots off, still chewing. Each time, I wait to blow the whistle until he's gone farther than before. Now he's going more than halfway to the little tree.

Then, on the next try, he stops before I blow the whistle. Uh-oh. He is new to the game and hasn't had enough experience to know that a missed marker doesn't mean the game is over, but simply means that you should try again. If I give him a whistle while he is standing still, he might develop the behavior of going out just that far and stopping. And if I don't give him a whistle at all, he might quit altogether. I watch him, praying he'll take another step forward so I can reinforce moving, not just standing.

Instead, he turns around and makes eye contact with me. His yellow eyes look into mine with a focus so intense that it feels as if he were seeing right into my brain—which, in a way, he is. That penetrating stare is literally breathtaking: I hold my breath and look steadily back.

Deciding, I think, that the game is still on, D'Artagnan turns away from me and heads straight off toward the tree again, breaking into a canter for the first time. I blast the whistle to mark that bold decision. His loping stride brings him abreast of the little evergreen. The wolf wheels around the tree and comes back down the other side at a gallop, screeching to a halt right in front of me, making my brag come true. Quit while you're ahead! I push a double handful of kibble through the chain link and leave him to enjoy that jackpot. Thanks, wolf! You saved my neck.

One experience was all D'Artagnan needed. Now, when Klinghammer takes visitors around Wolf Park, he can drive up to D'Artagnan's pen and blow the horn to call him. The wolf comes to the fence, sizes up the situation (Klinghammer, Jeep, whistle, kibble, got it), then turns away, gallops out and around the little evergreen, hears a blast of the whistle, and comes back for his treats. This new skill also ends his aggression display. Training people to give you kibble is much, much more satisfying than the old game of Get the Guest.

That single demonstration with D'Artagnan was also all Klinghammer needed to convert Wolf Park to the new technology. The staff and volunteers began using treats and acoustic markers, either whistles or clickers, to handle and move wolves and to give medical care. Staff ethologist Pat Goodman mitigated her border collie's irritating habit of staring at her incessantly by teaching him to turn his head when she whistled "Dixie" ("Look away, look away . . ."). Klinghammer, meanwhile, had fun using the same principles to coach a Purdue girls' volleyball team.

That demonstration paid off for me, too. I learned that wolves, or at least this wolf, enjoy a bit of fun: his game of scaring people was on the rough side, but it *was* a game. Then, that memorably powerful look into my eyes told me something more: compared to dogs, wolves are grown-ups. He was not asking for help, head down, forehead wrinkled, as a dog might: "Is this right? What do you want?" Instead, head high, gaze level, he was assessing me, like a poker player: "Are you in or out?" Judging that I was in, he made his move; and we both won.

Two Scientists, Two Sciences

Two tremendously innovative scientists have influenced the development of this kind of training: Konrad Lorenz and B. F. Skinner. Both started out in the 1930s and achieved their greatest prominence in the 1960s. Lorenz identified innate, evolutionary patterns of behavior in whole species of animals, work for which he and two other ethologists ultimately won a Nobel Prize. Skinner discovered basic laws of nature governing the way individuals, regardless of species, learn or acquire new behavior. Both of them gave us new understanding of the mechanisms underlying behavior.

Both of them also gave rise to new schools of behavioral science. The study of innate behavior, Lorenz's field, is called ethology, or just animal behavior. On any university campus you'll find these folks in the biology buildings. The study of learned behavior, Skinner's field, is called behaviorism, or behavior analysis. On most campuses you'll find these people over in psychology.

Often the people in those buildings tend to specialize in their own view of behavior and trivialize or dismiss the other. They typically don't talk to each other, don't read each other's papers, and don't go to the same meetings. This is annoying for those who are using this new technology. What we do involves both processes: what Mother Nature gives the animal, and what the individual discovers for itself. Yet if we have a question for a scientist, whichever kind of behaviorist we quiz can probably give us only half the answer.

The New Technology

We tend to think of "technology" as involving a lot of machines. How can this training be a technology when no machinery is involved beyond an event marker such as a whistle or a toy clicker? Hey, lots of technologies don't involve complicated equipment. The alphabet, when it first surfaced, was a new technology, too, and all you needed to use it was a stick and some clay.

A technology provides *repeatable* solutions to a problem. It is a replicable, transferable, and reliable system by which lots and lots of people can do something that has previously been difficult and chancy, requiring vast individual skills.

A technology does not limit you to one use: to dogs but not horses; to gymnasts but not pilots. A technology can have as many applications as there are people to think them up. Once you know how to build bridges, you can get across lots of different rivers.

As with any good technology, with this training the advantages are obvious the minute you see it in use. "Wow, how'd you do that? Let me try." Like any good technology, it is easy to get started. You can get results in the first few minutes. You can learn and use just as much as you want; total mastery of the whole system is not required. Also, like using a cell phone or any other new electronic gadget, you can pick it up from friends or even get started (sometimes) from written instructions.

A Contagious Idea

In my 1984 book, *Don't Shoot the Dog!,* I describe the mechanics of training with reinforcement instead of punishment. It was mostly about people, not animals; but the title (chosen by the publisher over my violent objections) gradually attracted the attention of dog trainers. Though the book said next to nothing about dogs specifically, it did explain how this new kind of training worked in general. Many dog owners, offended by traditional systems using choke chains and domination, were drawn in by the title and then intrigued by the possibility of training a dog without the traditional use of force.

Skinner himself had suggested that a cricket or toy clicker would make a good marker for dogs. In the early nineties sturdy, cheap clickers came on the market. I started distributing them by the hundreds, first at scientific meetings, then at seminars for dog trainers. On Internet lists and groups the technology spread in the dog world. Horse trainers also began to read my book and to convert traditional horse training to positive reinforcement.

Zookeepers turned their attention to these new ways to handle their animals. Medical care for large zoo animals used to be difficult. If you needed to sew up a cut or pull an infected tooth or give a vaccination to a tiger or a polar bear or a gorilla, you had to immobilize the animal with physical restraints or shoot it with a tranquilizing dart. Both procedures are scary and dangerous for the animals and the people, too. You did that only in emergencies.

Thanks to positive reinforcement training, keepers today can train their animals to come when called, to go in and out of doors when asked, and to accept medical treatment voluntarily, even daily. Lives are saved, animals are much less stressed overall, and the training is interesting and fun for both the keepers and the kept.

It's Okay for Animals, but We're Not Animals!

Both Skinner and Lorenz were roundly attacked and vilified during their lifetimes and since. Skinner, in particular, remains the personification of evil in many people's minds. In my opinion what mainly causes the hostility is resistance to the concept that what these scientists discovered doesn't just apply to animals: it applies to people, too. It's unnerving to some people, even to some scientists, to think that we, too, might be subject to the instinctive, automatic behavior patterns studied by ethologists. It's even more ruffling to think that we, like laboratory rats, might be controlled by mysterious systems of rewards and punishments, against our will and without our knowledge, as behaviorism seems to imply.

I think it's largely a religious issue, even if the person doing the huffing and puffing would not consider himself religious. In any case it's ridiculous. We no longer object to the fact that we share with the animals products of evolution such as digestive systems, skeletons, eyes, circulating blood, and so on. Why not give the same respectful understanding to things behavioral?

We all express our emotions through behavior, much of it innate (blushing, for example). The laws of learning also apply to all of us. Of course we humans differ from the rest in our ability to think and talk, to make things, and to accumulate learning through cultural means. We are a notch up, no doubt about that; but the anxiety we seem to feel about *any* possibility that we are also "animals" is, I think, misplaced.

Animals are more various in their behavior than it was fashionable to assume in the past, and we humans are more programmed than we used to think. So what? Every species has some behaviors dictated by its genes and some not. Every species can discover and enjoy new ways to make the universe pay off. The new technology, blending two behavioral sciences, is a highly enjoyable way to explore the possibilities.

What I Do

As a scientist, a writer, and an entrepreneur, I've been busy developing this technology and explaining it to others for about forty years. However, plenty of people in my life who know me as a writer, or as a businesswoman, would be astonished to hear me calling myself a scientist.

I certainly don't fit the normal picture of a scientist. I'm not a professor. I don't work in a laboratory. I'm not easily identified as one or another kind of specialist. I also don't have what has become the defining asset of a scientist: a Ph.D. I have, in fact, a good scientific education, but I acquired it bit by bit and unnoticed by the people around me, including family and friends.

Both my scientific education and my scientific career have occurred more or less underground. As a freshman at Cornell I realized that majoring in biology, my natural bent, would force me to take many premedical courses that I knew would be useless to me and a huge waste of strength and time. So I majored in English and took the science courses I actually wanted—a year of ornithology, a year of entomology, a nice little dip into botany, and so on—as electives.

In the years I was raising my children, I sandwiched in some graduate work whenever time and money permitted. The education was crucial; the degrees themselves were not. I could not afford to waste a single hour on those department requirements, such as organic chemistry or German, that were not germane to my interests or to the research I was already doing and publishing. And I definitely did not want to be a professor, so I didn't need degrees to get a job. Over the years, my peculiar specialties have brought me a steady stream of consulting contracts in areas ranging from commercial fishing to autism; and my clients never seem to care whether I am Dr. Pryor or just plain Karen.

What Is *She* Doing Here?

My low-profile scientific career has produced occasional honors, too, sometimes to the bewilderment of onlookers. For example, I sit on the board of the B. F. Skinner Foundation, which serves as an archive of his work and a resource for researchers. I have met more than one distinguished professor whose pained expression made it clear that he thought he would be a much more suitable member of that board than some woman who doesn't even have a degree in psychology.

In the 1980s I was appointed by the White House to a term on the Marine Mammal Commission. The commission oversees the well-being of all the marine mammals in U.S. territory and waters. It has been a powerful agency for good in marine conservation in general. I'm sure some marine mammal scientists assumed this dolphin trainer was picked largely because the White House needed to find female appointees (I thought it likely myself).

However, in addition to my scientific work, I had gained considerable business experience helping to develop Sea Life Park and some other commercial projects. I had then built a successful information-technology business of my own. The combination of scientific training, marine mammal expertise, and a business background allowed me to bring some common sense to many of the commission's activities, from drafting legislation to evaluating research proposals and funding. Meanwhile, if people ask me what I did on the commission, I tell them what the writer part of me accomplished: during my tenure, outgoing Marine Mammal Commission documents and correspondence were no longer riddled with split infinitives.

Animals without Big Brains

Explaining what I *do* depends on who's asking. Nowadays, since everyone seems to have heard of clicker training for dogs, many people think of me as a dog trainer. I never contradict them. But there's a lot more going on here than that. One of the wonderful aspects of reinforcement training is that it can open a connection with any animal, not just big, smart ones like wolves.

When I was still living in Hawaii, someone gave my kids a big hermit crab for a pet. It was the size of my hand. It lived in a turban shell as big as a baseball, in a saltwater aquarium in the living room. One afternoon, dropping some food in the water for the hermit crab, I wondered, what can *you* learn? Skinner's associate Richard Herrnstein once told me that he had trained a scallop to clap its shell for a food reward. I won't say I doubted him, but I did wonder how on earth you deliver food to a scallop, and what does it eat, anyway?

Well, I'm thinking to myself, here is another invertebrate, with a vigorous appetite for (what else?) crab meat. Maybe it can do something on purpose. Maybe it can ring a bell. I find a little brass bell in the kitchen drawer, glue a string to it, and hang it from a stick laid across the tank. I rig up a counterweight consisting of a thimble filled with candle wax. A pull on one end of the string tilts the bell over so the clapper hits the side, and the weighted thimble, stuck to the other end of the string, pulls the bell over the other way. Ding-dong.

Contriving the apparatus is the hard part. Teaching the crab is easy. In the kitchen drawer I also find a pair of ten-inch-long dissecting forceps left over from my graduate-student days. With this I can pop a bit of food directly into the crab's weird little waving mouthparts. The crab is receptive to being fed this way and eats fast, too.

I hang the string into the tank, hold the forceps in the water about three inches from the crab, and keep the forceps absolutely still until a waving claw accidentally touches the string. Then I pop the food in. The crab can see and probably sense through water pressure the quick movement of the forceps. I'm hoping and expecting that the movement of the forceps will serve as an event marker, communicating to the crab that its own action, touching the string, makes the food arrive.

I guess it's working, because in about five tries the waving claw arm is hitting the string repeatedly. Now the crab is full and doesn't seem to want any more food; so we stop.

The next day, I begin shaping for stronger behavior by marking behavior selectively, moving the forceps only when the claw is swinging strongly at the string, and letting smaller movements go unrewarded. Sometimes the string happens to fall inside the open claw, then the claw closes; that's probably almost a reflex, an automatic event. I start marking only the actual closing of the claw on the string. In another session or two, the crab is downright reliable at reaching for and grabbing the string on purpose. While the forceps moving is the marker, telling the crab it's doing the right thing, the string itself is the cue, telling the crab "Grab here" and "Grab now!" I am careful to put the string in the water only when I have the forceps in position, ready to mark the behavior and deliver the food. I don't want it to respond correctly to the string and not get results!

Pulling stuff toward its mouth with a claw is a natural movement for the crab, so by the fourth day I up the ante and reinforce only downward pulls. Again, it takes just a few reinforcements to get the goal behavior: a pull that is strong enough to ring the bell. Ding-dong. Yes, this crab can learn, and learn fast. Learning in this fashion is not a product of IQ but of the whole nervous system's alertness to the environment, and the hermit crab has plenty of that.

In building behavior step by step like this, I am discovering what the animal can do. The animal, meanwhile, is discovering new and better ways to make *me* deliver food. "The animal's training *you,*" people say with an uneasy laugh. Sure. That's the point. But I don't think that's how the animal sees it. The animal is not bossing me around (although, like D'Artagnan, it might initially try that). The animal has discovered, in me, a new resource, like a new water hole or berry patch. Thus it takes a new and intense interest in what I do. That opens up huge opportunities for understanding.

I take particular pleasure in the people who have tried this kind of training with their dogs, not just the serious competitors and fanciers, but regular pet owners, with typical pets, who have perhaps found a good clicker class in the local park or pet store. Their first reaction, as the dog begins to offer them behavior, is a thrill of personal success: wow, finally, look, he did what I wanted! And the second reaction is from the heart: I had no idea I had such a smart dog. I used to think he was such a nuisance. I *love* this great dog!

What's the Potential?

Positive reinforcement training, using the marker signal and the rest of this modern technology, certainly benefits a lot of animals. But the big potential for this technology is with people.

Used correctly, a marker simplifies the learning of any physical skill. The good tennis coach or golf pro knows exactly what five or ten different things you are doing wrong. Make him or her narrow the focus down to fixing one mistake at a time, hand over a clicker for instant feedback to your nervous system when you do the move right, and your game will actually start to improve.

The first public application of clicks to human muscle moves was in children's sports, particularly gymnastics and track. Human applications are now being developed in industrial settings, in physical therapy and rehabilitation, and in speech and language training. Nonverbal marker-based techniques are also proving useful in work with children or adults with language deficits and other developmental disabilities.

A Shift in Perception

More profound than any specific application is the change the technology brings about in the people who are using it. When you stop relying on aversive controls such as threats, intimidation, and punishment, and when you know how to use reinforcement to get not just the same but better results, your perception of the world undergoes a shift.

You don't have to become a wimp. You don't have to give up being in charge. You lose nothing of yourself. You just see things you didn't see before. One man said to me, "I stopped jerking my dogs around; and then I noticed what I was still doing with my kids." It's not a moral question. He was trying to be a good parent before. He is still trying to be a good parent. It's just that now he sees an alternative way.

The shift reminds me of those puzzles that came in comic books when I was a child. There's a line drawing of a landscape, say, showing a river and a leafy tree. Then, when you look for a while, you see it's also a woman's face. The two birds are her eyes, the leaves are her hair, the clump of flowers is her smile, and the river is the wrap around her shoulders. You can still see the landscape, but now you can also see the portrait; and once you've seen it, you can't unsee it. You might still be doing what you did before, but now you know it; and you can envision doing things another way.

I have heard professors of behavioral science, who should revere positive reinforcement, boasting about how tough they make life for their graduate students. As if that would help them learn better. Oh, come on, folks! I have watched the highest officials in my government bickering about different forms and degrees of torture, still relying on the primitive tools of fear, dominance, and injury without any recognition of what any dolphin trainer knows: that aversives stop behavior, they don't start it; and that fear and pain produce completely unpredictable and usually highly undesirable side effects, including being both exciting and reinforcing to the punisher. I have a faint but undying hope that the new technology that is the topic of this book might help to bring us all just a *little* bit past the behavioral Stone Age we are still in.

It seems to me that people are still jumpy about being compared to animals (in spite of acting in these primitive ways themselves). One way to tiptoe around the issue has been to focus only on really, really smart animals, individuals that might be assumed to be interesting special cases. Over and over one reads the same old stories about the same species and even the same individuals: Alex the parrot, Koko the gorilla, Washoe the chimpanzee, a collie that knows a hundred words, and so on.

These are indeed remarkable individuals, and the mentors who elicit their abilities have done remarkable work. To me, though, this emphasis on animals that seem to share our cognitive skills misses an important point. The mind has, at least, two parts: the cognitive part that thinks, consciously, in ideas and words, sometimes referred to as the left brain; and the part that senses, feels, and acts without that deliberative process, the right brain. That nonverbal part of the brain controls and learns movements, learns and recognizes scents and sights and sounds, is engaged when we dance or laugh or make music, and runs our emotions. We dismiss it unfairly by focusing on the cognitive side. That other part of the mind is far from stupid. It's aware and good at learning. It's that part of the brain that's engaged when we learn through reinforcement.

That's the kind of brain function that animals have, too. My goal is to show you the depth of awareness in many animals, not a special few; to identify the processes that can let you experience real communication with whatever animal is sitting in front of you; and, finally, to show you how you can use reinforcement-based technology to reach and communicate with the nonverbal side of the human mind.

I am going to avoid regurgitating both the work and the opinions of others. I intend, instead, to share with you mostly events I participated in personally, with many different organisms, revealing a huge range of preferences, intentions, and capabilities.

I don't want you to think that these kinds of events are unique to me. Everyone who uses this technology has had similar moments of astonishment, communication, recognition, and joy. In describing my own observations and what I think they mean, I speak for all of us.

Once, years ago, I glimpsed Jonas Salk on television. He was tall, thin, and balding. He stood quite motionless. His eyes didn't move. He seemed, I thought, as cold and still as a lizard: a formidable personality.

The interviewer asked him to sum up his illustrious career in science. Salk said nothing for a beat, then gave a gentle, even humble answer: "My job is to tell people what I see; and if they find it useful, good."

Hey, I thought. That's what I do, too.

So here's what I see. Come and have a look. If you find it useful, good. I'm pretty sure you will find it fun.

Chapter 2

Shaping

Becoming a Trainer

In 1963 I had been married for ten years to Tap Pryor, an entrepreneur who was building Sea Life Park, an oceanarium and research facility on Oahu, about fifteen miles from Honolulu, in the new state of Hawaii. Sea Life Park was, and is, a unique institution. Facing the sea and the wind, Sea Life Park sits on a desolate, treeless slope of old, tumbled rocks and lava, at the base of a long, thousand-foot-high cliff. As a visitor, you enter the park at the highest point, the entrance to a living coral reef. From that entrance you look across Sea Life Park to the main performance areas, Whaler's Cove, a lagoon with a reproduction of a whaling ship anchored at one end, and the Ocean Science Theater, a circular glass tank under a circular roof. Around them, fitting quietly into the curves of the land, you see the wood and stone of other exhibits and research buildings, landscaped with beach grass and Hawaiian plants. Everything lies open to the breeze, and open to the view. It is a view you can never see from continental shores. Here the great depths of the ocean butt right up against the land. Between and beyond two wild and barren little islands just offshore, and serving as the backdrop to every jumping whale and diving dolphin in Sea Life Park, is the dark blue, wind-churned, open Pacific. It's a view to please, certainly, but also a view to give you a chill: this is the real thing. Here we are part of the deep.

Sea Life Park was the first oceanarium planned and developed not by businesspeople but by scientists. One reason the State of Hawaii allowed us to build on this wild site was that the park would also be supporting and contributing a research organization, the Oceanic Institute, whose study projects, such as fish farming, would benefit the people of Hawaii.

Naturally, to attract paying customers, Sea Life Park would have dolphin shows; but they would be different from the circusy performances in the cement tanks of mainland aquariums. At that time, most trained-dolphin shows consisted largely of someone on a high platform holding out a fish and tempting dolphins to jump. Tap Pryor and his scientific adviser, a biology professor and onetime oceanarium curator named Ken Norris, wanted dolphin shows that went beyond that.

Norris told Tap about a new concept for training dolphins, based on the work of Harvard psychologist B. F. Skinner. Skinner had developed something he called operant conditioning. This was different from the classical conditioning of Pavlov's drooling dogs. First, Pavlov paired the sound of the bell with the arrival of food. Then, whenever Pavlov's dogs heard the bell, they expected food and salivated. Salivating was an automatic response; the dogs neither knew nor cared that they were drooling.

In operant conditioning, some sound or other stimulus is again paired with a natural reinforcer such as food, the way I paired the whistle with kibble for D'Artagnan the wolf; that part is classical conditioning. But then this newly reinforcing stimulus is used to teach animals to do specific behaviors intentionally. It was my using the now food-related stimulus as an event marker that taught Klinghammer's wolf to run around a tree and my kids' hermit crab to ring a bell. Skinner used the curious word *operant* for this kind of learning, to indicate that the animal is the "operator." In contrast to Pavlov's dogs, the animal is aware of what it's doing, and offers the behavior deliberately.

While working as curator at Marineland of the Pacific in California, Norris had used one of their bottlenose dolphins to accomplish some of the earliest research in dolphin sonar. He'd hired a psychology graduate student, Ron Turner, to train the dolphin for these studies; and Turner turned out to know all about the new science of operant conditioning. Norris had been very impressed. Operant conditioning, Norris said, was so clear and simple that any intelligent person could learn it and start training dolphins. Norris asked Turner to write a training manual for Sea Life Park on using operant conditioning with dolphins.

Sea Life Park built training tanks, caught a bunch of dolphins, hired three bright young people, and gave them Turner's manual. Unfortunately, they found the manual pretty impenetrable. Three months before the park was to open, there were ten dolphins, two prospective show arenas, and no shows. Tap joked that the dolphins had trained the trainers to give them fish for nothing. They needed a "real" trainer. Norris suggested me.

One reason I was an obvious choice was that since I was the boss's wife I could be expected to more or less donate my time. The main reason, though, was that I was the only person in the founding group who had actually trained anything.

So what animals had I actually trained? One dog and one horse. When we'd first moved to Hawaii, where Tap was completing his required military service in the Marine Corps, we lived in a cottage on a beach, a long way out in the country. I decided I needed a dog. I bought a Weimaraner puppy and named him Gus. Gus grew up to be a large dog. When he began knocking down children passing by on the beach to get their ice cream cones, I realized he needed training. We signed up for obedience classes.

The obedience classes consisted of traditional training using choke-chain collars. We were to command the dog with "Hccl!" and start forward. If the dog lagged behind, rushed ahead, or moved away from us, we were to "correct" the error with a severe snap and release of the choke chain. However, we were also taught to first use "No!" as a warning. When the animal made a mistake, instead of just nailing it, you said "No!" and paused, giving the dog a chance to correct itself. If it did, you said "Good." You would jerk the leash only if it failed to correct itself after hearing "No!"

I used "No!" a lot with Gus. Suppose, during a precision heeling exercise, Gus swung wide on a turn. Instead of jerking the collar, I said

"No!" If he immediately pulled in tight against my leg in the correct position, I said "Good." The dog escaped the punishment, and the well-timed "Good" also told him how to stay out of trouble on the next turn.

Gus did learn the meaning of those commands. I almost never had to jerk his collar in punishment. Gus was a gorgeous dog, and he worked briskly, with his head up, his eyes sparkling, and his stub of a tail wagging continuously. Judges loved that. We competed in dog shows with considerable success, both in obedience trials, where dogs and owners perform a series of prescribed moves as precisely as possible, and in the breed ring, where dogs are judged for their breed type, build, and way of moving.

I didn't like jerking the leash; but I did it because we were taught that you had to, especially with a big, strong dog like Gus. What I didn't learn until thirty years later was that those jerks can easily damage the trachea. Many elderly pet dogs wheeze and cough not just because they are old but because their windpipes are collapsing from years of being diligently yanked on a leash.

The success with Gus encouraged me to take on a bigger project. We had a bit of pasture around our cottage, so I acquired a Welsh pony. Much to my surprise, when the pony, a gray mare named Starlight, arrived, she had a little brown colt skittering along behind her. I named the colt Echo, for the first American satellite that was then chugging across Hawaii's night skies. Starlight already knew her manners, but Echo of course knew nothing. I taught the colt to wear a halter, follow a lead line, pick up his feet for hoof cleaning, and stand still to be brushed. As he grew, I did seek help to finish training Echo to be a riding horse and also to pull a cart. Echo was a lively young stallion, and the traditional trainers I consulted were quick to resort to the whip. Echo remained rather excitable and not something I could let little children sit on. I eventually sold Echo to breeders in California.

With this rather minimal background, the training of one dog and one pony, I was expected to understand Turner's manual and get some dolphins trained before the park opened to the public in three months.

My children were now three, six, and seven. I dreaded the idea of taking on an outside job, but I agreed to take a look at the manual. Oh, boy, this new way of training was a revelation. Here was the key to training without the punishment of leash and collar, whip and bits, and without the hard-to-learn physical skills and forceful personality seen as necessary with dogs and horses.

Here was an elegant set of laws, as explicit and prim as mathematics, for building behavior with what the manual called positive reinforcement. "Positive reinforcement" didn't refer to just any nice reward you thought the animal *might* like, or ought to like (such as praise), but only to certain kinds of items or events, identified by their results. A positive reinforcer is something the animal likes enough to work for, that strengthens a behavior *in the future,* making it bigger, stronger, and more apt to happen again.

Turner's brief if complicated document, expressed in this peculiar new vocabulary, seemed to contain everything I needed to know to start training not just a dolphin, but any animal, without punishment.

Operant conditioning made wonderful sense. I was dying to learn how to use it, and the dolphins would be perfect practice animals. There was no historical precedent, no "approved way" to train dolphins. No one could tell me, as I'd heard so often with my dog and my pony, "Oh, you must *never* do that" or "You *have* to do it this way." Furthermore, dolphins are big animals and eat many pounds of fish a day, so one could make a lot of training mistakes and still get good results before they got so full of fish they didn't want to eat any more. I couldn't wait to get started. I went to work the next day.

Dolphins That Aren't Flipper

Sea Life Park had built a dolphin-training facility outside the grounds of the park itself, where animals could be trained until the show pools and tanks were completed. Anyone who wasn't actually a trainer was under orders to stay out of that fenced area, and that definitely included the boss's wife. As I'd hoped, when I walked in the gate that first morning, the three existing trainers were cordial and welcoming. Perhaps they were relieved to have someone else responsible for figuring out what to do to get shows ready by opening day.

The big surprise for me was the dolphins themselves. I had assumed our dolphins were just like those in other oceanariums, the Atlantic bottlenose dolphin, *Tursiops truncatus,* good old Flipper with his squeaky voice and built-in smile. Until the day I went to work as head trainer, I had not noticed that the three training tanks held three completely different and unfamiliar species of dolphins.

In the 1960s there were no regulations restricting the catching of dolphins and whales. To fill the training tanks for Sea Life Park, Tap had bought a fishing boat, hired an experienced Hawaiian skipper named Georges Gilbert, and sent Georges and his crew off to catch and bring home some dolphins. A University of Hawaii professor told the newspapers that Sea Life Park would be a failure because the waters around Hawaii contained "a very impoverished cetacean fauna," but that turned out to be far from true.

The waters around Hawaii teemed with whales and dolphins, most of them mid-ocean species that had never before been kept in captivity. Using a dolphin-capture noose designed by Ken Norris, during the Park's first five years Georges and his crew brought in healthy specimens of thirteen different species of dolphins and small whales. Some, at the time, were known to science only from skeletons in the British Museum. None of them were good old Flipper.

We did have two bottlenose dolphins, but they were the Pacific bottlenose dolphin, *Tursiops gilli,* twice the size of the Atlantics, much more heavily built, and quite different in temperament. Besides these gigantic bottlenoses, we had two kinds of much smaller dolphins: Pacific spotted dolphins, *Stenella attenuata,* black and silver and covered with polka dots; and dainty, long-beaked, little spinner dolphins, *Stenella longirostris,* gray on the back and white, sometimes pink, below.

No oceanarium had ever kept spotted or spinner dolphins in captivity before. No oceanarium keeps them now; they are open-ocean lifeforms, not easily caught by mainland oceanariums and considered too specialized, too flighty, and thus too difficult to keep alive. We were naive; no one told us these species weren't suited to captivity. By giving them lots of individual care and attention, we kept them very well.

➤ **Watch the "Sea Life Park" slide show in chapter 2 at www.reachingtheanimalmind.com.**

New Kinds of Shows

I could have thought up behaviors for the animals to do, but I needed to design procedures for training those behaviors, too. Food, of course, was the primary tool. However, according to the manual, the key tool was not the food itself but something called a conditioned reinforcer. Conditioned just means "learned." The conditioned reinforcer was a signal we would teach to the animal, meaning "food is coming." (Turner did not use the term *event marker,* which was coined by Ogden Lindsley, a protégé of Skinner's, some years later; but Turner's conditioned reinforcer, besides heralding the arrival of food, was in fact an event marker, too, telling the dolphin exactly what behavior earned the fish.) This stimulus needed to be brief, noticeable, and different from everything else in the environment. The manual recommended a police whistle, which dolphins can hear clearly underwater. One could use the whistle to reinforce, or strengthen, accidental behavior that the dolphin might do on its own. The whistle was in some ways equivalent to the single word *good,* which I had used for both dog and pony, to identify when the animal was doing the right thing. It wasn't praise, exactly: it was information.

One could also use the whistle to shape totally new behavior, things the dolphin might never do by chance. The manual gave just one brief example of a shaped behavior: lever-pressing. Pressing a lever is the basic behavior taught to rats in laboratories, to enable them to earn reinforcement from an automatic feeding machine. Turner wrote that one could create a whole dolphin show around the behavior of lever-pressing. One lever enables the dolphin to play a drum, another blinks a light, and so on. Hmm. Not much of a show, but that was okay: show design was not what I needed to learn from this manual.

Shaping: Kahili Learns to Jump

My own first shaping experience occurred in those first few weeks with a Pacific spotted dolphin named Kahili. Spotted dolphins are built for speed. They are streamlined and slender—attenuated, as their species name, *attenuata*, points out. They are beautifully patterned, in designs that change with age. Kahili, a mature male, had a dark mantle over his back, sprinkled all over with little gray spots, and a pale gray underside, sprinkled with dark spots. His slender, sickle-shaped fins were black, and a handsome black mask covered his face, set off by a gleaming white tip on his nose.

Pacific spotted dolphins are prodigious jumpers. Out in the ocean our collecting crew had seen male spotters spring eight feet into the air, arch themselves into an S-curve vertically above the water, and soar horizontally several meters before splashing back down. Ethologists would call this a display behavior, usually seen in courtship or male-on-male conflicts. This large, dramatic behavior would take advantage of the ocean background and wide space in Whaler's Cove. Tap had asked the trainers to try to get spotters to do that behavior on cue.

Teaching our big male spotted dolphin, Kahili, to jump over a bar seemed like one place to start. One of the trainers, Chris, had initiated this project. He isolated Kahili in his own tank, intending to teach him to jump over a hurdle, a horizontal bar of plastic plumbing pipe fastened to a sliding bracket on an upright piece of pipe clamped to the tank wall.

Chris was having no luck. Kahili would willingly swim over the bar as long as it was underwater. But as soon as the bar was above the surface, even a couple of inches, he quit. There seemed to be no physical reason why Kahili could not jump over the bar. When I arrived, Chris confessed he was stymied. I suggested he turn Kahili over to me and concentrate on the spinners, which he seemed glad to do.

I immediately ran into the same problem. Put the bar underwater, even an inch or two underwater, and Kahili jumped over it, clearing it nicely. I blew the whistle at the peak of the jump and tossed him a fish afterward. He seemed to understand the arrangement; after eating his fish he swam right over to try again. But when I raised the bar just a couple of inches out of the water, he stopped. Why? I thought I might know. Perhaps, from his standpoint, the bar had disappeared.

When you are underwater, if you look up at the surface, you don't see the blue sky; you see a flickering silver mirror stretching into infinity in all directions. That is why so many fish are white or silver underneath. If a predator, deeper down, looks up, a silvery-bellied fish is nearly invisible against that mirrored surface.

As a diver, however, I knew that you can see through the surface in one place: directly overhead. Right above you the surface becomes transparent instead of mirrored, a circular porthole to the sky. On many a dive trip, having decided to return to the boat, I have looked up through that window to see the faces of people already in the boat leaning over to help me climb aboard. They could see me just fine; from above the surface you can see down in any direction. Underwater, I could see up only through that small circle.

Physicists call the circle Snell's window, after a seventeenth-century Dutch mathematician who identified the laws of diffraction of light through mediums of differing density. His discovery, Snell's law, explains why a pencil seems to bend when you poke it halfway into a glass of water. Snell's law also explains the famous green flash you can sometimes see, on calm days at sea, at the instant the sun sets and its rays bend through the atmosphere. (It's rare, and in my experience so fleeting that all who gather to watch for it bicker about whether they saw it, and whether it even exists. It does. I have also seen it from airplanes.)

Out in the ocean Kahili probably never in his entire life needed to look up through the surface, except possibly when chasing flying fish for breakfast. Therefore jumping over some obstacle that was located on the other side of the silvery mirror of the surface was simply incomprehensible to Kahili. However, directly over his head, he should be able to look through Snell's window and see the bar.

I'm thinking, Maybe I can make that happen.

Crossing the Bar

I get a bucket of delicious freshly thawed smelts from the freezer room, put my whistle in my teeth, and go over to Kahili's tank, next to the bar jump that Chris rigged up. The tank wall is about hip high, putting the water surface and the animal right under my hands, convenient for training. Kahili promptly swims over to me. I don't try to pet him. Some dolphins love to be stroked, but our spotted dolphins tend to quiver or move away when we touch them, as if putting hands on their body is rude; so we have respected that and don't try. However, Kahili gives me a cordial glance and is glad to eat a free fish.

I position the bar an inch or two under the water. Kahili, seeing me ready and standing by with the fish bucket, offers me his learned behavior: he circles away, comes back, and jumps over the bar. I mark the midpoint of the jump with a chirp of the whistle and pay him with a fish. We do this a few times, so that he feels confident about what this new trainer is doing.

Now I raise the bar just to the surface, where the little waves caused by his movements sometimes reveal it and sometimes not. This time, instead of letting him jump and marking the jump with a whistle, I use the sound to mark the moment before he jumps, when he is under the water near the bar and looking up (probably wondering where his bar went). I am hoping to identify for him that precise action, looking up through the surface, through Snell's window, and seeing the bar even though it's mostly in the air. Trainers call this use of the event marker "capturing" a behavior: with luck, the animal will identify what he did for that whistle, and do that new thing again. Using a marker in this way is the first step in shaping actions the animal might never do on its own.

Kahili startles when he hears the whistle and hesitates. Before he makes up his mind to jump anyway, I toss the fish he earned behind him. He turns and takes it. Now, since he had to move away from the bar to get the fish, there's a good chance he might repeat the behavior I'd marked: hesitating under the bar and looking up.

Indeed, he comes right back and takes up the same position under the bar again. "Look up, Kahili," I pray, and he does. As he orients his black beak with its starry tip upward and looks directly at the bar above him, I again mark that instant with the whistle and throw the fish behind him again. Once more, he will have to leave the "lucky spot" to collect his reinforcer. Thus he will have another opportunity to find the spot again by his own initiative.

Couldn't I help him? Couldn't I put a fish where I want him to go? Sure. Beginners are always tempted to use food to lure the animal into the place where they want it to be. Then, guess what? The shaping is over. The animal is thinking about getting a fish in that spot, and he's perfectly willing to go there and wait, forever if need be. He is no longer even considering what else he might do, in that spot, to make the whistle blow. So tempting him is useless. It's up to him now.

The third time he positions himself under the bar, I don't whistle. What will he do now? I hold my breath and wait. He looks up. Will he look through Snell's window and see the bar? Will he get the point?

Then, sticking his head in the air next to the bar, which is now almost entirely in the air, Kahili pumps his tail and kind of slithers headfirst across the bar. Intuitively I do something with my whistle that breaks the rules in our manual. Instead of blowing the whistle during the jump, I chirp it during the first powerful tail thrust that committed him to the crossing. I have marked not the act itself but the decision to go. *Yes!* You got it, buddy. Good thinking! Kahili gets a jackpot treat, five fish scattered across the water instead of the usual single smelt. He has to swim hither and thither to collect them all. He does that, and with speed.

The chance to reinforce a good decision arises rarely, often only once during the training of a new behavior. That single chirp sends a direct message to the animal's mind. It's an immensely powerful tool and one we operant trainers relish, since it can be wildly exciting for the animal, and also truly thrilling for the trainer when it works.

Meanwhile, by moving my marker from one part of the behavior to another, first marking the jump, then the earlier stage of looking for and locating the bar in the air, then the intermediate stage of committing to doing the jump, I have "shaped" a new behavior. In just a few chirps of the whistle, I have explained to Kahili how to recognize and jump obstacles even if they are in the air.

While Kahili is cleaning up his jackpot, I move the bar upward about two inches so it is completely clear of the surface. Again Kahili stations himself where he can see the bar through Snell's window. He pauses, then hops neatly over the bar: no slithering this time. This time the whistle marks the middle of the jump, and he gets another fish. Taking a chance, I raise the bar again. It is now four inches above the water. Kahili comes up from below, looks up, and, presto, launches himself confidently into the sky over the bar. He has it!

I raise the bar to about a foot over the water, about waist high for me since I am standing on the pavement outside the tank. Yes, he can do that, and he does do that. I raise it to two feet. Yup, that is also easy for this master jumper. Maybe he couldn't see through the surface without being educated about where to look; but he seems to know a lot about how to launch himself a specific distance into the air. He clears the jump skillfully and accurately each time, with a comfortable six or eight inches to spare.

This part of the process is not shaping, exactly, but something Skinner named successive approximation: increasing the scope or strength of a behavior, not by selecting new criteria to reinforce but by making a series of small changes in the environment. In this case, the changes are in the height of the bar.

In the next four tries I raise the bar as high as I can reach my arms upward, and Kahili continues jumping with élan. I have the distinct impression that Kahili is enjoying this exercise; I'm not the only one having fun here. Just then Chris comes into the training facility. "Chris, look," I call out, "look at Kahili!" Kahili is gathering speed underwater, and now he soars over the bar way above my head. Chris looks, nods, scowling, and disappears into the freezer room, slamming the door behind him. Oops. That was not reinforcing for him!

A Dolphin King Meets His Subjects

With the bar behavior conquered, and knowing that most dolphins like and need company, we decide to put Kahili with two other spotted dolphins, Hoku and Kiko. These two, a male and a female, are very attached to each other and always swim in perfect synchrony side by side, often "holding hands," overlapping their inside pectoral fins and pressing them together. Kahili seems to me to be benign, gentle, and polite; but Hoku and Kiko do not care for him a bit and avoid him as much as possible. He respects that and swims behind them, or apart from them. As this goes on day after day, it seems a lonely arrangement for him, so I have him moved again, this time into the training tank with the six spinners.

Oh, my goodness, what a happening! It's as if I'd thrown some famous rock star into a high school lunchroom. As Kahili cruises quietly around the perimeter of his new quarters, the female spinners prostrate themselves across his bow, lying sideways or upside down on the surface so he has to dip politely underwater just to get past them. Meanwhile the males mill around in the middle of the tank in confusion. Haole, the largest male and, until that moment, the alpha animal of our spinner tribe, floats vertically in the water, nose out, tail down, sinking tail-first now and then, a behavior dolphins do when they are totally overwhelmed: "I give up." He has been deposed without a fight.

Poor Haole was never king again. It made him, to my surprise, much more interested in socializing with people, and he became a favorite after-hours swimming playmate for trainers, for visiting scientists, and for me and my children and sometimes their friends. Kahili, though he was in their opinion in charge of the spinners, joined them in all their trained behaviors but remained socially aloof as far as I know.

Dumping the Laboratory Rules

The operant conditioning information in Turner's training manual was solid gold, but I disagreed with some of the management guidelines. The first management tool I tossed out the window was *food deprivation.* This is a normal laboratory procedure with experimental animals. To make them willing to peck buttons or press levers by the hour, they are commonly kept at 85 percent of normal body weight. Turner, in training dolphins for Ken Norris's sonar research, did not advocate making the dolphins thin (which is dangerous for dolphins), but he was not afraid of using temporary food deprivation as punishment. He recommended reducing the dolphin's rations sharply (to 30 percent of normal) for a day or two if the dolphin showed signs of what he dubbed "peskiness," i.e., disinterest in training. He advised that the dolphin treated with what he called "the strong rule" (cut the rations the minute the animal slacks off) would "work like a madman" the next day. It was routine, to him. It seemed a bit cruel, to me.

Besides, we were dealing with wild-caught, often timid animals. Sometimes the trainers had their hands full just getting them to eat a normal amount. Food deprivation as a training tool was out of the question. In any case, it proved to be quite unnecessary. Turner advocated one long training session per day; I threw that rule out, too. I knew from my dog, Gus, and my horse, Echo, that brief training sessions were easier on the animals and on the trainer, too. By doing our dolphin training in several fifteen-minute-to-half-hour training sessions a day, trainers could stay focused and dolphins had time to get hungry again. At the end of each day any dolphin who had not earned his normal amount got the rest of the day's rations for free.

Shaping Group Behavior

Our biggest training task was the spinners. Because the spinners were small, timid, and dependent on each other, I planned a show for Sea Life Park's big, outdoor arena, dubbed Whaler's Cove, in which they could all perform in unison, like a corps de ballet. Ron Turner's manual didn't have a scrap of information about training six animals at once, but we just started in anyway.

First, I wanted to capture the spectacular maneuver for which these animals are named. As well as just leaping in graceful arcs across the water, like most species of dolphins, spinners are given to exploding into the air and whirling like a top two or three meters above the water surface. They do it at sea; Melville described them as "the lads before the wind, moving in hilarious shoals, tossing themselves to heaven like caps in a fourth of July crowd."

I took to keeping a whistle in my teeth and a small fish in my pocket all day long (replacing the fish with a fresh one from time to time). That way if a spinner tossed itself to heaven, whirling like a top on its long axis, I could mark the behavior while the animal was still in the air and then get a fish right to that spinner.

By and by one or two spinners began spinning on purpose whenever a trainer walked by. Soon, if a passing trainer reinforced a single spin with the whistle and fish, other spinners would begin spinning madly and earning fish. Our champion, a male named Akamai (Hawaiian for "smart"), occasionally accomplished seven full revolutions in one jump; we counted them on film. (Kahili did his best to spin, too, but he was *terrible* at it; we settled for a tail-over-head aerial flip from him, which seemed to come more naturally.)

The spinners also frequently did a high, arcing jump we called "porpoising." We thought it would be nice if all the animals did this together, too. We reinforced Akamai for doing this jump. When he was offering it repeatedly, others began to try it, too. The trainer blew the whistle for Akamai. Everyone heard the whistle, but only those who had done the same kind of jump got a fish. Dolphins copy each other's behavior easily, so we were hoping the animals that did not get a fish would figure out how to do better next time.

The problem, however, was to get a fish to just those dolphins who had done a porpoising jump like his. I had a sort of lifeguard's tower built beside the spinner tank. Here one could perch above the tank and see all the animals at once. We could recognize them individually by sight, but still, if they were all zooming around, it was hard to keep track of who was where at any given moment.

The dolphins themselves evolved a system for improving their individual chances of getting the fish they'd earned. At the end of the jumping, when the whistle blew, the animals scattered, and each dolphin went to its own part of the tank and stayed there: Haole on the near left, Mele in the middle, Akamai in the upper right corner, and so on. We came to know where to deliver each fish; and we developed extremely good aim, because Akamai, not named Smartie for nothing, was a genius at nipping in and stealing other fish after he'd gotten his own.

Raising Criteria: The Path to Perfection

At first when Akamai started porpoising, we rewarded all the animals who jumped with the same arcing leap, no matter in what direction. Then I added a new requirement: only animals that jumped right to left, like Akamai, would get a fish. Trainers refer to this kind of standard or requirement as a criterion. If you want to improve behavior, in one animal or many, you choose a new criterion, then only reward behavior that meets that new standard.

To be fair to the animals, it has to be something that's already happening some or most of the time, so the animal can continue to have a good chance of reinforcement. Raising criteria in easy steps also gives the animal a chance to discover what specific behavior is working now and what no longer works. The spinners could handle that; in another day or two, they were all beginning to jump right to left, in the same direction as Akamai.

Then we added another criterion: jump exactly when Akamai jumps; no sooner, no later; then jump at the same height; then jump side by side. These three rules resulted in the elegant sight of seven animals—six spinners and Kahili—jumping about ten feet in the air in tight formation.

We raised criteria with patient attention. If one animal needed a few more chances to catch on to one particular new condition, fine; we didn't go on to a new criterion until every animal was secure about the old ones. These specific criteria were helpful to the trainers, too, especially when we started doing shows for the public. Everyone had in their mind's eye a picture of what the perfect group porpoising looked like. If, during shows, one animal took to jumping a little late, you noticed it. Then, by withholding that animal's fish after the next jump, you could communicate that its jump wasn't meeting the conditions; and if it corrected itself in the next show you could salute that good effort with two or three fish instead of just one.

Cues and Cuing: The Benign Alternative to Commands

Now we had two glorious spinner behaviors: a six-animal precision jump in formation, like military jet planes, and a scattering of whirling animals, like fireworks all going off at once. But getting one behavior or the other going depended on whatever behavior started up first. Spin? Leap in unison? Right now, the animals were just guessing. How could we tell them ahead of time which one to do?

The whistle, or event marker, is a form of communication, but it says the same thing every time: "Yes. You win. Go eat." That's probably enough if you're only going to teach the animal one behavior. D'Artagnan was a one-trick wolf; "run around the tree" was his way to get people to produce treats, and it always worked; he didn't need Klinghammer to give him any special instruction, and his cue to begin was probably just the arrival of Klinghammer's Jeep.

As soon as you want two or more behaviors, however, both the trainer and the animal need some way of telling them apart. You need to be able to communicate to the animal, *before* it starts doing anything at all, which behavior you will pay for at this particular moment. You do this by giving each behavior a name, an identifying sight or sound or other stimulus that conveys two messages at once (a noun, so to speak, and a verb): "This is the behavior to do" and "Start now!"

Turner's manual had a technical term for the name part of the message: he called it a "discriminative stimulus." A stimulus, of course, is anything the animal's nervous system can perceive: a sight, a sound, a touch, a change in temperature, and so on. *Discriminative* means a stimulus that distinguishes one particular item or event from others and allows your learner to tell them apart.

For practical purposes a trainer needs to choose some type of discriminative stimulus that's easy for both the animal and the trainer to perceive, and easy for the trainer to deliver. For dogs, we often use human words: *Sit. Down. Come. Speak. Roll over.* Dolphins didn't seem to hear our words very clearly, and not at all when underwater; so for dolphins, spoken words wouldn't do. Laboratory researchers working with rats and pigeons often use colored lights, but dolphin color vision is limited, and little lights are hard to see, even for people, in bright sunlight.

Today dolphin trainers usually use gestures, which dolphins can see well, as cues, telling the dolphins "Do this now." In fact, an international language of gestures for dolphin trainers exists, passed on from one to another around the world. A sideways sweep of the arm is the word for *jump.* Patting the water surface is the word for *come here.* Waving your hand means *wave your flipper.* But gestures have drawbacks. The animals have to be looking at you all the time, which you might not always want; and trainers give gestures in different ways, which can confuse the dolphins.

Fortunately, Ken Norris had been thinking about this problem. Since dolphins live very much in a world of sound, rather than a world of sight (although they see quite well), Norris had arranged custom-built equipment for us that could broadcast twenty different electronically generated sounds underwater. We would pick a different sound for each spinner behavior, then use those sounds as the cues for doing particular behaviors.

How do you explain that to a dolphin? You choose a sound: "This beep-beep-beep sound will be the spin cue." You put a label saying SPIN under the switch for that sound, flip it on, and go up onto the training platform. The spinners see you up there and start spinning. You step on a foot pedal that sends the sound through the underwater speaker.

You mark spinning with the whistle, turn the sound off, and feed each animal that gave you a spin during the time that the sound was on.

Then you pause. No sound is playing. The spinners spin again. You do nothing. At first they are perplexed; no whistle, no fish: what's wrong? Then you turn the sound on again. They spin. Again you reward every spin while the sound is playing. Soon, instead of spinning as soon as the trainer reaches the training platform, the spinners wait for beep-beep-beep to begin. Hearing the beep-beep-beep sound becomes exciting to the spinners. "Oh, boy, now I can spin and that will make the trainer give me a fish!"

We chose a warbling ooo-eee-ooo-eee sound for the group leap and repeated the training procedure with that cue. Soon all the dolphins would porpoise in unison on the ooo-eee sound, spin in unison on the beep-beep sound, and wait between sounds for the next opportunity to do the right thing and make us deliver fish.

In their free time, when playing or courting or doing whatever they were doing, dolphins could jump or spin at their own discretion. During training or performance, however, we could control those two behaviors perfectly with these two cues.

From the beginning, I junked the dog-training term *command*, although that's what the manual used. These cues were not orders to be obeyed. The dolphins were perfectly free to *not* do them. But they *wanted* to do them. The cue became more than a discriminator, a name, for this behavior or that: it also became a green light, a permission to Go! Now! The dolphins waited impatiently between cues, hovering, excited: May I do it now? May I? Hurry! They responded with enthusiasm: Oh, boy! At last I can do my thing and win my prize!

In contrast to a command, which is a veiled threat, a cue is a promise: if you understand what I'm saying, and you carry it out correctly, you will definitely win. We soon saw that once an animal really understood the cue, and would wait for it attentively, the cue became a desirable, even thrilling event. It became, in fact, a new kind of conditioned reinforcer, a promise of happy outcomes, like the event marker, like a dolphin trainer's whistle or a dog trainer's click.

As a form of communication, these cues differed profoundly from the commands I'd learned to give to Gus the dog and the messages from reins and whip and legs I'd been taught to use with Echo the pony. No punishment or threat of punishment followed for not responding correctly. The dolphin who did not respond to the spin cue, or who did a jump during the cue to spin, just lost that opportunity for reinforcement. Instead of being frightened or chastened, the dolphin was eager to try again and to see what might work this time.

These cues, in fact, gave us true control over the dolphins: not our superior brains, not our social dominance (get in the water with the dolphins and you'll soon find out who's really dominant here), but the elegant, almost mathematical laws of reinforcement that allowed us to establish this communication system. It was different from anything I'd used in the past; but boy, did it work!

We did not limit ourselves to underwater sounds for cues. We also used gestures, touch, and sometimes objects as cues. "See this hoop? Swim through it." When an animal knew a few cues, you could begin to communicate without doing any training at all: "See this rope? Bite on it and carry this end"—and here the trainer points—"to that trainer over there." Oh, okay, says the dolphin, and does it, sometimes just for fun.

Shaping Adventures

Now that we knew how to control new behaviors with cues, we could safely shape as many behaviors as we could think up. The trainers became fascinated by shaping. We tried shaping any behavior we could imagine. The Sea Life Park team taught a pair of beautiful sleek, black, tropical false killer whales, *Pseudorca crassidens,* to jump a hurdle simultaneously, but in opposite directions, crossing in midair (yes, they did get careless one day, resulting in a midair collision; it took three months of careful retraining to get the behavior back). Trainers shaped the whales to swim side by side at the surface with a person Roman-riding, standing with a foot on each whale's back. We often shaped new behavior right in front of the audience, such as two dolphins trimming an underwater Christmas tree during the holidays.

For our Hawaiian Village exhibit the trainers shaped behavior in the ancestral Polynesian domestic animals, first brought to Hawaii on long-distance canoe voyages from Tahiti: village dogs, wild pigs, and jungle fowl (*Gallus gallus*), the pretty little red-and-black ancestor of all modern chickens. We shaped behavior in the extremely rare native Hawaiian monk seal (*Monachus schauinslandi*) and free-flying, native seabirds, including red-footed boobies (*Sula sula rubripes*), frigate birds (*Fregata minor*), and two species of terns. Some were hand-raised at Sea Life Park, under federal permits. Some were volunteers from the ocean right outside our gates and the sky over us, drawn in by the sight of other seabirds circling the trainers, and quite willing to find ways to earn fish for themselves.

In the training facility we had plenty of fresh, running seawater, so I filled up a bathtub and got our collectors to bring us a few little fist-sized Hawaiian reef octopi (*Octopus cyanea*) for the trainers to play with. The trouble with an octopus, we found out, is that if you give it a food reinforcer, a small piece of crab, say, it wants to retire to its rock pile and eat it, which can take twenty minutes or more. This of course slows down the shaping considerably. One of the trainers got around that by teaching an octopus to take several pieces of crab, one after the other, tuck them under its mantle, and *then* go back in its cave and eat. Having built this opportunity to give several reinforcers quickly, the trainer taught the octopus to swim into his hand, turn upside down, let itself be lifted to the surface, then squirt water into the air from its siphon: an octopus fountain. I'd have said it was impossible if I hadn't seen it for myself.

One day I passed the open door of a laboratory in the Oceanic Institute and noticed a tank with a single fish in it, hovering in the middle of the water. It was roundish, about the size of a tennis ball. It had big triangular fins on the top, sides, and bottom. It was the exact color of a chocolate bar, unusual in a fish. It was decorated with a big white spot on each side and another on its forehead: thus the name, the three-spotted damselfish (*Dascyllus trimaculatus*). It's a favorite species of mine. Diving around Hawaii, you can sometimes see a whole family of twenty or thirty baby three-spotted damselfish, colored and shaped just like the adults but the size of a nickel, hovering around a little staghorn coral head. If something frightens them, a swimmer's shadow, say, they dive into the coral head and disappear. Then they instantly bounce out again as if they just couldn't bear not to see what's going on. Very alert fish. Now here before me is a captive adult *trimaculatus.* I wonder, could you train one of these?

It's lunch hour. No one's around. No notebooks or equipment suggests that this fish is currently in an experiment; maybe it's just being kept for its good looks. I open the lab's refrigerator. Aha, here are a couple of fresh raw shrimp in a dish—definitely damselfish food. A bit of air hose lying around can quickly be bent into a hoop, and here's a piece of string, too. I make a hoop and dangle it in the tank. By flicking bits of shrimp onto the surface, I can mark the behavior of looking at the hoop, approaching the hoop, and swimming toward the hoop. With perhaps a dozen little bits of shrimp and in three minutes or less, this damselfish is swimming back and forth through the hoop. Hey, a trained fish. Or, from the fish's standpoint, a trained person.

I have to confess, some of the behaviors we thought up and shaped didn't actually work. I decided it would be fun to set up a water polo game between Hoku and Kiko, our bonded pair of spotters, and our two big Pacific bottlenose dolphins living in the adjoining tank. I taught all four animals to knock a ball into a goal, spotters aiming for goalposts set up at the south end of their tank, bottlenoses aiming for a goal at the north end of their tank. Then I put the two teams together in the same tank and gave them the ball.

The spotters began batting the ball south, getting reinforced for that. The bottlenoses began batting the ball north, getting reinforced, too. Then Hoku, the male spotter, realized that the bottlenoses were deliberately taking his ball away from him. They were twice his length and five times his weight, but instead of nimbly stealing the ball back, which is what I expected, he flew into a temper and began attacking both of the huge bottlenoses. They quailed before him and retreated to the far side of the tank.

Wow! It was not totally surprising that Kahili would automatically reign over the smaller and timid spinners. But here was another spotted dolphin, and not a very big one at that, charging at two adult male bottlenose dolphins who were not just much bigger than he was, but pretty bossy themselves. Hoku, you have some nerve! Water polo was obviously not a good plan. I took the ball back and quickly separated my two teams before the bottlenoses came to their senses and open warfare broke out. Water polo was one idea that would not make it into the Sea Life Park shows.

Chapter 3

Communication

Lots of things can be reinforcers: food, play, air, water; warmth if you're cold, coolness if you're hot; and so on. Lots of things can become conditioned reinforcers, too—virtually anything you've learned to associate with the opportunity for reward. These might be considered two different levels of reinforcement: the real thing that, on arrival, you can now stop and enjoy, or the message about the real thing.

Skinnerians refer to these two levels as primary and secondary reinforcers. Unfortunately for the nonscientist, the labels are misleading. I've heard marine mammal trainers explain to the public that primary reinforcers are the necessities of life, such as food, air, and water, and that secondary reinforcers are things their dolphins enjoy but can live without, such as toys and petting. But that's not what Skinner meant at all. What he called a primary reinforcer is any good stuff that the learner wants. The secondary reinforcer is the message that the good stuff is on its way. The cues or signals that indicate which behavior will pay off and when to do it are a third level of conditioned reinforcer, even further removed from the primary reinforcer, which some trainers call a tertiary reinforcer.

Markers and cues can become more valuable to the animal than the primary reinforcer itself, because they contain information. They tell you something about how to get what you want in the future, not just now. As we've seen with the wolf, the hermit crab, dolphins, and even damselfish, living creatures can catch on to this kind of information with amazing speed.

The Lightbulb Moment

Sometimes the animal's awareness that its own actions make the marker happen seeps in gradually, and sometimes it comes suddenly. That's what trainers call the lightbulb moment. Biochemist Joan Orr sent me a video of a ferret's lightbulb moment. In the video, the trainer, on a visit to a friend with several pet ferrets, is sitting on a living room couch with a red ball beside her. She's holding some bits of meat in one hand—ferrets are carnivores—and a pocket noisemaker, a clicker, as the marker. Since the early 1990s clickers have become favorite secondary reinforcers, meaning food is coming, for many modern trainers.

The ferret, a white female, jumps up on the couch and sniffs the ball. Click! The ferret gets a small piece of meat, investigates it, and eats it. Soon the ferret sniffs at the ball again. Click! Treat! The ferret eats that treat and wanders off behind a pillow and out of sight. There's a pause; the animal has stopped back there.

Then she makes the connection. Wow! I made that happen! Bursting into view again, her four legs stiff like pogo sticks, she bounces up and down all over the ball, falls off the couch in her excitement, runs around the room twice, then scales the couch from behind and jumps down on top of the red ball again, grabbing it with all four legs. "*My* ball!" She then in rapid succession bumps the ball when it's held out and chases it across the room and through a cardboard tunnel, getting clicks every time.

When animals realize that the click gives them control over good things happening, they have made a permanent shift. It's as if the animal used to see the "portrait"—the single thing in front of it—and now it sees the landscape as well. Their environment begins to make sense. They want to know more.

You can't make this change with food alone; animals get fed every day and it doesn't do much to alter their outlook on life. You can't easily make this transformation just by trying to be nice and affectionate to the animals, either. Many don't understand and many don't care. It's the discovery of the marker, and the information it conveys, that makes the animal attentive to its environment in a new way.

The marker, however, is not the same as a cue. Clicks identify any and all winning behaviors, but they do not differentiate between them. That's the job of the cue, something which indicates what particular behavior will work at this particular time.

Once the ferret understands that sniffing the ball makes clicks and clicks mean treats, the red ball itself becomes a cue. The ball is now the name for a behavior: "Sniff here." Right away, a trainer, by holding out the ball, can bring the ferret over to her hand, and by rolling the ball, can send the ferret through tunnels and across the room. In a matter of seconds the ferret not only learned a new behavior, but also a secondary reinforcer signifying success, and a tertiary reinforcer, a cue for the new behavior, too.

➤ **Watch the "Happy Ferret Dance" video in chapter 3 at www.reachingtheanimalmind.com.**

Debarking a Kennel

A friend has asked me to give a talk on clicker training to the volunteers and staff of an animal shelter in a nearby town. It is a small place, with about thirty dogs, but they are making an incredible racket. In the first ten minutes I am totally fed up with trying to talk over the incessant barking.

Let's fix this, I think, and head into the kennels with my clicker and a bowl of diced hot dogs, trailed by the shelter's staff and volunteers. I will not have to plan out some kind of fancy approach for training thirty dogs at once. Even in an insanely noisy kennel, individual dogs do stop barking now and then, if only to breathe, and what you click is what you get. I can start by capturing the behavior I want; I will click any individual that's being quiet.

I walk up and down the aisle, looking at each dog, clicking any dog in front of me that is not barking, and passing a treat through the wires. Sometimes the treat drops on the wrong side, or some other dog in the same kennel grabs it first. Not a problem. The thief learns nothing, but the dog that thought it deserved that treat just tries even harder to earn another one. Sure enough, as I go up and down the aisle clicking and treating, one by one the dogs shut up, until only one barker is left.

A barker in the middle of the row has gone on automatic pilot and is just circling and yapping, circling and yapping. That repetitive pattern is stereotypic behavior, an unhealthy by-product of stress in some confined animals. I click and treat the nice quiet dog on the yapper's left, and the nice quiet dog on the yapper's right, two or three times each. The yapper looks puzzled and shuts her mouth for an instant. I've got my eye on her, and bingo, she gets a click and treat during that pause. She starts circling and yapping again, but now pauses, with a glance at me, more and more often, giving me more chances to click for moments of calmness.

Now some of the dogs are beginning to sit as I walk by; so they get clicked for sitting as well as for silence. In ten minutes even the yapper has settled down and is waiting quietly, tail wagging, gazing hopefully at the nice clicker lady. Good girl; click/treat. The job's done. The barking doesn't start up again. I finish my evening of clicker talk in peace and quiet.

The nice thing about this process is that anyone can do it; no skills are needed, just timely clicks and treats. The next day a teenage volunteer who had always hated the barking repeats the process and the shelter becomes quiet for good. What has happened? *Any* passing person becomes the cue for "Be quiet and look friendly." If clicks and treats don't happen every day, or with every person, so much the better; the dogs learn to keep themselves quiet on the *chance* that a passing person might click and treat, and that actually promotes even more quietness than certainty would. And these quiet, friendly dogs are much more appealing to potential adopters than the dogs that were frantically barking and jumping.

This procedure has been adopted by many shelters around the world. Peace and quiet is much less stressful for the dogs and for the staff, not to mention any cats the shelter is holding. Barking is contagious; perhaps attentive silence is, too. Even though dogs come and go and staff and volunteers may change, too, once a shelter is "debarked" it tends to stay that way.

Communicating with a Cue

Dog owners new to clicker training sometimes get so excited to see their dog learning with the clicker that they shape or capture a dozen behaviors, one right after another, without thinking about adding a cue. The result is a dog that knows you will pay for things it has learned, but can only guess which one. So when the owner seems available, the dog starts "throwing behaviors," eagerly running through its whole repertoire (sit, spin, wave, down, bow, back up, bark, sit again, bark again, down, wave, etc.) trying to guess what might make the person click this time.

This spectacle is disturbing to the conventional trainer; the dog seems not only totally "out of control" but idiotic besides. It is, however, just a beginner's glitch, easily repaired. The cure is to teach a cue, or name, for each of those behaviors, just as we taught the spinner dolphins to jump on one sound and spin on another.

The Extinction Curve

At Sea Life Park we taught the meaning of each cue by alternating "Cue ON" periods, when the behavior being currently rewarded will work, with "Cue OFF" periods, when it won't. By experiencing the oscillation between these two conditions, the dolphins learned to give the right behavior when they heard the cue and to do nothing if the cue was not present. The behavior fades away in the periods when no cue is given. In Skinnerian terms the behavior extinguishes, like a candle flame dying down and going out. During this process (called an extinction curve, because that's the shape it makes on a graph) the animal doesn't forget the behavior; it just gradually gives up trying to make it work.

Being put into an extinction curve is extremely upsetting. We've all been there. What used to work just fine no longer works at all. The printer jams. The car won't start. The phone is dead. The ATM won't give you money. Animals and people all get the same feeling from extinction: anger. How unfair! It's more than disappointing, it's infuriating. The common practice of punishing ("correcting") the animal for making a mistake—for innocently trying the behavior anyway—just makes that disagreeable situation much worse.

How to Teach New Cues without Pain: Shaping

Here's one way to teach cues without putting the animal through the pain of extinction. You get the behavior going at a high rate. Then you give the cue, firmly and obviously, right after the animal eats its treat, and just before it does the behavior again. Now, on the third or fourth repetition, just when the animal has finished the treat, you distract the animal briefly: speak its name, or move a step to the side. Interrupted, instead of just doing the behavior, the animal might look up questioningly, or perhaps move with you. Now you give the cue, and wait, doing nothing. You don't help or coax or repeat the cue; you let the animal figure it out.

Often you'll get a tentative response. You're trying to teach sitting, and the dog has been sitting fast for a click; but now, in this new circumstance, he just crouches a little. That's okay. You don't need to wait for the whole good behavior you've already trained. If you get even a whiff of the desired behavior, you click and treat generously. You are *not* reinforcing the behavior itself, you are reinforcing a response to the cue, by clicking the decision, however dubious, to try the behavior. You have thus reinforced a new criterion: do that behavior when you perceive this particular cue. The next response should be more confident. The word or gesture or object is becoming the name—the cue—for that particular behavior.

As soon as a dog (or other animal) has learned three cues in this fashion, it seems to generalize a concept: "Behaviors have cues. Each behavior has a cue of its own." When that happens, you no longer need to go through a long shaping procedure to establish new cues. If the dog learns a new behavior, it's prepared to notice and remember a new cue for the new task almost from the start. Oh-ho, here's a new thing that earns clicks, and that's the cue for the new thing? Okay, got it.

Cues can be attached to objects, too, not just to behavior. That's the mechanism by which a cue-savvy dog can learn, say, the name of a new toy or a new person on the first hearing. Furthermore, the number of cues an animal can learn seems to be pretty much open-ended, just like the ability of the average human to learn new words.

I suppose there are upper limits depending on species. One of my own dogs, without any exceptional training on my part, understood more than a hundred cues, perhaps forty of them spoken words or phrases, and the rest gestures, actions, and household events such as known versus unknown cars pulling into the driveway. If you really count out the verbal, gestural, and pressure cues used in training and riding a dressage horse, a Lipizzaner, say, it comes to more than a hundred. Irene Pepperberg's African Grey parrot, Alex, had a *speaking* vocabulary of more than a hundred words of which he demonstrably knew the meaning, and probably many more he understood but didn't say. Alex not only responded to many instructions, some complex, but gave them out with great accuracy, both to people and to other birds (Alex had no scruples about using commands). My choice for uninvestigated animals that might have far more capacity than previously imagined for using this kind of learned information would be the octopi and their squid cousins.

Controlling Misbehavior with Cues

One of the objections clicker trainers hear all the time from traditional trainers is this: I don't see how you can possibly use totally positive methods to stop bad behavior once it's started.

Well, we do it all the time.

The easiest way is to replace the bad behavior with a behavior you like better and put the new behavior on cue. Then you can ask for it as an alternative to the old, unwanted behavior (and pay for it generously, of course). Often the old behavior will then extinguish by itself (that's what happened with D'Artagnan's aggressive display).

Developing an alternate behavior is a great way to get rid of nuisance behavior in a pet. My friend Bill has been feeding his cat tidbits from his own dinner plate; not a good idea. Pretty soon the cat is hanging around through the whole meal, mewing and clawing at his leg for treats, especially if chicken or fish is on the menu.

Bill decides to use a clicker to shape a paw gesture, the behavior of giving a "high five," in which the cat presses Bill's raised hand with its own raised paw. When the cat has caught on to the idea, Bill's raised hand becomes the cue. He then begins asking the cat for a high five at meals, by holding up his hand and clicking and treating the cat's paw touch on his palm, each time.

The cat quickly discovers that there is no point in offering the behavior until Bill's hand is in the air. Soon, at mealtimes, instead of clawing at Bill's trousers, the cat sits quietly nearby, waiting for Bill to raise his hand in the high-five sign so it can raise its paw, touch Bill's hand, and get that longed-for bite of chicken.

At first Bill gave the cue at random intervals during the meal. Today he gives it just once, at the end, when the plates are taken to the kitchen; and the cat never bothers him in the dining room anymore.

This cue has also enabled the cat to communicate better with Bill. Now, when the cat needs to go out, it looks at Bill intently, gets his attention, and then gives the front *door* a high five. Is that cute or what? Of course Bill jumps up and lets the cat out, every time.

➤ **Watch the "Cat High Five" slide show in chapter 3 at www.reachingtheanimalmind.com.**

Using Two Cues to Get Rid of Nuisance Barking

Here's a dog behavior that people hate and that's hard to stop with punishment: incessant barking. How on earth could you stop this with positive means, other than by just feeding the dog incessantly? Well, you can establish two cues: one for when barking is a good thing, and one for when the opposite behavior, shutting your mouth, is a good thing. A great shortcut for this is to teach them both at once.

I'm visiting the University of North Texas for a scientific conference, and I notice a student sitting on a bench out in the sunshine, accompanied by a young Rottweiler. The dog is repeatedly barking. Everything he sees, especially every other dog, makes him start barking. I speak to the student and find out it's not her dog but her boyfriend's, and the barking is driving her crazy. "Can you bring the dog to my lecture tomorrow? Maybe we can do something about that barking." She's delighted at that idea.

The next day, I'm talking to an audience of a few hundred people, and since it's a lecture about training, some of them have brought dogs. By and by the Rottweiler arrives and is led onstage. Seeing strange faces and other dogs, he of course begins to bark.

I click and pass him a little piece of hot dog. Yum. He has to shut up to eat it, so since he's not barking, I click again and give him another treat. Then I wait. He looks around and begins barking. I distract him by raising my hand palm out, in a traffic cop's "Stop!" gesture, which causes him to look at me with his mouth momentarily shut. Click, treat for keeping your mouth shut, dog. Now I take my hand away and introduce a new cue, "Bark!" He begins barking again. Click, treat.

While he's eating the treat, and before he starts barking again, I put my hand up, in the "Stop" gesture, which I'm shaping into a cue for "Be quiet." Since he currently has his mouth closed because he's chewing, he's being quiet anyway, so I click and give him more to eat. What he's *doing* is what I click. Why he happens to be doing it at this moment is irrelevant. The nervous system will learn from each reinforcement.

Probably in his two years of existence he has sometimes been yelled at and even swatted for barking. Now, after earning about ten treats while he's barking, and ten treats while he isn't, his eyes lose focus and his brow wrinkles. People close enough to see his facial expression begin laughing. He's obviously struggling with an unfamiliar experience: mental activity. "She's feeding me for barking. I did have the impression . . . somehow it seemed to me . . . that people don't usually actually *like* me to be barking." Apparently he can't think and bark at the same time, as he has now been quiet for a good three seconds. So I tell him, "Bark!"

All that difficult thinking has paid off. He tries, for the first time, to give the behavior on purpose. Although he can bark all day reactively, it's apparent that he does not in fact know *how* to bark with conscious intent. Out comes a single hilarious cross between a groan and a yelp. Hey, it's a good try! Click, treat.

In three more tries he figures out how to give a decent, pleasant "Woof" on purpose when he hears the "Bark" signal. And on the "Be quiet" hand signal he is shutting his mouth so tightly you can see his lips pinching together. Without being deprived or confused (with extinction) or scolded or swatted (with punishment) he has learned how to control a piece of his own behavior. Now he can deliberately bark on cue, and also deliberately refrain from barking, on cue.

That's a lot to learn in ten minutes. I teach the two cues to the student, give her a clicker and some treats, and urge her to take the dog right home and let him rest. I know from experience that he will be exhausted after all that thinking, and a good nap will help the learning sink in, too.

The Power of Cues

We are apt to assume, from long habit, that cues, especially for dogs, have to be actual words, that the main way to control a dog is by speaking to it. The dog doesn't make that distinction. Anything in the world that means "This is the action that will now get results for you" can become a perfectly good cue for the animal. A spoken word can be a cue, but so can a hand gesture, a sound (the doorbell, for instance), a sight, a smell, a touch. I know trainers with disabilities who can cue their service dogs to move left, right, close, and away, depending on the direction of the trainer's eyes. The trainer can call the dog, send it to its mat to rest, or move the dog from the left to the right side of a wheelchair in a crowded room, just by a deliberate glance.

One can easily clicker train almost any dog to search for a particular scent, then sit next to it when he or she finds it. To us, one scent might be the name for "explosives" and another for "cocaine" and another for "agricultural products not allowed in this country." The dog just uses the scent cue as useful information identifying some behavior that will earn benefits for itself: "Go search for that scent cue, and when you find it, do the sit behavior, and you win."

No matter what kind of cue you are using, once it's established, the cue itself becomes a reinforcer. Here's why: cues identify a particular behavior that will lead to reinforcement. When you name that behavior, you also give the animal permission to do the behavior and get reinforced. Think about that little sense of joy or relief you feel when the traffic light turns green: that's a cue, identifying a behavior that you want to do. Every cue is a green light, permission to *go* do the thing it names. The cue thus becomes reinforcing in itself. Any time you give a well-learned cue, you are actually reinforcing whatever else the individual you are cuing happens to be doing at the time.

There's a downside to this: people who yell "Come, come here, boy," when their dog is running in the opposite direction, may actually be reinforcing going away. But there's also a big, big plus: by timing when you give a cue, you can use it to reinforce other behavior, exactly as if it were a click.

Here's an example: I am teaching a workshop for the British clicker trainer Kay Laurence, in England. I want to show people how to replace an old cue with a new cue. Why would you want a new cue? Maybe you adopted a shelter dog who came in with the name Devildog or Cujo. You don't have to live with that; change his name to Sparky. If Sparky means "Come here, I've got something nice for you," he won't mind a bit.

Sometimes you might need an extra cue just for convenience. You might want to use a quiet cue around the house for the behavior "lie down," but a really loud whistle for the same behavior if the dog is far away. That student with the Rottweiler need not stick with my hand signal for "Stop barking"; she could change over to a word, no doubt more convenient if her hands are full.

Replacing one cue with another is fantastically easy to do, if you are precise with the timing of cues and reinforcement. I look around Kay's group of students for a demonstration animal. A huge German shepherd is watching me. "What about him?" I ask Kay. "Yes, fine, all right," Kay says.

The owner, however, is dubious. "I don't think he'll work for anyone but me." Well, we'll find out. I ascertain his name and invite him over. He has been lying there all morning watching other dogs get hot-dog treats. He gets to his feet and comes gladly.

I confess I am suddenly a bit daunted. This is a large, shaggy, and formidable-looking dog, reminiscent of D'Artagnan the wolf, except of course this dog has pointed ears and a real wolf's ears are round. His face is guarded, his eyes shuttered. If I were training him in a shelter, I would want a kennel fence between us, at least at the start. However, I trust Kay's dog sense. Let's see what he can do.

To demonstrate replacing a cue, I need to find a behavior and a cue the dog already knows. "Sit," I say, and he dutifully sits. Okay, we'll use that. I click and give him a treat. Ouch. His teeth pinch my fingers. Kay can fix this in a few clicks, by shaping the behavior of taking the treat with lips and tongue instead of teeth, but I'm not that deft. So after the next click, instead of handing the dog the treat, I toss it to the floor.

Wow! The dog catches it on the way down. He's a good catcher! So we arrive at another arrangement: "After each click I'll toss the treat, and you catch it." Okay, says the dog.

He quickly demonstrates that he can sit reliably on a verbal cue, so I proceed to the second part of the lesson. I grab a blue plastic bowl from the equipment table and show it to him. This is going to be the new cue for "Sit."

I hold out the blue bowl, say "Sit," the dog sits, and I click, put the bowl behind my back, and toss a treat. We do that again a few times. Then I hold out the bowl and say nothing. The dog, dubiously, crouches a little in back. Hurray! He's hesitant, but he's offering the sit: click/treat. In a few more tries the dog is sitting, promptly and confidently, as soon as the blue bowl appears, and I'm not using the verbal cue at all.

But the job isn't quite done. Now the dog starts sitting as soon as he's finished his treat, not waiting for the bowl to be presented. The bowl turns the sit on, but the absence of the bowl does not yet keep the behavior turned off. We have to clean that up, and without having the dog just suffer through extinction, trying to sit and not understanding why it doesn't work.

The next time he sits before he gets a cue, I don't click; instead I move to the left a few steps. The dog gets up to come with me, and while he's standing, I pull the blue bowl out from behind my back and show it to him. He sits. I click and toss the treat a little away from him.

He has to stand up to reach the treat. This time I wait for a couple of beats, then offer the bowl cue. If he sat before I did that, if he anticipated the cue, nothing bad would happen, we'd just move and start again. But if I deliver the cue when he's been standing a second or two, I have actually used the presentation of the blue bowl to reinforce a new behavior: "Stand and wait." I gradually lengthen the duration by holding the bowl out only after he's been standing two seconds, then three, then five. Now, after each treat, he stands and waits.

Of course I make mistakes! Sometimes I hold out the bowl when I meant to put it behind my back. Sometimes I click late. But shaping is a matter of probabilities; if a large percentage of the connections are right, you'll get the job done. When I finally feel sure that the dog is deliberately controlling himself, standing, not starting to sit, as he waits for the blue-bowl cue, I stop the training and end the lesson by letting the dog dive into the actual treat bowl for one big final mouthful.

All this time, as I toss the treat here, there, and everywhere, the dog has been getting better and better at catching. He jumps up and snatches his reward in midair with an audible chomp from those impressive jaws. It's like training a killer whale; it's rather exciting to have all that energy and all those teeth flying past in midair right in front of you, and yet to be perfectly safe.

A couple of days after that workshop Kay has booked me for a public lecture in a big hall. That owner and that German shepherd are in the front row. The dog clearly wants to be onstage. This time the owner gives me permission with a big grin; and this time I have no moment of doubt about this big, scary dog. I call him. He comes galloping up the steps. Of course he remembers his blue bowl, his sit, and his four-star midair catches, too. He earns not only treats but a big round of applause.

Cues and Trust

I might not have been quite so comfortable with that German shepherd if I'd known his history or, rather, his lack of history, before I started. That night in a pub I found out that the shepherd was not a family pet. He'd been adopted two weeks earlier, and no one knew anything about him. Who knows what event had made him homeless, or what misbehavior might lie in his background? He had come to trust his new owner a little, but she was quite right when she said she didn't know if he'd work for someone else.

Clicker training, however, doesn't require a personal relationship or personal trust; it builds it. That had certainly worked, this time, and in both directions: dog to me, and me to dog.

If you're not familiar with the process, it's easy to misinterpret what's going on. Later that year, at the annual conference of a big dog-training organization, I gave a lecture on transferring cues. Before I did a demo with a live dog from the audience, I showed a video of this episode with the German shepherd and the blue bowl. From the camera's angle the shepherd's catches are awesome, too awesome for one woman in the audience. She comes up to me afterward in the hall and rebukes me: "You *taught* that dog to jump up. You *taught* that dog to snap."

No, he already knew how to do those things, I thought, but I understood her dismay. Just exhibited at random, these are not nice behaviors, especially from a dog of that size and strength. But this was not random. Not only his sitting was on cue. By the end of our session his leap/chomp behavior was on cue. The click and my hand movement as I tossed the treat was the cue for look, leap, and chomp. Those teeth would not come in my direction spontaneously. He was waiting for that cue.

➤ **Watch the "Blue Bowl" video in chapter 3 at www.reachingtheanimalmind.com.**

Cues Turn Behaviors On—and Off

Cues turn specific behaviors on, and their absence turns that behavior off. By establishing both aspects of the cue, we are "bringing the behavior under stimulus control." Behavior that is under stimulus control tends to disappear in the absence of the stimulus. Bill's cat stopped clawing him when he put raising the paw on cue. The Rottweiler would now bark less because he had learned to bark and to shut up on purpose. When I used the blue bowl to mark "stand and wait," the German shepherd learned when to sit—when the blue bowl is held out—and *also* learned when to deliberately "not sit": when the blue bowl is not there.

The dramatic leap and catch that so upset this particular spectator were likewise done in response to a cue, the click, my arm movement, and the treat's flight in the air. Consequently, I knew that this dog, even if he had a past record of aggression (which we will never know), was actually far *less* likely to snap spontaneously, or to leap at people uninvited, than he may have been before this learning experience.

Clicking with Cues: Behavior Chains

A cue, once established, becomes a conditioned reinforcer, too—so you can use it, like a click, to reinforce some other behavior—which opens up some interesting possibilities. By using cues both to name the next behavior and mark the previous one, you can string many behaviors together into a long sequence or chain and just give one "real" or primary reinforcer at the end. Lots of human activities are really behavior chains, learned in small units and then executed as one long flow, each behavior giving rise to the cue for the next: brushing your teeth, playing a musical instrument, driving a car, flying a plane, typing this sentence. These skills may have been laborious to learn, but now we can do the whole chain, and our skill is maintained not by a parent's or instructor's approval but by real-life reinforcers, the end results.

Several modern dog-related activities differ from traditional sports not only in being based on positive reinforcement, but also in relying heavily on behavior chains. One example is agility compctition, in which the dog races around an obstacle course against the clock. Cues can be words, hand signals, body moves, the obstacles themselves, or combinations of all these. Properly done, the run becomes a treasure hunt of secondary and tertiary reinforcers for the dog. Hear your owner's cue, "Tunnel!," you find the tunnel and run through it; that behavior gets you a cue to go over a jump, and so on until you reach the end and are rewarded by a big food treat or an exciting game of tug with your owner. The run is exciting in itself, and the repeated news of what to do next makes it even more so.

➤ **Watch the "Agility Cat" video in chapter 3 at www.reachingtheanimalmind.com.**

Dancing with dogs, sometimes just called Freestyle, is a newly popular sport in which a person and a dog perform together to music. A performance of three minutes or more may constitute one long chain in which each of the dog's behaviors are reinforced with a cue from the handler for the next move. Success in both of these two sports depends greatly on the clarity of the cues and on maintaining the chain, a fact not always understood by competitors.

Learning to Learn

Learning a variety of cues, including learning to substitute one cue for another, and learning to do behavior chains, teaches more than just the specific cues involved. It teaches the animal a concept: cues are very good information with highly beneficial results. This generalized understanding of cues produces what behaviorists call fluency, the ability to learn cues easily and to give confident and brisk responses to many cues with high levels of reliability.

The fluent animal's whole behavior differs from that of a traditionally trained animal, controlled with commands and punished for mistakes. That conventionally trained animal may know exactly what to do when it receives commands, and it may respond well to the commands it has learned, but trying new things is a sure recipe for trouble. The animal is cautious, inhibited, and afraid to make mistakes.

Animals trained in the new way are apt to be curious and friendly, instead of reserved and evasive. They take an interest in what you are doing. They are always willing to experiment and to learn new things. This is true of all species, from guinea pigs to lions; but the difference is perhaps particularly obvious in domestic species, such as horses, that are usually trained largely with dominance, force, and punishment.

Training Horses, Dolphin-style

B. F. Skinner had foreseen that horses could be handled by other than conventional means. He once visited a riding stable, bent on sharing his insights. However, when he started explaining about positive reinforcement, he was cut short by an expert horsewoman, who said, "Dr. Skinner, the first rule you have to learn with horses is '*Never* be nice to the horse.' " This discouraged Skinner permanently from further forays into equestrian circles.

Well, once you become an operant trainer, the first rule you have to learn about conventional trainers is to watch out for those words *must, have to, should, always,* and *never.* When those words crop up, you know you are hearing tradition, personal opinion, and/or superstition, not laws of nature.

In my years in Hawaii I had enjoyed training my Welsh pony stallion so much that I went into the pony business. My father-in-law, Sam Pryor, owned some pastureland on the neighboring island of Maui. I acquired some Welsh pony broodmares and another stallion and installed them on Sam's pastures. The plan was that the breeding stock and growing youngsters would live on Maui. Each fall that year's crop of two-year-olds would be shipped to Honolulu so I could train them and sell them to new owners.

From the dolphin work I was now sure that horses do not have to be trained with whips and pain-inducing bits and physical or psychic mastery. You can shape the behavior you want. You can use food as a reinforcer. You can teach the horses to look for and respond to cues and skip the whole business of punishment and dominance altogether. In fact, children could do the training, and I can train children to do so.

I find a horse farm a couple of miles from my house where the first bunch of ponies can be boarded and trained. I round up several fifth- and sixth-grade children, including my own oldest, Ted, to be the ponies' teachers.

The children all have some riding experience but no experience of training at all. The ponies are in a similar state of innocence. They've been handled a bit, to be cleaned up and shipped, and they can be haltered and led, but that's about it. It's an excellent starting place: neither children nor ponies have any bad habits or frightening past experiences to overcome.

I establish a good primary reinforcer: pockets full of molasses-flavored feed, to be doled out in small amounts in the palm of the hand. I establish a conditioned or secondary reinforcer, the phrase "Good pony," to be said each time the food is given. That phrase will be our whistle, our marker, to be used at no other time. Three days a week I picked the kids up from school or at their houses and drive them out to the farm to do what they call "playing ponies."

The children are scrupulous about using the conditioned reinforcer phrase, "Good pony," only as a marker, never dropping the words into casual conversation. A visiting child, someone's older sibling, is patting one of the ponies. As she has no doubt heard the other children doing, she tells it, "Good pony." Two of the other pony children round on her: "What did you say that for? He didn't do anything!" I am thrilled, privately, at this evidence of how well they understand the power of those words.

The ponies also understand that they get a treat only if they've heard the magic words *Good pony.* They never nuzzle pockets or nip at hands, the traditional reason to avoid using food with horses. Instead of looking for treats they hold themselves quietly at attention, listening to the children, a good thing in itself.

I break down the behaviors the horses need to learn into separate training tasks, then break each task into even smaller behaviors that can be shaped and reinforced one step at a time. I write down each week's behaviors and steps and tack the paper up on the barn door as a guide.

Here's what happens, with each pony. First the children carefully shape the behavior of standing quietly to be groomed, always using the marker "Good pony." Each pony learns to hold its feet up one at a time to have its hooves cleaned out; a tap on the leg and the word *foot* is the cue. The children teach the ponies a verbal cue for coming when called. They teach each pony to stick its head in a halter voluntarily when you hold it out, to stand quietly when tied to the fence, and to let itself be squirted with the hose to get the pasture mud off. In leading the ponies from pasture to barn and back, the children also use treats (the molasses feed) and the marker, "Good pony," to teach them some useful verbal cues for the behaviors of turning left, turning right, walk, trot, back up, and stop. ("Whoa.") Then we proceed to riding and driving.

Saddle-breaking, Clicker-style

One way to introduce a young horse to, say, a saddle is to just gradually expose the pony to more and more contact with this scary item until it stops being scared, a process called desensitization. That can take days, depending on the fear level of a particular colt. But since these ponies already understand reinforcers, shaping, and cues, you can use the marker and treats to bypass that slow procedure.

Let the pony smell the saddle, say "Good pony," give a treat. Touch its side with the saddle: "Good pony," treat. Put the saddle all the way on the pony's back: "Good pony," treat. Do up the girth, flapping the stirrups around to show the pony they are harmless: "Good pony," treat. Lead the pony around a little so it can get used to the feeling of moving under the saddle: "Good pony," treat. (That the pony sees other ponies wearing saddles at the same time is also reassuring.)

From then on, that pony is calm about saddles. The next day you can proceed to shaping and reinforcing calm acceptance of a rider. Since the children can easily reach forward with a handful of grain and reinforce from the saddle, the ponies take being ridden as a splendid new way to make children say "Good pony." Long before the ponies are actually ridden, they have learned verbal cues for *go, left, right, come here, walk, trot,* and *stop.* Transferring these behaviors from verbal cues to the tactile cues of gentle pulls and pushes from reins and legs involves no pain, just more "good pony" experiences. All the ponies have to learn now is to juggle the weight on their backs so it stays balanced; ponies and children learn together how to move in all directions and speeds without the riders accidentally falling off.

The ponies also learn to wear harness and pull carts, with children driving. They learn that children do many strange but harmless things. They sit on you backward. They slide off over your head or tail. They braid flowers in your mane. They teach you to drink Coca-Cola out of the bottle. None of this involves punishment or causes fear. All of it is fun, and all of it is reinforcing. Soon I don't need to supervise the training. I just drop the kids off with a list of what to work on now, then pick them up later to take them to their various homes in time for supper.

Only in Hawaii...

This freedom leads to something that isn't on the training agenda. One day I come home to my house on the beach and am startled to find my front yard full of ponies, each with a child on its back. They have no business being here! To get from the farm to my house the children would have had to ride down the side of a busy highway. This is absolutely forbidden. Not only that, the children are riding bareback, and they don't even have bridles, just halters and lead ropes. Oh my goodness, how dangerous! I have never scolded or rebuked the children, but I am about to do so now when the oldest girl interrupts me. "Mrs. Pryor, Mrs. Pryor, come see the ponies surfing!" And they all go cantering around the side of the house onto the beach. Well, I have to shut up and go look, don't I?

My house is right on the beach. Each of the ponies, with a child aboard, wades out into the water and heads toward the long line of gently breaking surf. As the next wave rolls in, the white water foams right over child and pony both, so they completely disappear. They pop into view again on the far side of the waves, where it is too deep for the ponies to touch bottom. There, the ponies begin swimming back and forth parallel to the beach. All heads are turned out to sea. The children and the ponies, too, are watching for a good wave.

When a bigger wave comes, the ponies turn toward the shore. The wave, breaking around them, whooshes them toward the beach. When they feel the bottom, they canter up onto the sloping sand. The children jump off. The ponies drop onto the sand and have a great roll, then stand up, shake themselves, and wait. The children jump on the now sand-coated ponies and back they go into the water, out past the break, to catch another wave.

The children explain that the ponies are without bridles and saddles because they didn't want to get the good leather tack wet. However, the ponies are so calm, so willing, and so interested in whatever is going on that the children can steer them, stop them, and urge them forward with words and gentle shifts of weight. They have no need for bits and bridles and all the usual punitive accoutrements of the equestrian world.

The resulting communication level between children and ponies is phenomenal. Nobody is saying "Good pony." No molasses feed has been brought along on this excursion; that is no longer necessary. Children and ponies have a mutual language that they can use for anything they want, including surfing, which they are doing together, by agreement, and for fun. I really do have to put a stop to future beach visits because of the highway hazards; but it is a wonderful sight.

Of course, to the eye of a traditional equestrian, such as the one Skinner ran into, everything the children and I seemed to do with the ponies was incorrect. Once at a horse show I overheard someone in the next stall say, "Mrs. Pryor doesn't know a thing about horses, but she has the smartest ponies."

I did at the time think that Welsh ponies were an unusual breed and I had especially good ones, and maybe that was true. I never stopped to think, however, that horse training wasn't supposed to go this way, and certainly hadn't gone this way with Echo, my original, traditionally trained Welsh stud colt, who had been resistant and often excitable (and often "corrected").

I know now that we created, through this kind of learning, truly normal horses, friendly, calm, curious, sociable, and ready to learn more: the way they were meant to be. Instead of correcting the ponies, we taught them specific behaviors and cues. For a pony, carrying a rider became one long behavior chain, full of conditioned reinforcers. By and by the reinforcers were not markers and food, but exploration and new fun, such as going surfing together. The results were quite different from the expectations of the traditional trainer. The results of this kind of training might be quite different, too, from the scientific view of the behavior of a given species. Scientists, too, have their musts and shoulds, their always and never, their conventions and traditions. But the rich communication, the mutual understanding, the mutual sense of trust, are a natural outcome available to anyone. Animals and people alike can have new insights from this new path to the mind.

Chapter 4

Feelings

Reading the Animal

Right from the first days at Sea Life Park, with a whistle in my teeth and a fish bucket in front of me, I started finding out things about animal communication that had not yet made it into the scientific literature.

For example, most species of dolphins and many species of whales frequently jump all or partway out of the water. Why do they do that? The experts and the textbooks say that marine mammals jump in the air to herd fish (yes, sometimes they do, I've seen that); to discharge excess energy (virtually *any* vigorous behavior might be explained away in those words); and, a common explanation, to dislodge parasites. (Doesn't that last reason sound plausible? Yes, until you actually meet a marine mammal wearing a few external parasites. Believe me, you need wire cutters or a scalpel to get those things off; mere jumping around wouldn't bother them at all.)

The multiple species in our tanks at Sea Life Park showed us, first, that they all had many different kinds of jumps. One jump was common to all the animals: the smooth arcing jump we called porpoising. This is primarily a way of conserving energy at high speeds by leaping instead of swimming, thus reducing friction briefly. Out in the ocean whole schools of dolphins may jump this way when they are going somewhere in a hurry.

Some species also have different, highly conspicuous unique leaps of their own. The spin of the spinners is one example. The spotted dolphin's high, long, horizontal leap (which we never saw in captivity) is another. The Pacific bottlenose occasionally executes a dramatic teardrop-shaped leap in which the animal comes straight up out of the water, arcs at the top of the jump, and goes smoothly back in through the same hole it came out of. These conspicuous acts are probably social display behaviors, like a peacock spreading its tail, or a horse rearing. Display behaviors are visible and identifiable from a long distance. The display communicates the size, prowess, mood, and possibly the intentions of that particular individual.

Meaning of the Breach

Then there's a jump whaling men called breaching, something that both whales and dolphins do quite often. The animal propels itself partially or wholly out of the water, turns on its side, and comes down hard on the water surface, making a big, noisy splash. This is the jump particularly likely to be blamed on the animal trying to remove parasites. To me, however, it fits the definition of display behavior: it's big, noisy, and obvious from a distance. Like all display behaviors, it's a way to communicate; and sometimes the message is specific.

I'm standing at the side of a training tank, training a big Pacific bottlenose to wear blindfolds, two soft rubber suction cups, over his eyes. Dolphins can make focused beams of brief sounds that they aim at objects in the water. Listening to the returning echoes enables them to perceive what's out in front of them, including prey and predators, even in the dark or if the water is murky. I'm planning to teach the animal to demonstrate this dolphin sonar by picking things up underwater using this echolocation ability instead of his eyes.

I reinforce the animal several times for wearing the suction cup on different parts of his forehead. Then I try putting it over his nearest eye. The animal moves out of reach. I call him back by slapping the water, but when he returns, instead of making the job just a tiny bit harder, perhaps by touching the cup near the eye, or by holding the cup over the eye and then pulling it away again, I keep trying to cover the eye.

I am accidentally frustrating my dolphin by asking repeatedly for a behavior he has not yet learned (let this thing go over your eye) and by *not* reinforcing behavior the animal continues to offer (wear this thing on your forehead). Finally, instead of offering his forehead again, the dolphin swims away, leaps partway out of the water, and comes down on his side, breaching. He makes a huge splash, which, strange to say, comes right in my direction so that I am neatly soaked with salt water from head to toe. As I'm wringing the salt water out of my hair, the dolphin pops his head out and looks at me with a glint in his eye. Another trainer watching from the shade of the building nearby bursts into laughter. The dolphin has definitely given me the finger.

Here's another form of unfavorable comment. Spinners are gabby and make a lot of whistles; they also sometimes make the buzz that is their echolocation sound, or sonar. Nothing in the literature implies that echolocation could also be used for communication, but we found out that if you are swimming with spinners, and you hear (and feel) a loud blast of sonar nearby, *zzzzzzZZZT!*, like a dotted line going through you, you have been given a rude message. Spinners never "aim" their sonar accidentally at each other; doing it deliberately is a challenge or a threat. You would be wise to turn around and stare down the animal who is zapping you. The spinner might follow that threat with a blow on the arm or the leg from a fin: not a dangerous blow, but hard enough to bruise. In the wild, spinners sometimes ram each other head-on, leaving permanent scars (and no doubt sometimes causing internal injuries); a threat even from these relatively small dolphins needs to be respected.

A lot of attention was being paid by the U.S. Navy and others to the many kinds of communicative sounds dolphins make in addition to echolocation buzzes. Meanwhile, why was no one paying attention to bubbles? To dolphins, bubbles are not only visible to the eye, but as conspicuous as a neon sign to their sonar. Bubbles are a great way for a marine mammal to communicate. We saw bubble streams used, along with matching whistle sounds, to identify and locate the whistler; bubble globs expressing surprise; bubble smoke screens used to escape behind; and bubbles as toys, by catching and releasing them, and making lines and shapes. I have also seen dolphins blow a perfect torus, or smoke ring, both in captivity and in the wild. I don't know what that means, but I'm sure it means something.

Could an Animal Say Thank You?

One day I was working in the training facility with an animal of an unfamiliar species, the rough-toothed dolphin, *Steno bredanensis.* You won't see this highly specialized, deep-water, tropical species in any other U.S. or European oceanarium. They are homely animals, brown, bulgy, with big, wide flippers, and covered with blotches and scars. No one knew anything about their biology or their behavior when we began collecting them.

The first one our collectors brought in amazed us all. We lowered her into a tank with a bottlenose for company. The Steno swam around a little while a trainer kept the bottlenose busy pressing a lever to ring a bell and earn fish. The Steno, taken wild from the ocean just a few hours earlier, studied this situation briefly, then knocked the bottlenose out of the way, slammed the lever so hard she nearly broke it, and stuck her open jaws out of the water to get a fish for herself.

Stenos were completely unafraid of objects. Give them some strange toy, a beach chair, say, and they immediately start playing 101 Things to Do with a Beach Chair. If you put a net in the tank to move animals into an adjoining tank, most dolphins will move away from it, allowing you to herd them through a gate. A pair of newly caught Stenos, seeing their first net, not only refused to be herded, but they took turns lifting up the bottom of the net and letting each other swim back and forth under it. When they finished playing London Bridge, they politely swam into the adjoining tank without being herded at all. Still, they didn't know all the training rules yet; and as I found out, they hate being wrong.

I am standing at the side of one of the Sea Life Park training tanks, working with a newly caught adult female Steno named Malia, reinforcing leaping. She's caught on and is readily leaping, hearing the whistle in midair, and eating the fish I toss her. Then she makes a sound, a little mew or squeak. That surprises me; up until then our Stenos have all been silent. So I reinforce the sound, and she makes it several more times.

Now I make a training mistake. I am so interested in the sound that I decide not to reinforce leaping anymore. Leaping, after all, is a common Steno behavior; I could catch that any time. I wait for more sounds and ignore the next four leaps.

Malia has not yet experienced failing to be reinforced for something that had previously paid off. I have carelessly put her into extinction. Malia is furious. After the fourth unreinforced jump, she breaches twice (away from me, not on me), then retires to the side of the tank that is farthest away from me and turns her back. There she stays, ignoring people and refusing all fish for two days.

Going without food is dangerous for dolphins. On the second day I go in the water and take Malia's temperature and sniff her breath to see if she is sick. No, her breath is sweet, not fishy, and her temperature normal. She's not sick. Nevertheless if she goes a third day without eating, we will have to force-feed her, which she wouldn't like much, nor us either.

On the third morning I show up with my whistle and the fish bucket one more time before gathering up a team to strand Malia on the bottom of an empty tank and put a tube down her throat. Malia makes a small leap, which I hasten to reinforce. She eats the fish.

Whew! We're back in business. I reinforce several more leaps, then set about building a cue, a raised hand, to explain to her when jumping will work and when it won't. Any leap that occurs when my hand is in the air will be successful. If I put my hand down, leaping won't bring a whistle or a fish.

Malia soon catches on and begins leaping as soon as my hand goes up, getting her whistle and fish. Even more important, she begins watching my hand and waiting *until* it goes up before leaping. In one of these brief waiting periods, Malia makes the noise again. I immediately blow the whistle to mark the noise. Then, instead of throwing a fish, I raise my hand in the new jump cue. Malia makes a nice leap, which I reinforce with whistle and fish. I have reinforced the sound-making with the cue for the jump. This not only increases sound-making but also strengthens that jump cue, making it clearer than ever.

The bucket is almost empty; Malia has eaten her full meal. I give her the last few fish all at once, my personal signal that the session is over, and put my arms in the tank to wash the sticky fish scales off my hands. While my arms are underwater, Malia swims over to me and strokes my nearest arm, gently and repeatedly, with the front edge of her pectoral fin. It's a gesture of affection that one sees quite often from dolphin mothers to their babies or from one dolphin to another. But I have never, before or since, seen a dolphin do this to a human. It's as if she is saying, "Okay, stupid, I get it now, and I forgive you."

I published a description of this exchange in a scientific paper and filed it away in my mind as one of those amazing things dolphins do. It never occurred to me then that a dog—a mere dog!—might do the same thing. And for the same reason: "Thanks for helping me out."

A New Social Signal in Dogs? Dog #1

Although my children and I had a number of dogs over the years, I wasn't particularly involved in the world of dog lovers until long after the children were grown, when my book about positive reinforcement, *Don't Shoot the Dog!*, became so popular with dog owners.

Considering how long dogs and people have been living together, it's amazing how thick most people are when it comes to reading the domestic dog's emotional signals. Even some dog experts may misinterpret dog threats or be totally oblivious of blatant signs of stress and fear. Still, I assumed, when I stepped into the dog world, that at least the scientists, the ethologists, would have identified most, indeed all, of the innate or genetically governed social signaling behavior of the domestic dog and its relatives; nothing new to learn there. Well, wrong again.

At an annual conference of dog trainers and other professionals, I am giving a talk on problem-solving with the clicker. A woman with a handsome, young black Labrador comes onstage. She is having trouble with the obedience exercise of retrieving a wooden dumbbell. Obedience competition rules say that the dog must hold the dumbbell quietly; but whenever the owner hands the dog the dumbbell, it immediately begins chomping on it, spitting it in and out, and rolling it around in its mouth.

I can see what has gone wrong. The owner is clicking too late. Over and over, her clicks have fallen on moments when the dumbbell is moving; so that's what the dog thinks it's supposed to do. Now, onstage, while the owner keeps trying to wait the dog out and catch a quiet moment, the dog tries ever harder to move the dumbbell around in some successful way. The dog finally lies down on its back and throws the dumbbell into the air and catches it while upside down! Wow, this dog is ready for Hollywood! But definitely not for the obedience ring.

I don't usually like to take the clicker out of the trainer's hand, but it seems time to intervene. "Let me try." I am going to reshape this behavior from scratch. I hold the dumbbell out to the dog and click the instant I feel the teeth touch the wooden bar, without letting go of the dumbbell myself. I progress to clicking as the dog begins biting down, then to clicking for a split second of holding on. When he's holding on tight, not moving, I shake the dumbbell gently, as if I were trying to take it away from him. His eyes sparkle, and he holds on even more firmly; "tug" is a favorite dog game. Click! "Great job hanging on tight, dog."

Now, will he do it without my holding the dumbbell, too? "The game is, take the dumbbell and hold on to it, dog; that's all you have to do." I give him the dumbbell, take my hand off, and wait, with my heart in my throat, for two beats. He holds it, motionless and firm, until the click.

He's got it! He now holds it absolutely still for three seconds, then for six seconds. "Is that all I'm supposed to do? That's so easy!" I quickly transfer the behavior to the owner. Now that the dog is clamping down firmly for a few seconds, she is able to insert a click while the dumbbell is perfectly still, so the problem should be resolved. Hurray! Students dismissed.

The next day that owner and her Lab pass me in the exhibit hall and she stops to talk, with her dog standing quietly next to her on a leash. After a moment the dog walks over to me and licks the back of my hand, just once, but firmly, then walks back to his owner's side. The owner doesn't remark on this, nor do I, but I am puzzled. It wasn't a greeting. There was no eye contact. The dog's tail never moved. The dog didn't solicit petting, I didn't speak to him, and I hadn't even looked at the dog. Why did it do that?

Dog #2

A year or two later, at a training seminar, another dog does the same thing to me, under similar circumstances. The owner comes onstage with a collie to deal with a heeling problem. This owner, I see, is asking for two different things at once: "Walk beside me" (on the sidewalk) and "Walk in front of me" (in the show ring). Like the Lab with the dumbbell, the dog is offering all kinds of variations, including walking on both sides and trailing behind her.

We straighten it out in no time with the clicker, not by shaping a new behavior, as I'd done with the dumbbell grab, but by reducing the choices to one at a time and then teaching a different cue for each condition, as with Malia, the Steno. The next day during the morning break as the owner stands near me, her collie walks over to me, deliberately licks the back of my nearest hand, and walks back to the owner. I remember the Labrador. This dog seems to be saying the same thing: "Hey, thanks for clearing that up, lady."

Of course, these dogs expressed themselves, if that's what they were doing, a day after the event. Is that so surprising? You wouldn't be amazed if a dog growled on Wednesday at someone who had frightened it on Tuesday. Why should dogs remember only bad things?

Dog #3

Then it happens one more time, this time with a traditionally trained dog, not a savvy clicker dog. My friend Sue Cone, a well-known obedience competitor, is in Seattle to compete in some big obedience trials with her Chesapeake Bay retriever, Abbie. I go downtown to watch the trials and meet Abbie for the first time. Abbie is reserved, almost aloof: no joyful greeting and waving tail like a golden retriever, no "Pet me!" nose pokes like a friendly Labrador. Abbie is here to work. The kindest thing I can do is to leave her alone, and that is fine with both of us.

Chesapeakes are a breed not often seen in obedience competition. With her powerful build, rippled liver-colored coat, and golden eyes, Abbie attracts attention. She, however, ignores her admirers. She doesn't really like people, I think, and I say so to Sue. Sue says that Abbie likes people okay; the one thing she really does not like is children, and she will avoid them if she can.

That afternoon, in the vast lobby outside the main arena, Sue commands Abbie to sit and stay while she goes to the ladies' room. Being left alone under command in public like this is something Abbie must be used to. Nevertheless it seems to me like quite a challenge. I stay nearby to keep an eye on her.

Then I see a boy of about eleven or twelve, with a big grin on his face, crossing the lobby and heading right for Abbie. An unattended dog, all his to play with! I quickly step to Abbie's side before he reaches her.

The boy stops. "May I pet your dog?" he says almost perfunctorily. He already has his hand out.

"No."

No? He looks surprised. "But I *love* dogs! I know all about dogs!" He grins winningly. Accustomed to getting his way, I think. "No, I'm sorry, you may not pet this dog. She does not like children." Even so, he takes another step toward Abbie. I step into his path and say firmly, "She might bite you."

I certainly don't think that's true, but I am quite sure she would hate being petted by this kid, whom I now dislike myself. The boy looks again at Abbie. Her head reaches the height of his shoulder. He absorbs the concept, backs up a step or two, and goes away. I move back to the wall and leave Abbie alone in her obedient sit-stay.

When Sue comes out of the ladies' room, she puts the leash back on Abbie and releases her from the sit. We head back to the arena with

Abbie walking between us. On the way we stop for a moment to take a look at the program. In that moment, Abbie stands up on her hind legs, puts her front paws on my shoulders, and licks me heartily, just once, from chin to ear. She then gets down and stands quietly next to Sue again.

Sue is flabbergasted, too surprised to even think of reprimanding. "I *never* saw her do that before; I never saw her do anything *like* that, *ever*!" I smile at Abbie and think, You're most welcome, glad to help. But I don't try to pet her. She hates that.

Anecdotes vs. Observations

So? Were these dogs saying thank you? Somehow it is easy to believe one has seen something unusual in the behavior of a dolphin; rather harder if it's a dog. We see dogs all the time, and they're forever licking people, for all kinds of reasons; how would this be different? I can hear people saying, about that Lab, that collie, and that Chesapeake, these are just anecdotes, and anecdotes are not science!

This has become a popular prejudice in the scientific community. If you don't have measurements of multiple occurrences of the same thing under deliberately varied circumstances, you don't have anything. Something that has been observed, but not repeated experimentally, is dismissed as "anecdotal," implying that it has no validity. In fact, observation is basic to science. If the observer is competent, observation and description make up the first step in forming a hypothesis, in designing an experiment, and in deciding what data to collect.

I now wonder if someone else had seen the same thing. Aside from Androcles and the lion, it would probably be a waste of time perusing the literature for studies of thankful animals; publishing on such an iffy topic would be a good way to get kicked off the tenure track. But if a gesture expressive of appreciation is a real, unreported aspect of canid behavior, one other group might have seen something like this: the folks at Wolf Park. I call Klinghammer.

"Yes, we have seen this, too, in the wolves," Klinghammer says at once. "It's a quick lick or gentle touch, with no other signs of affect such as eye contact or tail movements. I have seen it now in my own dogs. Pat Goodman has examples."

Here's one. Pat and Wolf Park photographer Monty Sloan are in the main pack's enclosure when Chetan, a young male wolf, finds himself in difficulties. Chetan has become the butt of some of the other males in the pack. They occasionally descend on him with rude pokes and jostles and snapping, trying to provoke him. They might rough him up a little, but they never actually hurt him. However, one of the females, Marian, sometimes takes advantage of this situation to sneak in behind Chetan and bite him in the rear; and Marian, most unfairly, bites hard enough to puncture.

Marian hears some commotion and comes sneaking toward Chetan's rump. So Pat steps in her way and says, "Marian, how are you, great to see you!" in a squealing voice, like a girl running into a friend at a party: a human social greeting. Marian lies down and rolls over to have her belly scratched, and Pat obliges. While Marian is thus distracted, the bullying males lose interest and leave. Chetan can safely get up and move away without worrying about sneak attacks from the rear.

Pat expects Chetan to leave, now that he is unmolested. Instead, he walks over to her and gives her a quick little lick on the wrist. Pat reports that she had the instant and strong feeling he was saying, "Thanks for fending off Marian!" I think she was right.

Like Klinghammer, I occasionally see that behavior now in my own dogs. Other people have reported it, too; once you know what to look for, it kind of jumps out at you. My friend Beth tells me her own experience. Her neighbor owns a pleasant American bull terrier named Ruby. One evening on her way home from work, Beth stops by with a present for Ruby, an especially wonderful chewy ball. The dog rushes off to play with it. Abruptly leaving the ball on the far side of the room, the dog comes back to Beth, licks her once on the hand, and returns to the new treasure. "Thanks for the great toy!"

"If I hadn't known about it, I'd have ignored it, but since I knew what it meant, I was thrilled," Beth said. It's an innate signal of emotion that has probably been happening, every once in a while, all along; we just didn't have the predictive tools to enable us to see it. Now knowledge taken from one science, behaviorism, has given us new information in another other science, ethology; and both benefit from the crossover.

Lorenz on Gratitude

The mystery of the licking dogs might have remained inscrutable to me had it not been for Konrad Lorenz himself. We first met when Konrad visited Hawaii and a mutual friend brought him out to Sea Life Park. I was excited, of course, and rushed up gushing enthusiasm. Konrad said, "I wish I were a timber wolf, so I could respond to your greeting properly." Meanwhile, sweeping one hand back and forth behind his back, he created the vision of a large, plumy wagging tail.

We became friends on the spot and exchanged visits and correspondence throughout the remainder of his life. He also wrote a prescient and generous foreword to my first book on training animals, *Lads Before the Wind.* The paper in which I described how Malia stroked my arm in forgiveness was published in a German journal, *Die Naturwissenschaften.* Konrad had read it and referred to it in his introduction to my book, remarking that it almost moved him to tears. My feeling exactly, I thought, and from then on I trusted more fully my own behavioral observations and the curiosity they sometimes arouse. Hence I noticed, and wondered at, those dogs.

Feelings in a Fish

As I begin teaching clicker training to dog owners, I realize they need to see examples of shaping behavior in an animal that's not a dog. I remember the bold damselfish I trained to swim through a hoop back at Sea Life Park; let's do that again!

I go to a pet store and buy a cichlid, *Astronotus ocellatus,* the species that fish fanciers call Oscars. Cichlids are freshwater cousins of the saltwater damselfish. Like the damselfish they are sturdy and fairly fearless, they eat a lot and grow fast, and they don't mind living alone. Thus they should be easy to train. This one is about two inches long and mottled brown all over. I install it in an aquarium on the kitchen counter. It eagerly eats bits of crab and shrimp. I make a hoop out of plastic tubing, as I'd done before, and start to train this fish.

First I need a secondary reinforcer to serve as a marker. I know the fish can't hear a click. What about a tap on the glass? I try it. The tap sends the fish diving for cover; that won't do! I settle for a little splash of one finger on the water surface to be the marker, followed by the primary reinforcer, a piece of food. Working in ten-minute sessions twice a day for a week, I reinforce looking at the hoop, approaching the hoop, and swimming through the hoop. Soon, each time I put the hoop in the water the fish goes through it, earning a splash and a snack. Every training session is videotaped.

Wondering sentimentally if my fish might be lonely, I get a few platies (*Xiphophorus maculatus*) and put them in a bowl next to the tank. The fish, seeing other fish moving around in the distance, is now revealed to be a male: he goes into courting mode immediately and stops eating for several days while he digs a nest in the sand.

Removing the platies takes care of the courtship problem, and the fish is eating again. Then I make a serious training mistake. I fail to realize that the hoop itself has become a cue to the fish. Instead of taking the hoop away when I'm not ready to train, I let the hoop stay in the tank while I jot down some notes.

The fish goes toward the hoop again. Instead of going through it, he goes around it on the outside, brushing along the hoop's left rim. Of course he doesn't get reinforced, since that's not the right behavior, and besides, I am busy doing something else; but now I'm curious. I write it down and go on watching.

He circles around and tries again, brushing his flank past the outside of the rim. Now I am really surprised. Could it be that this fish is deliberately experimenting? Is he testing the premise "I know what works here, let's see what else might work?" Cats and otters do that often, and so do ferrets; but it seems unusual in a mere fish!

Having tested out alternatives, if that's what he was doing, the fish rapidly spins around and dashes through the middle of the hoop. "Aha! Now I know what to do!" And again, nothing happens. I'm not ready! After two failed tries perhaps he was sure he was right this time. But he didn't get a finger splash. He didn't get the treat. And he has a fit.

He sinks to the bottom and lies on the gravel, half-tilted against the glass. He turns dark all over. He gasps, fighting for breath. I am stunned. I understand what has happened to him. He failed, three tries in a row, and that is enough to put him into the disappointment and anger-inducing experience of an extinction curve. All organisms find this aversive; but I truly had no idea a fish could get so *upset*. And the video camera has been running the whole time: we have it on tape.

In the next few sessions I arrange things so that *mostly* the fish wins, but once in a while, even though he goes through the hoop correctly, he has to do it twice to get his splash/treat. Even twice can sometimes be too much to bear; he collapses in the corner three more times over the next couple of days. I guess a fish doesn't have much mental resilience for enduring bad news. However, by and by he does learn that if you don't succeed the first time, try again and it will probably be all right.

I never take him beyond two tries. I don't have the need or the heart to see how hard I could push him. But the process does help him to become sufficiently resistant to extinction so that I can put the behavior on cue. My hand poised over the water becomes the cue to go through the hoop. The fish learns to watch and wait for that hand before trying the hoop. Finally he does the behavior beautifully, fluently, with high reliability, only on cue.

The resulting short video has become a bit of a classic, especially the part showing the fish collapsing in despair. Biology professors use it in animal-behavior courses, while psychologists use it in learning-theory courses. One social worker shows it to families at risk for child abuse and delinquency; she says for parents and children both it instantly teaches empathy.

➤ **Watch the "Fainting Fish" video in chapter 4 at www.reachingtheanimalmind.com.**

Faking It

Of course, if you *want* an animal to appear to show an emotion, on demand and regardless of what it is actually feeling, you can train it to do so. The best example I've seen so far of a totally trained apparent emotion in a dog was produced by biochemist Attila Szkukalek, a gifted trainer whose hobby is the new sport of freestyle, or dancing with dogs, which involves designing and presenting choreographed routines in which a person and a dog perform together to music. Cues and reinforcers are a vital tool in this complex process, and Attila is a top international competitor. In a medal-winning Charlie Chaplin routine in which Attila portrays Chaplin's Little Tramp, the dog humiliates the Tramp by jumping on his back, knocking him down, and turning around and kicking with the hind legs as if burying him. Then, with the Tramp still on the ground and looking bewildered, the dog stands on her hind legs, waves her paws, opens her mouth, lolls her tongue out, and "laughs" at her victim. How the audience loves it! The effect is totally convincing, but of course it's a shaped behavior, subtly cued every time. Furthermore Attila can milk the applause by letting the dog stand there, "laughing," until he (invisibly to us) cues something else.

➤ **Watch the "Attila Szkukalek's Charlie Chaplin Routine with His Dog, Fly" video in chapter 4 at www.reachingtheanimalmind.com.**

The Dastardly Dalmatians

I have succumbed personally just once to the temptation to fake an animal's emotional response. As any trainer can tell you, nothing is more difficult to deal with than the dog behavior problems offered by family and close friends. It's not that you can't see solutions, but that the loved ones who are asking for your free advice are unlikely to take any of it. Still, it's hard to just say no. My downfall is brought about by a pair of well-bred Dalmatians.

My friend Kristina has invited me to spend a weekend at her house in the country. When I arrive, her husband says, "I'm glad you're here, because I'd like you to train the dogs over the weekend. We're having a little trouble with them."

A little trouble! I'll say. The dogs are two-year-old sisters from the same litter (the couple went to get a puppy, and the dogs were so cute they came home with two). The dogs have the run of this big country place and can go in and out freely. But neighbors are complaining. These dogs sneak down the road, go into people's yards, and steal children's toys: a favorite doll, a new baseball glove. They bring the possessions home and bury them in the woods. Hmm. I could appreciate that this would be annoying.

The dogs don't bark unduly, but I have already observed that they can certainly make a convincing threat display at visitors' cars. They have totally cowed the UPS man, who refuses to leave packages at the door if the dogs are outside. Of course, if the dogs are away, burying stolen goods perhaps, and the UPS man does leave a package, when the dogs come home, they make short work of it. The children in the family tell me (with some pride, I think) that the dogs recently made their way through a stout Styrofoam shipping container and helped themselves to an entire side of smoked salmon.

On Saturday morning I am in the kitchen helping make sandwiches for lunch. As I'm buttering a slice of bread, a sleek spotted head surfaces between me and the kitchen table, like a seal coming up through a hole in the ice. The dog grabs the piece of bread right out of my hand. She sinks out of sight again before I can do much more than gasp in surprise.

How long has this thievery been allowed, even in these dogs' own household? Quite awhile, apparently. Some construction work is going on in the back of the house. One of the Dalmatians comes quietly up behind a carpenter who is kneeling on the floor to measure a board. I watch in awe as the dog gently lifts a screwdriver out of the man's tool belt, tiptoes away, nudges the back door open, and slips outside (said screwdriver never to be seen again). And where is the other dog, meanwhile? Perhaps she is at that very moment inside the hall closet dragging my new winter coat, with its deer-antler buttons, down from a hanger to the floor.

In some ways they are nice dogs. They are perfectly housebroken, as far as I can tell. They usually obey verbal instructions. They don't jump up. They don't destroy the furniture, although they could. They are sweet and gentle with the children. They are absolutely beautiful to look at. However, if the father of the family thinks I am going to change their mischievous ways in a weekend, he has another think coming. Besides, reforming the dogs might require some changes in the behavior of the humans. Here, I thought, is a household in which the song "Who Let the Dogs Out?" needs to be taken seriously.

That's not to say I get no training done at all. Late in the afternoon I notice that the dogs have been confined temporarily to two wire crates in the hall. Hmpf. Just where they belong, in my opinion. And it gives me the opportunity, if not to improve the dogs, at least to improve my own state of mind.

I get a clicker from my purse and some bits of cheese from the kitchen. I sit down on the floor in front of the two dogs in their crates. I'm waiting for some little move I can find a use for. The left-hand dog dips her head. Click. She moves a paw. Click. She tries again. Click. She makes the connection between click and treat and between her moves and my clicks. She begins raising her paw higher and dipping her head more. Clicking the direction of the moves, I soon have a dog that is lowering her head and putting her paw across her face. Perfect.

I move to the other dog and catch her turning her head sharply, perhaps because of some noise outside. A few clicks later, she is doing it on purpose, and I am able to add a cue. For both dogs, the cue is my shaking my index finger in front of their faces.

In the evening, when the family gathers in the living room before dinner, I get some more cheese and ask the dogs to come into the room. They sit nicely side by side in front of me, watching me attentively. "All right, dogs," I say sternly, shaking my finger in their faces. "Who chewed the deer-horn buttons off my *new winter coat*?" And one dog ducks her head and covers her eyes with her paw, while the other one looks quickly away over her shoulder. Guilty!

Some years later this story appeared in a magazine and I sent a copy to Kristina. She wrote me the denouement. The two dogs looked so much alike that I had never bothered to sort them out, nor had anyone else, apparently, except the children, of course. Then at the age of six or seven one of the dogs, Chloe, died of some cardiac disorder. And the troubles stopped. It became manifest that Chloe, and Chloe alone, had been the perpetrator of all the Dalmatian malfeasance. The remaining dog, Zelda, was a perfect angel, the dream dog of all time, and lives on yet, cherished and admired by all.

Chapter 5

Creativity

The Creative Dolphin Experiment

In the late 1960s we did an experiment at Sea Life Park that has become quite famous. We taught a dolphin to think up its own tricks. We didn't set out to do that; we just wanted to show our audiences the basics of dolphin training. But the animal gave us more; she proved to be not only creative, but an artist.

The participants in this adventure were me; Ingrid Kang Shallenberger, an animal behaviorist who was at this time my second-in-command in the training department; and Malia, the same Steno who stroked me on the arm to forgive my stupidity back when she was a newcomer.

Malia was now a star in our glass-walled tank in the Ocean Science Theater, demonstrating dolphin sonar, her jumping skills, and pretty much whatever we asked of her. One morning, when I am narrating and Ingrid is training the first show of the day, in front of an audience of several hundred people, we decide on the spot to demonstrate to the audience the heart of the training, the first steps of capturing and shaping a new behavior.

I explain what we're going to do. Ingrid lets Malia into the tank. Malia swims about, waiting for a cue, and then, getting none, slaps her tail on the water in annoyance. Ingrid captures that with a whistle, Malia does it again, and in a few minutes Malia is motoring herself across the tank with a series of fast tailslaps. The audience applauds.

In the next show, Malia, getting no cues, offers the tailslap. When that doesn't work either (it is no longer a new behavior) she gets mad enough to breach, and Ingrid selects that.

There are four shows a day. We find something new to select—a turn, a wave of a fin, sticking the head in the air, something different at least—in each show, for a couple of days. But then we begin to run out of normally occurring behaviors to capture; and shaping something totally from scratch, using a prop, say, doesn't fit the rules of our new game. We endure a couple of shows in which Malia, just as frustrated as we are, swims around trying all the things we'd already picked, without results. Darn! Maybe we'll have to give this idea up.

The fourth morning, when we arrive before the first show, Malia begins breaching in her tank. What is her problem?! The show starts and Ingrid lets Malia into the main tank. She swims around a little, waiting. When she is sure she isn't going to get any cues and it is up to her, Malia circles the tank once, building up speed. Then she rolls over on her back, sticks her big wide tail into the air, and coasts, without power, so to speak, about forty feet, from one side of the tank to the other. Look, Ma, no hands.

Ingrid and I and the audience, too, burst into laughter and applause. Malia has come up with something we have never seen another dolphin do, something she could not have practiced in her little holding tank, and something so amusing that we immediately add a cue to it and put it in the show. She has created a new behavior.

Malia continues coming up with new ideas, not in every show, but quite often. Sometimes, as on that first breakthrough day, when we first arrive in the morning, she breaches and tears around in her overnight quarters, bursting to try out something else she's invented. She thinks up wonderful things: all kinds of aerial flips and twirls; a beautiful upside-down jump, again something we've never seen or heard of a dolphin doing; a spiraling "corkscrew" swim underwater, revolving on her long axis as she circles the tank.

To me the most imaginative idea of all is Malia's art project. I didn't realize it, but the cement floor of the tank is covered with a thin layer of silt, settling out of the seawater that passes continuously through the system. But Malia knows about the silt. One day her new invention is this: she turns upside down, swims in circles above the bottom, and with the tip of her dorsal fin makes beautiful looping lines on the floor of the tank. Dolphin skin is thin and sensitive; you can draw blood with a fingernail. How Malia is able to create those long, graceful lines on cement without abrading the tip of her fin, I don't know; but dolphins have fabulous underwater balance; they are masters at knowing where they are in the water, and she manages well.

I invite scientist Gregory Bateson from the adjoining research institute to see Malia in action. He gets some Navy scientists interested in this example of dolphin cognitive abilities. The Office of Naval Research gives me the money to repeat the experiment. Luckily we have another female Steno, named Hou, at the Ocean Science Theater. Doing one session a day, in the early mornings before the park opens, Ingrid and I put Hou through roughly the same experience we'd given Malia, with two assistants collecting research data on every session so we can report exactly what happens.

Hou, too, eventually made the breakthrough, got the picture, and started inventing new behavior; but her creations were rather dull. Spitting. Nodding. A flip or two. Leaning her chin on the tank edge. Hou was able to innovate, but Hou was not Malia. Malia, face it, was an artist.

➤ **Watch the "Creative Porpoise Experiment" video in chapter 5 at www.reachingtheanimalmind.com.**

Gorillas

I wrote up a paper about these events, "The Creative Porpoise: Training for novel behavior," which appeared in the *Journal of Experimental Analysis of Behavior.* The U.S. Navy dolphin trainers began using creativity training to relax and refresh their dolphins after their research tasks. I also described the experiment in a book about my dolphin-training years, *Lads Before the Wind,* which brought it to the attention of people in the zoo world.

Zookeepers now use a version of the creativity experiment as a game for gorillas. They call it Show Me Something New. Here's a typical session, with an adolescent male who needs something to think about (besides new ways to get into trouble). The keeper says to the gorilla, "Show me something new." The gorilla waves a foot. The keeper clicks and treats, then again says, "Show me something new." The gorilla puts his arms over his head. The next time, he stands on all fours. Then he crosses his arms. Then he lies down. Click/treat for each new behavior. Then the gorilla starts to put his arms over his head again and looks chagrined. His facial expression is so clear—"Oh, no, I did that one"—that it makes the keeper laugh. The gorilla pulls his arms down and waves his hands instead.

Some gorillas can take the creativity game further than that. At Disney's Animal Kingdom in Orlando, Florida, the keepers invite me to see their daily training program. At the time of this visit, DAK has a gorilla family of seven. The keepers have developed a routine for briefly separating all the gorillas into individual quarters. Nine keepers are taking part in the maneuver this morning. Equipped with clickers and treats, they will open and shut doors and move the animals about in such a way that each one gets personal attention, some training, and (incidentally) a brief separation from the others. This daily exercise is actually preventive maintenance. If, someday, an animal must be isolated for medical treatment or removed from the group, that can be accomplished quietly during the routine training without throwing the whole gorilla family into a panic.

We all go together into the corridors that surround the gorilla family's indoor quarters. The head of the family is a big silverback named Gino; his training station, as befits his status, is right by the main entry door. We stop there, and the head keeper tells me to stay directly behind her. "Gino already knows you're here, and he'll be more comfortable if he can keep an eye on you," she says.

Gino sits peaceably at the bars, face-to-face with his trainer. The trainer runs through a few of what zoos call husbandry behaviors, trained responses that make his routine medical care easier, ranging from presenting a haunch for a practice injection to showing his healthy teeth. Gino obliges, receiving a click and a grape each time.

Meanwhile a young male is being shifted through the back of Gino's space, in through a door in one corner, out through a door in the other corner. It's always a slightly hazardous moment as, being temporarily alone together in one room, either male might take the opportunity to get in a whack at the other.

How do you prevent a four-hundred-pound gorilla from moving? The keeper gives Gino two wooden pegs to hold, each with a thick plywood disk around the middle, like the hilt of a sword. When Gino takes hold of his ends of the pegs, the keeper lets go of her ends. To earn his click, Gino has to hold the disks tight against the bars; if he lets go, the pegs will fall on the keeper's side. So he can't turn around and beat up the other guy passing behind him. Clever! Meanwhile, from his standpoint, holding his pegs is yet one more way to bend the keeper to his will and get her to give him another grape.

"Do you play Show Me Something New with him?" I ask.

"We already did that this morning," the keeper says, "but I'll try." She relieves Gino of his "hold still" props and says, "Show me something new." He claps his hands. Click/treat. She asks again. He waves a foot. Click/treat. She asks again, and this time he does something utterly amazing to me: he makes a face. He bulges his eyes, sticks out his enormous black tongue, and shakes both hands rapidly up and down beside his ears. It is fleeting, over in a second. It is hilarious. It is almost unbelievable.

I have often seen and enjoyed moments of facial expression in animals, but this was a little different. I'd never seen an animal make a *joke* face before. Did Gino really make up that funny face on his own, or did he copy it from someone? I ask the head keeper. "Oh, he made it up," she says. "He does that all the time. He made up a different new face yesterday, opening his mouth really wide and clapping his hands. He's just a fun-loving guy," she adds fondly.

I was washed with a curious sensation. I am used to thinking of animals as individuals, which of course they are; but this is a little different. A *person* is inside that huge creature; a primitive one, but a person. Furthermore, he's a comedian.

➤ Watch the "Gorilla Game" video in chapter 5 at www.reachingtheanimalmind.com.

101 Things to Do with a Box: Creative Dogs

One can see how a game demanding novelty might work well with noticeably intelligent animals, such as dolphins and gorillas. But do you really think you could train innovative behavior in more ordinary animals, such as dogs? I thought not, for many years.

Oops! Wrong again. As clicker training spread, the dog trainers were teaching dogs to be creative. A group of trainers in Virginia thought it up first. Based on a joke about Stenos in my book *Lads Before the Wind,* they called their version of the game 101 Things to Do with a Box.

You put a cardboard box on the floor and click for any interaction the dog has with the box: looking at it, approaching it, sniffing, pawing, touching it, and so on. By choosing what to click, you can strengthen an action. You might get the dog to pick up the box and carry it around, or to flip the box upside down, or to shove it around the room. You could shape the behavior of standing inside the box. That's an easy goal if the box is a cardboard carton and the dog is a nimble fox terrier, but more of a challenge if the box is a shoe box and the dog is a German shepherd.

The box game has spread over the Internet to dog trainers all over the world. I cherish a series of photographs from England of a twelve-year-old schipperke, a small, black, barge-guarding dog from Holland, playing this game. The dog's name is Peggy, and Peggy's owner is using the challenging gorilla version of the game: after every single click, the dog must change the behavior to something new.

Out on the lawn in the sunshine, with a cardboard packing box in front of her, the little black dog offers and gets paid for one different behavior after another. She noses the box, bumps the box, steps on the box, stands on the box, jumps on the box, jumps off the box, goes inside the box. For the final behavior she lies down beside the box. Schipperkes are in my experience rather solemn little souls. What makes the photos moving, to me, is the dog's radiant, laughing face; this is *so much fun.* The photos don't show us the owner, but I bet the owner is laughing, too.

➤ **Watch the "Peggy's Box Game" slide show in chapter 5 at www.reachingtheanimalmind.com.**

A lot of conventional dog training is aimed at suppressing spontaneous actions. The aim is to give control to the owner. The ideal result is a dog that does just what it's told to do and no more. The box game is especially valuable in loosening up these traditionally trained dogs—retired police dogs, for example—and teaching them to interact more informally. When you bring initiative back into the picture and make it rewardable, you get a different sort of animal: confident, focused, cheerful, and relaxed. And the experience is *fun.*

People aren't quite used to animals that can combine self-control with fun. In the middle of teaching a big two-day seminar on clicker training in England, I drag a chair onto the stage, describe the creativity game, and ask if someone from the audience wants to demonstrate the game using this chair. A woman volunteers and comes onstage with a border collie. I let the audience suggest the behavior. We decide the dog should crawl through the legs of the chair from one side to the other.

The owner takes off the dog's leash and waits. The dog looks at the chair: click/treat. The dog goes over to the chair at once and nudges it with his nose. Click/treat. That tells the dog that the game has something to do with the chair. The dog puts a paw on the chair. No click. The dog puts both paws on the chair. The dog goes around the chair. The dog jumps up on the chair. The dog jumps down. The dog stands up and puts his paws on the back of the chair. Nothing.

The dog looks at the owner. The owner is motionless—still waiting, clicker and treats in hand. The dog goes back to work, guessing and trying different things to do with the chair. The audience becomes restless, then noisy: "Help the poor dog!" "Show it what to do!" "Stop this!"

The dog, as far as I can see, is enjoying the puzzle; it doesn't slow down a bit. "It's her dog," I say. "She knows how long the dog is willing to work. Let her decide." A cross-brace is between the two back legs of the chair, a few inches under the seat. The dog sticks his nose under the seat, between the seat and the brace. Click/treat. Immediately the dog does that again. Nothing.

The dog pauses, then lowers his head a couple of inches and sticks his nose beneath the brace, instead of between the brace and the seat of the chair. Click! Two click/treats in a row, after all that effort! The dog's tail begins to swing gently. "I'm getting closer!"

He collects his treat, comes back to the chair, and sticks his head all the way under the brace. Click. Now the dog can see through the legs and under the chair. Instead of going back to the owner to collect the treat for that click, he scuttles under the whole chair (hearing another click). He comes out the other side, prancing, tail waving like a flag: "That was it! I got it!" He is greeted by the owner's smile, a big treat, and a roar of applause from the audience. This dog, by experimenting creatively, has won the challenge, and his exhilaration shows.

But why do this with dogs? More than a few dog trainers have told me that playing the box game with dogs is pointless; it's artificial in the first place, and it might teach the dog to be unpredictable, the last thing you want from your police dog or your hunting dog or even your household pet. Besides, regardless of how far one can "push" the animal with training, isn't this all rather unnatural, a human-induced distortion of normal animal behavior? Why not let the animal live a more undisturbed, "normal" life?

I think that's a rather sentimental view of what's normal. From the evolutionary standpoint, if many animals, when "pushed" this way, seem to be able to think and experiment and explore, then certainly the capacity is genetic and occurs for a reason. Maybe it happens in the wild, sometimes even routinely, and we just don't know about it. Maybe the box game is just one way to get a look into an already-existing mental capacity of animals.

The Fish

Let's consider that upset fish. The fish, his video chores completed, becomes part of my household. He grows to the size of my hand. I get him a fifty-gallon tank and set it up at the entrance to the living room. The fish hangs out in the middle of his tank and watches everything that happens. He likes to play. If visiting children put their noses against the glass, the fish puts his nose against theirs on the other side. If they put their hands on the glass, he will put his nose to hands, too. They can get him to swim back and forth by putting their hands on one end of the tank, then the other. Sometimes I let the children feed the fish a snail. He crunches it up in the gular jaws inside his throat (you can hear that through the glass), then flushes the bits of shell out his gills, a thrillingly revolting event.

The fish likes to have his own way. Sometimes, if you walk by without giving him something to eat or at least looking at him, the fish jumps up and slams into the tank cover hard enough to make a clatter and splash water on the living room rug. That usually makes you turn around and come back, of course reinforcing future similar displays of temper.

Hardwired vs. Softwired

I know the fish likes worms and snails, but I sometimes give him beetles and other oddities, just to see what his limits are. Once, I offered the fish a woolly caterpillar. Some of these caterpillars have irritating hairs. This one doesn't bother my hands, so I assume it is safe for him, but the fish feels otherwise. Fishermen like to say that fish don't feel pain, but I no longer believe that. The fish takes the caterpillar in his mouth, startles, spits it out, and rushes frantically to the bottom to rub his gaping mouthparts against the stones and gravel. Ouch! That was unpleasant. He will never eat one of those things again!

For any species to survive, some behaviors must be carried out in a certain way, while others can be acquired by trial and error. While the fish was willing to gamble on caterpillars, when I present him with a (dead and destingered) wasp, with its distinctive yellow-and-black warning coloration, he responds with fear, turning pale and hiding behind a rock until I take the wasp away. Fear of wasps is hardwired.

From an evolutionary standpoint, hardwiring is costly. Once something has been programmed in and happens automatically, it's hard to change, even if the environment changes and the old program becomes a handicap. Nature's way around that is to hardwire only those things that are absolutely life-threatening and to leave as much as possible softwired. This is true of people, too. Swallow something the wrong way and you will cough and choke it back up; that's hardwired, you don't have a choice. Take in something that tastes bitter, and you might swallow it once, by accident, but you'll learn not to put it in your mouth again; nature can leave you to discover on your own most of the things that are not good to eat.

Programming a fish to "know" without previous experience the edibility of every single insect in the Amazon that might fall in its pool would be unwieldy and, really, unnecessary. The fish had to learn about caterpillars, but he "knew" about lethally venomous wasps. For those, the fish has a built-in warning system, not unlike some people's hardwired fear of snakes and spiders. It is a function not of intelligence but of genes and evolution.

When the fish, once the size of a matchbook, arrives to full adulthood, about five by eight inches and weighing perhaps a pound, it becomes easy to imagine him in his natural habitat somewhere in the Amazon River drainage. At this age he might be owner and king of a little pool of his own, root-walled, tree-shaded, lined with dead leaves that he matches perfectly in coloring. He might have a book-sized female sharing his den, and, once a year or so, a hundred or more little babies to herd and tend.

For at least part of the year his pool would connect with a larger stream or flooded area from which trouble could come: big vegetarian fishes that might dig up his nest; nosy, white river dolphins that might eat a fish his size. Lots of intruders could attack his babies. During times of low water, predators could also come from overhead, such as herons and ocelots (who are fishing cats). A fish has to be on guard.

Perhaps a fish like this one, with many responsibilities, has to be able to adapt, and perhaps to do more than adapt, to innovate.

Of course I taught this fish to learn; I trained this fish to make humans deliver. But did that create some kind of unnatural überfish, tainted by its long contact with humans? I think not. Playing, as the fish did with children, is probably a possibility for fish, or at least some fish; other fish clicker trainers are reporting what looks like play. On the other hand, training one's human to stop and say hello, by making noise and splashing water on the human's carpet, is not just innate; it's creative. Though a lot of fish behavior is hardwired, maybe even a fish has plenty of options.

The Polar Bear

It is my youngest grandson Nathaniel's sixth birthday, and his mother, my daughter, Gale, has agreed to take everybody to the zoo. As guests Nattie has commandeered his older brothers, Max and Wylie; his friend Tayla; and me, Grandma Karen. We like the giraffes and the elephants and the thorny devil (an Indonesian insect), but the hit of the day is indubitably the baby female polar bear.

When we get to the bear enclosure, the huge mama polar bear is snoozing on the rocks. The baby bear is in the pool. The pool has an underwater viewing area. We rush to the tunnel to see the baby swimming. The baby bear is underwater, looking through the glass at some children sitting on the floor. Nat and Tayla sit down with the others, noses and hands on the glass. The baby bear comes over to these newcomers, turns herself upside down in the water, and puts her nose against Nat's nose. Then she puts her nose against Tayla's hand. Tayla puts both hands flat on the glass. The bear turns herself right-side up and puts her own big paws flat against Tayla's hands, on the other side. This bear is playing 101 Things to Do with an Audience!

Now and then the bear has to go up and get a breath. Like a click and treat, that provides a sort of break in the action. Each time the bear dives down again, she does something new. She tries blowing different amounts of bubbles. She makes noises. She follows a moving child. She pokes at the children with her paw. Once she hangs from the pool ledge by her back feet for a while, her back against the glass, looking over her shoulder upside down.

Gale crouches down to the glass next to the children. The bear immediately rushes at her sufficiently aggressively to make her jump back involuntarily. "That's a great behavior," I joke. "Get Mom!" The bear cub likes it, too, because she goes on a riff of play attack. She rushes at a wadded-up shirt in a child's lap. Other kids immediately produce wadded-up garments and the bear darts at those. One boy unfolds a zoo map and spreads it on the glass. The bear feigns an attack on that, this time with an audible underwater growl (parents began to worry whether the glass is really thick enough).

By and by the bear tires of the children and leaves the window. We go outdoors again, to the top of the pool. The baby bear is now at the surface, practicing a maneuver that in my high school water-ballet days was called the submarine. Holding one hind paw up into the air like a periscope, the bear is slowly traveling in a circle underwater, keeping only that one furry foot above the surface.

This big baby bear has come up with approximately sixty behaviors in about ten minutes, about half of which involve getting the kids doing something, too. Part of being a successful polar bear must include developing initiative, imagination, flexibility of mind and body—and a sense of humor. That's what this baby is working on. Here is a wild animal, captive born but not trained, and she's exercising exactly the capacities that we bring out in other animals by playing the creative-training game.

The Creative Horse

Well, of course a polar bear needs a brain. It's a predator; it has to outwit its prey. Some people maintain that prey animals, therefore, such as cattle, horses, and sheep, have no need for this level of adaptability. Their food is easy to find, it's right under their feet, and all they have to do is eat it. Their one defense is flight; they don't need to think about that, either. Horse trainers, particularly, love this piece of sophistry. Since horses are prey animals, the theory goes, they can't learn from being given food; avoiding danger is the only thing they can really understand. Therefore, food-based clicker training might work for dogs, but not horses. Reactive, unthinking prey animals that they are, you have to train horses by dominance and, if necessary, force.

People are clicker-training horses all over the world now, so the horse punishers' plausible faux science is moot. But could horses be creative? Again, my first feeling is no, not horses. They can be taught, of course, without punishment, to do things horses don't normally do, as did my surfing ponies; but thinking up new games on their own? I thought not. But a horse, a very small horse, showed me that I was still being an interspecies snob.

Miniature horses are a special breed. Most of them are about the size of a large dog. Like some large dogs, they make great guides for blind people. How can that be? Well, first, yes, they can be housebroken. Like a dog, a horse can learn where and when to relieve itself, and how to signal when it needs to go out. A horse can easily learn to carry out all the functions of a guide dog: watching traffic; stopping and alerting the owner at curbs, steps, and stairs; avoiding obstacles; staying quietly next to the owner in restaurants and other public spaces; and so on. A miniature guide horse can ride in cars and on trains, and sometimes they are allowed on planes. And here's the money part. Miniature horses live a lot longer than dogs. Once trained, a guide dog has six or seven years left before it is too old to work. The owner of a guide *horse,* however, can expect to enjoy the services of this faithful friend for twenty years or more.

The guide horse I know personally is a black-and-white mare named Panda. She belongs to Ann Edy, a college professor in New York State who has been blind since birth.

Ann has owned several guide dogs during her life. She finds Panda to be more competent than any of her dogs. Panda never misses even difficult-to-see overhead obstacles such as dangling wires. Panda is also extremely good at predicting potentially hazardous movements of cars. I have seen Panda stop Ann at a curb when a car, driven by Ann's husband, as a training exercise, suddenly stops and backs up. Panda halts abruptly and backs up herself, telling Ann they cannot yet proceed. Then when the hazard is past and the pair do go forward, Panda tosses her head and prances a little. "I guessed *that* right!"

➤ **Watch the "Panda the Guide Horse in Action" video in chapter 5 at www.reachingtheanimalmind.com.**

Panda and ClickerExpo

In the early 1990s I started a business called Sunshine Books to publish and sell information about clicker training. Alexandra Kurland, who pioneered clicker training for horses and trained Panda to be a guide horse for Ann, became one of my first authors.

Other authors followed. My little company grew. The business I had started in my home, selling clicker-training books and videos on the Internet, became a corporation in the Boston area, with offices, employees, and wholesale customers. When a national chain store picked up some of our products and ordered items not by the dozen but by the thousands, I realized I was out of my depth, businesswise. Friends introduced me to a young business consultant, Aaron Clayton, with considerable experience in making small companies grow. Aaron started as my consultant, became the president of and then a partner in the business, and rapidly the company was not only profitable but expanding in new directions.

The more people learned about clicker training, the more they wanted to be taught, not through books and videos, but by live teachers with advanced skills. The company, now called Karen Pryor's Clicker Training (KPCT), began meeting this need by hosting a series of conferences called ClickerExpo, in which well-known operant trainers presented a wide range of lectures and hands-on workshops twice a year to the general public in various locations across the United States. Along with scientists; dog, cat, and bird trainers; and experts from zoos and oceanariums, Alexandra Kurland became one of our regular presenters, lecturing on marker-based positive training for horses.

In 2005, while we hosted ClickerExpo in Newport, Rhode Island, Alexandra Kurland brought her student Ann Edy and her clicker-trained guide animal, Panda. Four hundred human attendees and about a hundred and fifty dogs (and a few cats, rabbits, birds, and other clicker-trained beings) have pretty much taken over an elegant waterfront hotel. The assembled trainers are awed by Panda's calmness as she guides Ann through crowds and halls and past all sorts of dogs (some of which are distinctly upset at discovering a horse in a hotel). People enjoy Ann's eloquent comments on Panda's skills, and on the many ways Panda shows Ann that she is happy, from her greeting whicker in the morning to her happy gamboling on the lawn in the evenings. At the Saturday-night autograph party Panda even signs her own picture book, *Panda: A Guide Horse for Ann*, with a little, inky front hoof.

After the conference the fifteen members of the ClickerExpo faculty, including Alexandra and Ann, have gathered for a private meeting to plan next year's programs and to share news and events. Alexandra and Ann put on a demonstration we can all participate in, a game that Panda created.

The Panda Game

Each of us gets a handful of Panda treats: bean-sized alfalfa pellets, much enjoyed by horses. Alexandra shows us all how to make a click sound with our mouths and how to hold the treat out under Panda's mouth so she can eat it without nipping a finger by mistake. Alex spreads us out into a circle, about six feet apart. "What do we do now?" someone asks. "Panda will show you," Alex says, removing Panda's guide harness. She tells Panda to start playing.

In a businesslike way Panda sets off for the first person on her left, Emma Parsons. She circles Emma, comes up alongside in "guide horse" position, and halts. Emma's response is instant: click, treat. Panda then briskly moves to the next person, comes up alongside, and again earns a click and a treat. The third person is Britisher Kay Laurence. This time Panda comes in and halts at a forty-five-degree angle instead of straight. Kay instantly steps sidewise. "None of that carelessness from you, my girl." Panda corrects her own position just as quickly and gets a click and a treat.

Panda goes on around the circle, methodically getting each person to click and treat. Then she starts around the circle a second time. When Panda stops beside Ken Ramirez, marine mammal expert and training director of the Shedd Aquarium, Ken takes a step forward and stops. She matches him exactly with her own steps. Click/treat. When she gets to me, three people later, I try two steps forward. Panda comes forward with the precision of a high-scoring obedience dog. Click/treat. Then she comes to Aaron Clayton, president of our corporation. Ever the risk-taker, Aaron takes six steps forward. Instead of going with him, Panda tosses her head, switches her tail, and trots away across the circle to join Kay Laurence instead. Everyone laughs.

Panda begins crisscrossing the circle, choosing whom she will play with next. Those who are chosen began asking for more behavior—backing up a step, say—but tactfully, since we have now witnessed Panda's ability to express her opinion. Panda seems to prefer the most skilled trainers, but she also occasionally joins up with someone for whom this is new. She gives Aaron another chance. He takes her a modest two steps forward and clicks. Panda accepts her treat and moves on. Something about her compressed lips catches my eye: Does she look just a little smug?

Gradually people run out of treats and begin leaving the circle. Ken Ramirez and I are walking back to the meeting table together when Panda barges between us, circles behind Ken, and actually herds him back into the game. Ken, gently jostled by this determined little creature, looks at me with awe on his face: "I feel so flattered!" "Indeed, you should!" I tell him; and Alexandra gives Ken a few more pellets so he can play another round or two of the Panda game. Panda uses her brains every day in her job. Creativity is not just a possibility for Panda; it's her métier. Panda's game has earned from all of us not just our affection but our respect.

Chapter 6

Attachments

Animal Friends

We are a little presumptuous about individual friendships and preferences among our domestic animals. We assume that because we like each and every animal, they must like each other. A common complaint of pet owners is that they added a new cat or dog to the household and friction ensued. These two dogs hate each other. This young cat is pouncing on the old, tired cat with ever-increasing glee. What can the behaviorist or trainer do to stop that? While I sympathize with the issue, I sometimes sympathize more with the pets. Who asked them if they liked this new individual? Perhaps they were never meant to be friends.

Of course our domestic animals can indeed form intense attachments, not just with us (as we perennially hope and assume) but with other animals, both within and across species. Animals, like people, have preferences for other individuals that can only partly be explained by reinforcement, and for which we have no particular evolutionary explanation.

In about 1985 I acquired my first border terrier, named Skookum (a Northwest Indian word meaning "sturdy and useful but not beautiful"). When Skookum was just a puppy, he spent an afternoon playing with a half-grown German shepherd named Orca. A few months later Orca and her owner visited my house, and Skookum and Orca played again. That was it: two encounters. About three years later, I took Skookum to a lecture by a visiting dog trainer. The room was jammed with people and dogs. Skookum, normally respectably behaved in public, suddenly went berserk, pulling on his leash, whining, jumping up and down, trying desperately to get me to take him to something across the room.

"Look, it's Orca, Orca's here!" Indeed it was Orca. Orca was now a big, grown-up search-and-rescue shepherd, looking very different from herself when younger. Alas, she had zero time for him now; but Skookum, in spite of their minimal contact, would never forget her.

Back in Hawaii, one of my Welsh pony broodmares, Lyric, had several foals for me. Her first was a dark dappled bay filly I named Sonnet. When Sonnet was three years old, I sent her to California to show and sell. She was a sturdy, cobby Welsh with a pretty face and a fine big trot: the ideal pony, I thought. I did not know that the fashion in California was for longer necks and more hock action; no one bought her. I left her there with other breeders for a year or so, then brought her back to Hawaii to join my broodmare band again.

When Sonnet was unloaded from the truck, her mother, Lyric, two fields away, set up a tremendous uproar of screams and whinnying. Lyric had seen her second and third offspring come and go with aplomb. Her handsome son Telstar was probably in plain sight, another two fields over. Apparently, however, Lyric was strongly attached to this daughter. The two were reunited, with great joy and nickering from Lyric (and considerably less emotion on Sonnet's part).

Emotional attachments can happen between captive animals in zoos and oceanariums but are not always apparent until one of the animals is gone. At Disney's Animal Kingdom, the daily exercise of separating the gorilla family paid off when two adolescent males, who, in the wild, would soon be wanting to leave their natal band anyway, were sent to another zoo to join a different gorilla family. Separation went smoothly, as did the crating and shipping; at least one of the youngsters reportedly played clicker games with his keeper through the crate walls to pass the time on the airplane trip. The young males seemed to be delighted with their new family and fit right in; but back at Animal Kingdom the mother of one of them cried for four days.

We can accept that biologically determined ties exist in animals.

We don't feel surprised when a cow bellows for her weaned calf for a day and a night. We tell ourselves, however, that this distress, whatever its nature, is short-lived, and therefore not at all like human grief. My feeling is that emotion is emotion—handed out to different species in differing amounts, perhaps, but causing the same internal sensations while it lasts. We assume that the animal feels no real pain because it soon forgets. Is that true? Skookum and Lyric did not forget.

In Germany some years ago, a group of cattle, by some rich owner's whim, were allowed to simply exist and reproduce with no individuals being removed. Ethologists studied this herd for years, tracking the behavior and associations of individuals. One discovery was that the cows had particular friends, often (as with humans) dating back to their "school years." When they were all calves together, female calves associated closely with some age-mates and avoided others; and those friendships (and antagonisms) persisted throughout life. Isn't that a lot like people? Your best friend from the third grade may still be someone you enjoy; and the children you didn't feel close to then, you might not have much in common with now, either.

The attachment between cow and calf might also not always be as transitory as we like to suppose. Another interesting finding from that cattle-herd study concerned the dominant bull. In this undisturbed herd the lead bull was not purchased from elsewhere as bulls usually are, but arose to his position after growing up in the herd. The investigators noticed that this bull always grazed around midday next to one particular cow. Why? His favorite in the harem? Not at all. Turns out he was in the habit of having lunch with his mother.

Romance

While some mammals, birds, and fish form strong pair bonds that can last for years, even lifetimes, in most species sexual behavior is not necessarily based on individual relationships. Whales and dolphins, for example, do not typically form male-female pair bonds. In some species, one or a few mature males live among the females and the young and do all the breeding. In other species, females and males normally live in separate groups, meeting up only in the breeding season. Sexual encounters may involve a conflict between males and also aggression toward females. For example, ethologists in Australia have seen male bottlenose dolphins form temporary "alliances" of three or four males that actually abduct females by force from their all-female bands and steal them away for days at a time.

Sea Life Park offered one sole exception to this general plan: Hoku and Kiko. Their strong attachment was visible from the beginning. They swam "holding hands." They ignored all other companions. They enjoyed a decorous and on the whole private love life (only once, as far as I know, did they decide to copulate during a show).

Hoku and Kiko performed four times daily in the Ocean Science Theater, circling inside the glass walls while taking a series of hurdles in unison, demonstrating their speed and agility. As they dove down deep after each hurdle, then turned upward for the next jump, three beautiful lines of tiny bubbles streamed from the tips of their dorsal and pectoral fins, making long, waving lines around the glass tank, showing clearly how their sleek forms could shed turbulence better than any submarine.

When they got their whistle and fish at the end, Hoku was downright chivalrous to Kiko. Normally if a fish falls between two dolphins, the boldest animal grabs it at once. However, if a fish fell between Hoku and Kiko, he ceded it to her immediately, something absolutely unprecedented.

The finale of the spotter section of the show was Hoku's jump through a hoop high above the water surface. As he made the jump, he got a whistle and a scattered jackpot of several fish, in which Kiko, naturally, shared. If he missed the hoop, as he sometimes did, earning no whistle and no fish, Kiko would burst into disagreeable squawking sounds, shake her open jaws up and down, and chase Hoku around the tank. The audience always roared at this wifely snit, which they could not only see but hear through built-in underwater microphones.

Their romance ended when Kiko died suddenly, overnight, from an unsuspected kidney infection. For a week Hoku swam in a slow circle with both eyes shut, as if unwilling to look on a world that did not contain Kiko. Out of sympathy we gave him a new companion, a young female spotter named Lei. Lei joined up with Hoku immediately, swimming beside him but deferentially, a few inches behind. Hoku permitted that, but he never paid her any attention, then or later; and for many days he continued to keep the eye on Lei's side shut.

Hoku's behavior with Lei was quite typical of spotters in general. One of their oddest characteristics was an extreme standoffishness to strangers. They weren't aggressive; they just declined to associate. Even with a member of their own species, they could be snobs; it was as if they preferred to be alone rather than forced to swim with an unsuitable companion. I don't know that it was a question of like or dislike. It was more as if, like humans from some long-standing aristocracy, spotted dolphins are governed by rules more stringent than those of more ordinary beings. What in the world, I wondered, were their social arrangements in the wild? I would, in fact, have a chance to see for myself.

Seeing Spotters

Some years after I had left Hawaii and moved to New York, the National Marine Fisheries Service hired me to do some research on the behavior of dolphins caught in the nets of tuna-fishing boats. The American purse-seining tuna fleet had discovered that in the tropical Pacific off Mexico and Central America, valuable yellowfin and skipjack tuna often swim with schools of spinner and spotter dolphins. They began catching the tuna by encircling the dolphins with huge nets, called purse seines, drawing (or pursing) the bottom of the net shut, then letting the dolphins out over the top of the net and bringing just the tuna on board.

Initially the dolphin mortality was high. Animals that were not used to barricades could get a tooth or a fin caught in the netting and be unable to escape. Sometimes the nets closed across the top, drowning whole schools at once. The public outcry was enormous.

Ban the fishery! That was the first popular idea; but that was not a good solution. The Marine Mammal Protection Act could, of course, be used to stop American boats from fishing in this way; but fishing is a planetary business these days. Other fleets could and would move in, fleets over which the United States would have no control at all. A more realistic plan seemed to be to reduce mortality by designing ways to release the dolphins safely, then to share that technology with everyone doing this kind of fishing, using trade agreements and onboard observers to enforce compliance.

That is more or less what happened. By the time I got involved as a researcher, the mechanics of the problem had largely been solved. New net designs, new training for skippers and crews, new regulations, and new international agreements had made life a lot safer for the dolphins. Boats could fish all year and never drown a single dolphin.

But the Marine Mammal Commission was still worried. Although for some years the fleet had been successful in releasing dolphins unharmed, and dolphin reproductive rates seemed normal again, the populations were not rebounding as they should.

What was happening? Perhaps the dolphins were being stressed so severely that although they looked unharmed, they were succumbing later from shock, after their apparently safe release. But how could you tell if they were *that* scared? Government-agency scientists decided that someone would have to go and look.

No one knew more about the behavior of spotters and spinners than Ingrid Kang Shallenberger and I. My children were grown and flown, I was presently unattached, and my business plans were far in the future. I agreed to be principal investigator for an at-sea study of what the spinners and spotters were doing in the nets; and Ingrid agreed to come with me.

Ingrid and I would go aboard the tuna clipper *Queen Mary,* a ship specially fitted out to carry scientists as well as crew, for a month of fishing. We would be diving inside the vast net every time it was set, looking at the dolphins underwater.

I was worried, of course. I hate going to sea. I can't think why I've ended up doing it so often. In my experience, life on the open ocean is tedious, uncomfortable, and dangerous. This kind of fishing takes place a long way out in the eastern tropical Pacific, fifteen hundred miles from land. No friendly Coast Guard helicopter can evacuate you if, say, you break a leg or are bitten by a shark. Even the best of fishing boats (and the *Queen Mary* was a 180-foot beauty) have been known to sink. Even if nothing went wrong, we might never get close enough to the dolphins to see anything. And as some government bureaucrat saw fit to warn me, fishing crews had not always been cordial to visiting scientists, a fatiguing possibility.

I was, however, wildly excited about what I might learn. I was not concerned about answering the government's question of how scared the dolphins were; we'd know that at a glance. But I had that consuming personal question about the spotted dolphins. Scientists reported, and aerial photographs confirmed, that spotter dolphins sometimes gather in schools of thousands of animals. How on earth could they do that?

Ken Norris and others had discovered in Hawaii that spinner schools are fluid, with individuals and groups merging and separating easily from one day to another in the wild, just as they did in our tanks and pools. I could imagine spinners traveling with jillions of other spinners and not minding a bit if they were with strangers or friends. But how could spotters, these snobbish, clannish animals, *possibly* live in the schools of thousands reported on the tuna-fishing grounds? Maybe we could find out.

Thousand-hour Eyeballs

We were at sea for nearly a month. We didn't drown, we didn't get eaten by sharks, and no one on the vessel got seriously injured. Contrary to that bureaucrat's warnings, the skipper and crew were wonderful to us, treating us like favorite aunts or cousins, taking an interest in our work, and helping us whenever they could.

Our research task was a striking example of the value of using two behavioral viewpoints, that of the ethologist and that of the behaviorist, interactively. Ethologist George Schaller has written that to really understand what an animal is doing, you need thousand-hour eyeballs; that is, you must watch the animals for that long before trying to draw conclusions. As ethologists, Ingrid and I had the necessary thousand-hour eyeballs for these dolphin species; in fact, we probably had ten-thousand-hour eyeballs. As trainers, we also had thousands of hours of experience with these same species; and as trainers we had learned to understand and translate social signals such as a breach or a gape or a particular whistle. In our limited time at sea we could never have identified the social roles and relationships of spotted dolphins had we not already been looking at the animals' behaviors from both viewpoints simultaneously.

I think also that we could never have come to understand the remarkable role of the spotter males had we not also been exposed, through the training interchanges, to their specific limitations. These animals are not creative, innovative experimenters like Stenos and bottlenoses, but rather the opposite. They don't like change or novelty. They don't play with objects as bottlenoses do. They adapt themselves to novel circumstances with difficulty. Only because we knew them so well were we able to spot the places where the wild dolphins, especially the adult males, transcended those limitations and did things that were not only creative but positively heroic.

In the end, we solved three mysteries: whether the dolphins were being scared to death; how spotted dolphins manage to keep themselves united with acceptable friends in spite of being jumbled into huge aggregations of thousands and tens of thousands; and finally, a small but niggling mystery: how come Hoku and Kiko, members of a species that *never* pair-bonds, fell so totally in love?

Into the Net

We have traveled for days. Now we are fishing, and the vessel has set the net. It's early morning and flat calm. Ingrid and I are out in the net, floating and snorkeling next to our little inflatable Avon boat. We're each wearing mask, snorkel, and flippers, and, at the skipper's orders, jeans and long-sleeved dark shirts over our bathing suits, to cover flashing white arms and legs that might attract sharks. We're each carrying an underwater plastic slate on which to jot down the data we will take.

The water is an abyssal dark blue from the surface, and nearly transparent from below. Visibility is fabulous, the best I've ever experienced; it feels as if you could see forever. The temperature is blissfully warm; we could stay in for hours, but about one hour is all the time we'll get.

Each time the net is put in the ocean, the whole procedure of setting the net is the same. It must be deployed in a circle, pursed or pulled shut at the bottom, then slowly winched back aboard the ship, run up to a pulley high above the deck, and stacked neatly at the stern, ready for the next setting of the net. The huge net, half a mile long and six hundred feet deep, is heavy, and even heavier when wet. Once it's in the water, the boat is completely immobilized until most of the net is back on board. Each complete set and recovery of the net takes a couple of hours, sometimes longer. Ingrid and I are allowed in the net from the time that the entire net is in the water until the release of the dolphins, about an hour.

Toward the end of the set, if there were tuna in this particular set, the last bit of the net in the water forms a sack packed with fish (and sometimes a shark or two). The crew will use scoop nets to bail the fish out of that sack and into the icy brine in the hold of the *Queen Mary.* The speedboats will be winched back aboard, the fishermen will clean the ship, and the hunt will start again. On our voyage the *Queen Mary* made a total of seventeen sets.

Now, at the start of our time in the water on this set, we are floating about thirty feet away from a school of sixty spotted dolphins. They are not in the least upset. Some are resting at the surface, with just their blowholes out. Some are swimming slowly up and down in a sort of vertical column. Some are circling quietly around that column in little groups.

Every spotter school consists of several kinds of subgroups. In front of me right now is the simplest kind of subgroup: a female and her calf. The mother and baby are playing, touching noses and exchanging pats with their pectoral fins. I'm taking what's called a focal animal sample, recording on my slate every behavior I observe during five-minutes using the computer-friendly code we've devised: BR (breathe), DV (dive), PTB (pat baby), PTM (pat mama), and so on. These five-minute samples of the behavior of many different animals will give us data that can be analyzed and used to back up descriptions of what we say we saw.

Philippe Vergne, a tuna-industry biologist who has kindly become our boat handler, is patiently sitting next to the outboard motor in the Avon, amid our piles of data slates. Lifting my head from the water to deposit a completed slate and pick up a new one, I can see the white hull of the *Queen Mary* on the far side of the net. The net is huge, and the boat is far away. I can just make out the husky form of Chapo the cook leaning on the railing, looking at us through binoculars. He has been assigned to keep watch over us whenever we are in the net. Over the water (and under it, too) comes the noise of the engines and winches as the net is slowly being pursed and brought aboard.

Between focal animal samples, Ingrid and I take a few moments to visit some adult animals nearby that are completely at rest, rafted together at the surface with their blowholes in the air and their tails hanging down. We touch them, peer under them to confirm their sexes, even stroke them. They regard us calmly—no whites of the eyes showing, no chuffing breath; they are just looking us over, too.

I notice that one big male has several brown, jelly-bean-shaped organisms, probably parasitic copepods, attached to the trailing edge of his pectoral fin by thin, black stems. That must be a nuisance, I think, and try to pull one of them off. Ouch! Those wiry stems are rooted tight. The big male flinches, gives me an annoyed glance, and moves away. He doesn't mind my being next to him, or even petting him, but he can do without my well-meant veterinary attentions!

The Clan

We have already pinned down an important fact: spotters are divided into five basic kinds of subgroups, and every spotter school contains at least four of them. The first and smallest are mother-baby pairs. Then there are mother-young subgroups, consisting of three or four adult females, assorted young, and sometimes a larger, darker grandma: the playground set. In a miscellaneous, loosely swimming tumble of spotted-all-over young adults, a lot of casual, shifting interactions go on: the bar scene. Some schools have one or more groups of four or five little juveniles with few spots (probably males) that swim in tight formation all by themselves, acting like miniature senior males. Then there are the senior-male squads, the most conspicuous individuals in every school.

Adult males are easy to distinguish; besides being heavier through the shoulders than the females, they have a ridge under the tail section, called a postanal keel, obvious from the side view. The senior males are also the biggest and the darkest. The school that Ingrid and I are diving in this morning has three of these senior-male squads. They swim shoulder to shoulder, in tight formation and in unison. Wherever they go, the other dolphins quietly open up space and let them through. They have an air of menace, with their heavy shoulders, dark coloring, black masks, and the eerie precision of their swimming. Nevertheless, the menace has a sort of comic-opera feel. A squad may split off and zoom across the net in tight formation like fighter planes, prompting one to expect some kind of attack—but no. They're just checking out a weather instrument that's been lowered into the water. Having spiraled around it, they peel away in four directions and reunite in tight formation, again looking just like fighter planes in an air show, then come sedately back to the rest of the school.

As I'm taking data on my plastic slate, two of these gangs, circling in opposite directions, meet face-to-face right in front of me. They stop, open their mouths, shake their tooth-lined jaws rapidly up and down, and exchange furious bursts of insulting sounds. Then, honor apparently having been served, one squad goes down a little, the other crosses over them, and both groups proceed quietly on their way. I am not alarmed in the slightest: nobody is really angry and this ritual has nothing to do with me.

Releasing the Dolphins

The net is smaller now, I realize. Enough of the web has been brought back aboard to turn the net from a vast bowl into a long, narrow shape called the backdown channel, a corridor to freedom. The ship's engines go into reverse, to pull this final portion of the net through the water until the far end of it sinks, making a gate through which the dolphins can be sluiced out back into the ocean.

Philippe taps me on the shoulder; it's time to get back into the Avon lest we, like the dolphins, get sluiced out into sharky waters of the open sea. Ingrid and I hoist ourselves into the raft. Philippe ties the Avon to the top part of the net, near the marked section of the net where the dolphins will be released. Now, as the ship moves backward and the net is pulled through the water, this backdown section will narrow down and become the backdown channel. Finally the corkline at the far end will be pulled under the water, and the dolphins can see their way to freedom. Even if they don't swim out voluntarily, the net will pass underneath them and set them free. Around us the dolphins are lined up in little groups, heads facing the ship, maintaining their place in the moving corridor of netting by swimming slowly, as they wait to be let out. They are close to the net walls, where in the past many an animal has been snagged and drowned. Nowadays this part of the net is lined with special small-meshed netting, designed by one of the skippers, in which even the slender rostrum of a spinner cannot get stuck by accident.

Nevertheless the dolphins are careful not to move around much, except for a two- or three-month-old calf, a few feet away from us, that is dashing here and there around its mother in play. I see the mother gape her jaws at it. The calf zooms by, ignoring her threat. On its next pass she sticks out her tail and whaps that calf about six feet in the air. Whew! That's what ethologists call a reprimand. The calf comes down with a plop and presses itself against her flank in the travel position. Yes, ma'am.

Now the rim of the net begins to pass under the dolphins. As they clear the net, each pair or group turns and bolts to freedom, with some individuals jumping straight up into the air as they go. I've seen films of antelope jumping straight up like this while being chased by a predator. It's a conspicuous behavior; scientists call it stotting. I've seen sheep do it, too, after being driven through a gate. There's some argument about why an animal would do this, wasting time and energy going upward instead of just fleeing. Here, as Ingrid and I watch the departing dolphins stotting, it seems, at least to our eyes, expressive: "I'm free, I'm free, I'm free!" When they are all gone, we head back to the ship and begin the long job of transferring data samples from slates to paper, and getting our gear ready for the next set of the net.

The Schools

One reason we are focusing on spotters is that the spinners are much harder to observe. They are present in only a few sets. They travel constantly and in one huge mass, males, females, large, small, all jumbled together, often at the limits of our visibility. The spotters, on the other hand, are present in every set, make next to no effort to avoid us, and generally choose to stay put, conveniently for us. It's the spotters that are most poorly understood anyway; so we concentrate on them.

In one afternoon set we begin to get a picture of how the bigger aggregations that had mystified me might work. The net has encircled about four hundred spotted dolphins. From above water, the rolling backs and dorsal fins seem to belong to one big school. Once we are out in the net and under the surface, however, we can see three separate schools: one of seventy-four animals quite near us, beyond them another school of about a hundred and thirty animals, and yet farther away (too far to make an accurate count) a still larger school of perhaps two hundred.

The three groups are spaced out with open water between them. It's as if, like newly purchased tropical fish, they are swimming around in three plastic bags floating in a big aquarium. You can see them all, but they are completely separate: three closed social groups that apparently never mix. Are the animals in each specific group all related? Have they been together all their lives? Do they know each other as individuals? When groups get too big for comfort, do they split? How do they take care of genetic variation: do the male squads grow up in one school and then transfer to another? One could ask questions forever. I am joyful to have at least this one month of close looks.

The Chase

The tropical ocean is like a desert, empty for miles and miles, except for particular spots that are rich in resources: oases in deserts, upwellings of nutrients in the sea. In this ocean, as in the desert, no matter what you eat, you may have to search long and hard to find it; but when one kind of food is present, other kinds are likely to be abundant, too.

Spinners, with something like 250 tiny, sharp teeth, feed on minnow-sized prey, at night, and probably at considerable depth. Spotters have larger, fewer teeth and prefer eight-to-ten-inch-long, surface-swimming prey such as flying fish. Tuna may like small prey or large, or something in between. However, if one species finds food, the others probably will, too; so the dolphins and the tuna together constitute a hunting party, or what ecologists call a mixed-species foraging flock. In this case dolphins and tuna are not the whole party; several species of seabirds often accompany these travelers, along with occasional solitary predators such as sharks and marlin. You can witness exactly this phenomenon at your bird feeders in the winter. For a while there are no birds, then suddenly you have chickadees, a woodpecker, titmice, two cardinals, and a nuthatch. They eat different things, but they search together.

From dawn to sunset, day after day, the *Queen Mary* powers across this desert, a square of ocean a thousand miles long and wide, hunting for the hunters. In the old days, the guys say, you could just drive up to a school of dolphins and put the net around them. By now, however, when dolphins hear a ship's engines heading their way, they bunch up tight and stampede for the horizon, usually (but not always) taking the tuna with them (and the sharks and the marlin; the birds usually bail out when a chase begins).

The top speed of spotted dolphins is around 21.4 knots, which I know because I designed and supervised the training for a Navy speed trial using Hoku and Kiko. We taught them to follow a target down a saltwater canal at ever-increasing speeds. At speeds over 12 knots they began making low leaps across the water. By 18 knots they gave up jumping and hunkered down just under the surface, their powerful tail thrusts leaving big, circular "dolphin footprints" behind them. By 22 knots they couldn't catch the target at all.

The *Queen Mary* is fast, but the dolphins are faster; so the ship lowers speedboats, each with a driver, to race ahead of the vessel. Like cowboys, they will herd the dolphins back and hold them on the left side of the ship while the net is being set. It is exciting work for the speedboat drivers, especially in rough seas. During one chase on a rough day I watch a speedboat jumping from one huge wave to another, with the whole boat in the air all the way and just its propeller in the crest of each wave.

Going into the net on rough, windy days is hazardous and exciting for us, too. We never say no. If the captain does not forbid us, into the set we go. There are only so many opportunities. If the Avon is unmanageable, we just tie up to the corkline at the far side of the net and wait the set out.

In one rough set, as the Avon is half-swamped, Philippe struggles to keep the motor going. Ingrid and I scramble to grab flippers and slates that are starting to float away. The glassy face of an eight-foot wave rises up right next to us. A dozen spotted dolphins hang comfortably inside the wave, ranked horizontally and looking out through the face of the wave like people looking through the windows of a train. Their sparkly little eyes are aimed not at us but downward at the tumble of floating gear inside our boat. "Huh! Look at all that junk! Messy critters, aren't they!"

Escaping

Don't kid yourself that we are the first predators to disrupt the otherwise serene existence of the dolphins. Sharks are a constant danger. In the schools we often see individuals with missing fins, half a tail fluke, or huge shark-bite scars on their bodies. And the dolphins aren't built for speed for no reason. At a party after the voyage, another skipper tells me he once watched killer whales herd a school of spinners into a circle and then take turns helping themselves. He had a high-powered rifle aboard (most ships that go into obscure and distant ports carry some kind of armament), and he thought of shooting the killer whales. "But then I'd be in violation of the Marine Mammal Protection Act. But the killer whales were in violation of the Marine Mammal Protection Act!"

Dolphins have evolved several ways of eluding predators. Sometimes, during the chase, the stampeding herd suddenly splits into two or three groups, each going in a different direction. Which one has the tuna? Even the skipper watching with high-powered binoculars from the top of the mast can't be sure. Whichever group he decides to go after, the others will, of course, get away.

Ingrid and I are witness to another excellent escape technique. During a chase, one of the puffy little clouds that often dot the sky over tropical waters suddenly opens up and lets out a downpour. Instantly the dolphins turn, sprint toward that rain squall, and disappear into it. There is no way to guess which side they will come out on, or when; that chase is over. That ploy would probably work on killer whales as well as it does on a tuna-fishing boat.

How do the schools "decide" where to go and what to do? Is it a collective avoidance response, as with flocks of birds and schools of fish? Do the males play a role? Ingrid and I get a clue to the answer in the net.

It's a fairly rough day. Taking data has been possible, but wearing; we have tied up the Avon in the backdown area early. We're still in the water though, holding on to the Avon and watching through our masks as long as we are allowed.

A small school of about forty animals is spread out along the backdown channel, waiting to be released. Just one senior-male squad is in this school. As usual the others are giving the male squad plenty of room; though the dolphins are crowded together, they're leaving perhaps six feet of empty water around the big males.

Several speedboats are tied up nearby as well so the drivers can manually help the animals if necessary during backdown. One of the powerful speedboat motors suddenly starts up. It's a huge noise underwater. It startles us and really frightens the dolphins. Instantly mothers, babies, everyone, are physically plastered to that senior-male squad. You can't even see the males now: the school is one cohesive clump of dolphins, with those dominant males in the core. As we boost ourselves back into the Avon, Ingrid exclaims, "They're not going to let those guys go anywhere without them!"

We look at each other and realize we've just seen one mechanism for surviving the fishing, at least for spotted dolphins. It is not that the males are leaders, exactly; it's that everyone else depends on them. If danger arises, these guys *might* know what to do; and whatever action they opt for, everyone else, down to the silliest calf, will do it, too.

Dolphin Heroics

There's no doubt the fishing has put new kinds of pressure on the dolphins; but the spotted dolphins, at least, have found some new solutions. Probably, knowing spotters, if one bunch finds a successful escape method, they just use the same maneuver over and over. During the chase, the speedboats, like cowboys on horses, round up the dolphins and herd them back toward the ship. The school is driven toward the left side of the ship, where the net will go. Once they are in that zone, the end of the net goes in the water, temporarily tethered to a heavy flatboat, the net skiff, and the ship begins making a vast circle around the dolphin school, paying out net behind itself as it goes. Corks keep the top of the net afloat while weights sink the bottom rim six hundred feet down. Until the two ends of the net meet each other and the circle is closed, the dolphins could escape, and of course the valuable tuna would go with them. Only the presence of the dolphins keeps the tuna in the circle; and the tuna are what count. So while the net is being laid in a circle, the speedboats go back and forth across the gap, making as much noise as possible and creating a wide and deep barrier of bubbles.

Why don't the dolphins just jump out over the net? Because, like Kahili, they have never seen or imagined a solid barrier in their entire lives. Now and then Steno dolphins, also creatures of the open sea, are caught in a tuna net by accident; but the Steno is a very different critter: when it figures out it's surrounded, it just jumps over the net and leaves. Stenos can do that; Stenellas, spinners and spotters, cannot.

Nevertheless, while the net is being set in place, and before the bottom is pursed or drawn shut, turning the net from a corral into a bowl, some schools do get away. The crew tells us of some rare schools that dive six hundred feet down and escape under the lower rim of the net before the bottom is pursed shut. Others flee through the gap before the net is closed, no matter how hard the speedboats try to keep them in.

The bubbles from the speedboat wakes are not only a visual obstacle but also impenetrable to sonar; for dolphins such a barricade might as well be a stone wall. But some nervy spotter schools have learned to just power through the bubbles anyway. It's exactly the kind of decision I can imagine Hoku taking, faced with something that really, really annoys him. If he were a member of a male squad, his fellow musketeers would back him up; and when they plunged into the harmless bubble wall, of course the rest of the dolphins would go with them, and all the tuna, too.

Ingrid and I witness yet another brilliantly successful escape method. We are watching a chase from the bow of the ship. The speedboats have overtaken the dolphins and are herding them back toward the left of the ship, where the net has to be set. Just as the dolphin school comes abreast of the ship, however, some of them veer to our right and start streaming across the tuna vessel's prow.

The net must be set in its big circle on the left of the ship because that's where the winches are that bring in the net and dip the tuna fish aboard at the end. Part of the net is already in the water, and the ship is committed to a leftward circle. The dolphins can't escape behind the ship, because the net is already deployed there. Any animal, however, that gets across the bow to the right-hand side of the ship is free. The speedboats are too far away to turn them back. The mother ship can't change direction nearly fast enough to make any difference.

And the animals know that.

We can tell, because the dolphins that have successfully crossed the path of the ship are stotting. "Yippee, I made it!" Pop, pop, pop, in the air. Now we see a good biological reason for that odd behavior. If it's an expression of relief for the stotter, it's also a display behavior that other fleeing animals can easily see and thus know, themselves, which way to run.

The members of the school that are still to the left of the ship, where the net will be set, now also start racing toward the ship's bow. They are at maximum speed, hunkered down just under the surface, leaving a series of circular "footprints" behind them the way Hoku and Kiko did during their speed trials. This flat-out sprinting can't be sustained for long, but it's working. In moments, most of the school have made it to the safe side of the vessel. The captain, with a snort of disgust, cuts the engines and calls a halt to the set. The ship stops. The dolphins, and any tuna that may be with them, head for the horizon. The speedboats are called in. This particular set is over.

I think all of these escape maneuvers take guts, enormous daring on the part of the first little band of animals that overcome their fear and try a new solution, and often considerable effort and bravery from the followers as well. But to me that seems to be the essence of the spotted dolphin's nature. In a pinch, it's not so much brains that gets them by, it's courage.

Courage might be a hard thing to demonstrate in a laboratory—In fact, I shudder to think how people might go about trying to do so. But it's a real phenomenon nevertheless. Perhaps in spotted dolphins a whole set of attachments, a network of strong and long-term family and clan ties, have been built around that species-specific characteristic. They may be small but they have a lot of nerve.

I think of one more curious event I witnessed in the net: a message about connection. I am taking data on a senior-male group of four animals, cruising slowly beneath me, when I realize, by her slimmer build, that the central animal in the group is an equally senior and black-masked female. She is "holding hands," overlapping pectoral fins, with the male on her left, *and* with the male on her right. A third male swims slightly below and behind her; as I watch, she reaches down with her tail and pats that male gently on the forehead. The hussy! Or maybe, since they look to be age-mates, they all grew up together and were cousins. One thing I am quite sure of, though: she is truly fond of them all.

➤ **Watch the "Tuna-Porpoise-at-Sea Research" slide show in chapter 6 at www.reachingtheanimalmind.com.**

Mysteries Resolved

After this voyage I mashed all the data through the computer in various ways and presented it to the fishing industry, to government agencies, at numerous universities and scientific conferences, and in published form as a government monograph.

The government's initial question was answered. How scared were the dolphins? Except for one school in which the animals didn't seem to know what was happening and were visibly confused and upset, we saw no evidence of high levels of stress. And why? Because they had all been in the nets before, probably not once but many times, and they knew what to do. That in itself was rather alarming; but we did feel sure that whatever was keeping the numbers down, it wasn't due to fear in the nets.

The second mystery, how spotters could live in huge aggregations, was resolved as well. They seem to live in small, highly organized, and long-lasting schools of close relatives and long-term friends. The huge aggregations seen from ships and filmed from the air are just temporary convocations of many such clans or tribes.

And how about Hoku and Kiko? I think I know, but it takes a little discussion of physiology to explain it. Hoku and Kiko were young animals. I didn't realize this when we had them in our tanks, but they lacked the fully mature dark coloring and black masks of senior males and females (Kahili, however, was a fully mature male). In a wild school Hoku and Kiko would both have traveled in the hurly-burly young-adult crowd.

In a normal wild school the big, dark males do all the breeding. As long as they are around, younger males do not develop functioning testes; the presence of dominant, breeding males in the social group suppresses their fertility (this happens in some terrestrial animals as well). Fisheries' research showed that only during the period before dolphin safety procedures were developed, when dolphin mortality was still high and presumably many adult males were gone from the schools, did the scientists find young-adult males like Hoku in breeding condition.

In a wild school, a female Kiko's age would be old enough to come into season and might well become pregnant by one of the senior males. She would then move from the swinging-singles set to a mother-young group. However, a male of the same age might not actually mate productively until much later in life and the senior males might show aggression toward the younger male pursuing fertile females. I saw only one fight in the net, but it was between a senior black-masked male and a younger male, a wild circling skirmish that ended in the younger male blowing a huge smokescreen of bubbles and departing behind it.

Kiko and Hoku would perhaps have met in a wild school, but they would *never* have had a chance to enjoy each other's company or favors for long because they were simply too young to do so. In our tanks, with no social brakes on Hoku's development, and no pregnancy shifting Kiko into parenthood, they were a happy Romeo and Juliet.

One final mystery: what was still keeping the populations down? Current thinking points to the chase. It seems probable that babies can't keep up in the long stampedes. Mothers and calves get separated; we did see, a couple of times, a "lost baby," twirling and peeping sadly all by itself, underneath the rafting spotters. A separated baby has, really, no chance of survival. That invisible mortality may well be enough to keep the numbers down.

What will happen in the long run? The dolphins, in my opinion, are probably going to survive. This method of fishing depends on fast travel and lots of it, so for the fishermen, the cost of fuel is huge, with high prices already impacting this fishery and sending some boats into retirement. Another guess, and one that worried me then and now, is that what's really at risk are the tuna. This fishery takes many adult yellowfin tuna. Like the dolphins, they are long-lived, swim in closely related schools, and are more intelligent than you might think. By persistently catching the adults we are removing the breeding stock. Perhaps the fishing for tuna by surrounding dolphins will stop because the tuna population will be reduced too much to be worth pursuit.

Hoku's New Romance

After Kiko's death, Sea Life Park collected no more spotted dolphins. Hoku matured into a senior male and became, eventually, our only spotted dolphin, as old age took Kahili and a respiratory infection took little Lei. Hoku lived in Whaler's Cove, in a heterogeneous collection of spinners, bottlenoses, pilot whales (*Globicephala*), and false killer whales.

Although like other spotted dolphins Hoku snubbed the spinners, I don't want you to think he lived out his life as a lonely bachelor. He took a highly unlikely paramour: the star of the show, a false killer whale named Makapuu, the Hawaiian name of the point of land on which Sea Life Park is built.

The false killer whale, *Pseudorca crassidens,* is a tropical cousin of the great true killer whale, *Orcinus orca.* That better-known killer whale is a chunky, solid animal handsomely patterned in black and white; the false killer whale is long, slender, sleek, and completely black all over. Like their northern cousins, false killer whales are formidable predators, attacking fish weighing hundreds of pounds, such as marlin and tuna; but they don't eat other mammals, such as seals and dolphins, as the true killer whales do, so they can safely be kept in mixed company.

Makapuu was fourteen feet long and weighed about two thousand pounds. Hoku was a third of her length and weighed perhaps 130 pounds. Swimming side by side with his consort, he looked like a minnow next to a trout. Makapuu allowed him sexual favors, which he enjoyed often. Luckily, since Hoku's part of this activity required him to be underneath Makapuu, where he was completely out of sight from the surface, their amours went unnoticed by visiting tourists and groups of schoolchildren.

Hoku was by no means as chivalrous with Makapuu as he had been with Kiko. He bossed her around unmercifully. During the five daily shows the small dolphins usually got one six-ounce smelt apiece for each behavior. Makapuu's pay for her star turns—prodigious leaps, carrying a rider, pulling a boat, and so on—was a dozen or more smelt, which a trainer at the ship's rail tossed in one bunch into her bucket-sized, open mouth. Once, on a visit to Sea Life Park many years after I had moved to the mainland, Ingrid invited me to come onto the ship during a show and see what happened when Makapuu got paid. Makapuu did her stunt for the audience, heard her special whale whistle (a different one from the dolphins' marker sound), and came to the ship's side and held up her open jaws. Ingrid tossed in a double handful of little fishes. As Makapuu subsided with her reinforcers, Hoku pulled up alongside her, eye to eye, and shook his open jaws up and down, uttering dolphin curses and imprecations in a fine aggressive display. Makapuu, eyeing him back, then opened her vast mouth just an inch or two and let two little smelt slide out in his direction. Hmph! About time! said Hoku, snapping them up. He now had a girlfriend who earned *him* free fish, instead of the other way around. Ingrid had the feeling that Makapuu thought this was funny.

Chapter 7

Fear

Misinterpretation

I recognize fear in the dolphins. When I start working with dog trainers, however, I noticed that dogs, too, often experience fear in our thoughtless hands, and people don't even know it.

I'm passing through the lobby of a friend's apartment building in New York. A couple in 12D wanted a new dog, so they did the "right thing": they went to an animal shelter and adopted a puppy. People are crowding around to see the new arrival. "Oh, isn't it cute!" "How adorable!" I go to take a look.

The puppy, male, a short-haired, long-legged, whip-tailed mutt, is lying on his back, skinny legs sprawled, mouth agape, eyes rolled up into his head so far that all I can see is the whites. He is urinating straight upward in, I guess, an adorable little fountain. He is absolutely terrified.

The puppy is swamped with new sounds and scents. He's overwhelmed by the people bending over him like predators. Once he gets upstairs into apartment 12D, I daresay he will urinate frequently from fear, defecate everywhere (again from fear), throw up whatever he's fed, and spend most of his time hiding under the furniture. I bet this puppy won't last a week. Indeed, my friends report, the dog goes back to the shelter the next day.

When I work with dog owners and trainers, I am often struck by their failure to notice even the most clear-cut behavioral messages from their dogs. Some dog facial expressions are not easy to read unless you're looking for them, such as the lines and ridges that show up in the cheeks and around the base of the skull when the dog is alarmed and the skin draws tight. But domestic dogs also have many expressions that are similar to ours. Dogs, like people, can look visibly joyful, doubtful, puzzled, pleased, suspicious, annoyed, and sad. This is our doing; we didn't make the emotions, but over the millennia we have selectively bred dogs for highly visible eyebrows, big eyes with dark rims, and conspicuous, mobile lips and ears, all helping to make canine facial expressions more obvious to the human eye. And still, we mostly don't get the message.

Professional Blindness

It's not just naive, well-meaning city folk who misunderstand dog social signals. Professional dog breeders, handlers, and trainers can be equally blind. ClickerExpo gatherings include many lab sessions in which individuals can train their own dogs. Senior trainers bring dogs for workshops with clicker experts, ranging from clicker training your dog while you are blindfolded (as the blind learn to train) to arcane challenges such as the Ultimate Retrieve: teaching the dog to pick up, carry, and put in your hand a whole hot dog.

➤ Watch the "ClickerExpo" video in chapter 7 at www.reachingtheanimalmind.com.

Three days of nonstop lectures and workshops is hard even on the calmest animal. Sometimes I notice a dog lying down next to its owner, panting, with the whites of the eyes showing and the corners of the lips drawn all the way back in a grimace of anxiety. This dog has really had all the crowds and noise and strangers it can stand right now.

I stop to suggest to the owner that the dog should be put away to rest for a while. The clicker trainer might say, "I was thinking about that; I'll take him up to my room right now." It's the traditional trainer who will glance at the dog, look back at me, and say, "Oh, no, he's fine." The dog's facial signals are not useful information to this trainer, who either doesn't recognize them or is accustomed to seeing the dog in that state.

Perhaps traditionally trained animals, like veteran soldiers, sometimes deliberately keep their faces impassive. I was astonished to learn that a Hollywood trainer, in the middle of the production of a big multidog film, stated firmly to reporters that dogs have no facial expressions. What! Maybe your dogs never show what they're feeling, buddy; but not mine.

I think also that the coercive or traditional trainers learn not to look. It's partly the pervasive cultural fear of being thought anthropomorphic, and it's partly that they accept these signs of fear and stress as a normal part of training a dog. Maybe the dog isn't exactly happy now, but that will pass, so it doesn't matter. Once the dog becomes "obedient," those signs of "resistance" will go away.

Crossing Over

So what happens if you are already a traditional dog trainer and now you become an operant or modern trainer? Your methods change, of course, but so do your eyes. As with the portrait in the landscape, you can now see what was invisible to you before: the fear. This new clarity became poignantly apparent during a research experiment I helped design that turned out to be (in some ways, anyway) a complete failure.

Every experienced dog trainer who gets into clicker training soon discovers that it is faster than choke-chain training, often much faster; what used to take people and dogs six to eight weekly classes to learn is now all done in four weeks, and the instructors are scratching their heads finding ways to fill the remaining time the people have paid for. However, proving experimentally that "clicker is quicker" is a challenge. How do you compare different trainers, different dogs, different methods? There are just too many variables.

I and my friends and colleagues, social worker Lynn Loar and psychologist Barbara Bush, formed a nonprofit organization, the Pryor

Foundation, to promote research into just such questions. While this tiny foundation has no money, it proves useful as a catalyst in developing experimental programs. As one of our first efforts we meet with three experienced dog trainers who have crossed over from traditional, force-based training to clicker training. Together we develop a research idea. These three trainers are all skilled at traditional compulsion-based training and also modern reinforcement-based training. Perhaps the same trainers could take a bunch of naive dogs and each teach the same behavior, "down," both ways and see how long it took each way. Well, let's try.

The trainers make a deal with a local adoption organization. They have quite a few young, lively, untrained dogs available, many of them golden retrievers. The rescue organization is delighted that the dogs will be receiving some training at no expense.

Two of the trainers will work with the dogs while the third trainer runs the video camera. Nothing drastic will go on here, no choke chains, nothing involving pain. The traditional training portion of the experiment uses "modeling" or physical guidance. With each dog the trainer says "Down" and puts the dog gently into the down position, either with hand pressure on the neck, or by pulling the forelegs forward until the dog's elbows are on the ground. Each trainer knows from extensive past experience that eventually the dog will start cooperating and lie down on its own.

Some dogs are chosen for the first task, teaching "down" the traditional way. The experiment begins. Taking turns, the trainers give three dogs their first lesson. These crossover trainers have become accustomed to dogs learning to do a new behavior with joy and quick, glad participation. "You want what? I can do that, watch me!" Now, as they push and pull, they feel the stiffness in the dogs' muscles, as an automatic opposition reflex causes the dogs to push back against the pressure. They can also see, on the dogs' faces, increasing confusion and fear. In fact, the trainers can no longer *not see* the stress they are causing.

The dogs are suffering. Suffering! Extreme word for a little manual manipulation, isn't it? Ask the dogs; they are not struggling, they are trying to cooperate, but they are miserable. And so are the trainers. By the sixth dog the trainer behind the video camera is in tears and asks the others to stop. They do. They have to. Others might come up with different experimental designs in the future; this attempt is over.

What strikes me about this aborted experiment is not the behavior of the dogs, but the behavior of the trainers. Clicker training has turned them into much better observers of natural behavior. They can see the innate signals. They understand the training circumstances that elicited the signals, and they no longer feel comfortable causing that degree of discomfort.

Modern trainers, operant trainers, can't afford to ignore what the animal is feeling. While it's fun to share the moments of exhilaration and success, it's also crucial to spot any signs of stress or avoidance. If you see fear and doubt creeping in, you know at once that you are not communicating clearly and it's time to take a break and rethink the training plan.

Reducing Fear: Traditional Methods

The traditional tools for overcoming fear are three procedures psychologists call habituation, desensitization, and flooding. (I daresay there are more, but these are the ones people talk about most.) Habituation means just letting the organism live with the upsetting stimulus until it gets used to it. Although I was born and partly raised in Manhattan, when I first moved back to New York as an adult, I was unable to sleep because of the sounds coming from the streets below my apartment: fire engines, police sirens, garbage trucks, shrieks of laughter, car horns, and (only once) gunshots. In a month I didn't even hear the noise; that's habituation.

Desensitization, the second method, refers to exposing your learner to the stimulus in small and then gradually increasing amounts. This is the standard way of, say, tempting feral cats out of the bushes or teaching a dog to let you clip its nails or getting a pet bird to sit on your hand. Desensitization can take quite a long time, ranging from a few hours to forever; some wild animals would rather starve to death than come out into the open and take food from your hand. Another problem is that an accidental additional scare can send you right back to the beginning. The animal may become more wary of you than it was when you first showed up.

The third technique trainers sometimes use is flooding: exposing the individual to such extreme levels of the scary thing that it just gives up. I have witnessed a horse trainer's flooding technique called sacking out. You fill a burlap bag with empty tin cans. You tie the horse by means of a stout rope and halter to a heavy post in the ground, so no matter how it struggles, it can't get away. Then you whop it from head to tail on both sides with the noisy—but totally harmless—sack of empty tin cans. The horse bucks, bolts, falls down, urinates, defecates, and foams at the mouth, until eventually it just stops and stands there. Theoretically at least, absolutely nothing in the way of touch or sound can frighten it from then on.

All of these methods have been used for centuries, with all kinds of animals, including people. All three procedures have the major drawback of requiring learners to experience the scary thing over and over, being frightened by it again and again, until they accept it (desensitization), learn to ignore it (habituation), or retreat into learned helplessness (flooding). And you can, of course, set things up so that while current fears may still exist, your learner is more afraid of you than of anything else. This fear-inducing use of one's own skill at dominating others is a favorite technique of some sports coaches, drill sergeants, bosses, and many self-styled expert animal trainers.

Erasing Fears by Shaping

Modern trainers don't just avoid causing fear: we have powerful additional tools for overcoming fear that already exists. This gives us a huge advantage in working with wild species that cannot be tamed or trained in the traditional sense, and also in mitigating difficulties with individuals that are already frightened.

Here's an easy example from the fear-fixing tool kit: how to bring a loose animal close to you, quickly, so it can be handled or caught. Instead of baiting the animal into a trap, or luring the animal with food in the hope that greed may overcome caution, you shape the behavior. You explain to the animal: here's the deal, earn a click and I'll give you the food free.

My friends have found a feral kitten, about five weeks old. They'd like to keep it, but it's completely wild, hissing and scratching; so they put it in a dog crate while it gets used to civilization. It has retreated to the far corner and stayed there, crouched and unmoving, for two days. They think there's something wrong with it. What do I think?

I get a clicker and some tuna fish. I click and flick a tiny piece of tuna through the bars of the crate next to the cat. Then I step back and wait. The cat can't help smelling the tuna; it raises its head a quarter inch. I click that move and flick another piece of tuna near the cat. The cat eats those tuna bits. Hurray.

Now I do nothing. The cat stands up and takes a step toward me. I click the step and flick tuna near the cat again, and again it eats. I am wrapping a classical-conditioning process (being near people is a good thing) inside an operant-conditioning process: step forward, hear a click, get a fabulous treat delivered right to your safe place.

How long does it take this kitten to figure that out? In six clicks it's suddenly at the front of the crate, waiting indignantly for me to hurry up and click and produce tuna again. I produce a jackpot, which for this tiny kitten consists of about a teaspoon of food. End of session.

That afternoon when the friends and I show up again, the little cat comes right up to the front and accepts being petted with one finger for a click and tuna. The next morning it accepts being picked up. It starts purring, and guess what: it's a tame cat now, already well on its way to happily ruling a whole household of food providers.

➤ **Watch the "Feral Kitten" video in chapter 7 at www.reachingtheanimalmind.com.**

During this process, signs of fear, aggression, and avoidance can just vanish, never to be seen again. A nifty example of this permanent switch took place at the Philadelphia Zoo; and it may have been instrumental in saving a whole species.

The northern bald ibis, *Geronticus eremita,* is a critically endangered species. Once it ranged all over northern Africa and southern Europe. At present the wild population is limited to some eighty breeding pairs in Morocco and an even smaller remnant population in Turkey. More of these ibises are in captivity than in the wild.

It's hard to say why one would want to display this bird; it's certainly no beauty. Like all ibis the northern bald ibis is a tall, skinny bird with a long, thin neck. Some ibis are prettily colored, but this one is totally black except for its bare-skinned red face. It has a long, down-turned bill and a sort of sagging crest on the back of the head: the poster bird for depression. In captivity, at least, this bird seems to have a temperament to match, being nervous, suspicious, given to feather plucking, nasty to other ibis, and subject to serious skin problems.

The Philadelphia Zoo had a flock of northern bald ibis, some of whom had been in captivity for years. They never got over being fearful. Each time a keeper came into their enclosure, even if just bringing food, the whole flock flapped in all directions and took hours to calm down. Caring for such spooky birds is stressful not just for the birds, but for the keepers.

One summer the zoo hires a bird-training consultant. The ibis keepers are allowed to try out some training. First they get the birds used to many small meals across the day, rather than one big one. Then, using the word *good* as a marker, the keepers teach the birds to calm down and land on the ground even if a keeper is in the exhibit. Then, just as I did with the feral kitten, they shape the behavior of coming toward a keeper and taking food from the hand. They click for looking at the keeper, but toss the food where the ibis can reach it without being scared to do so. Then they click head moves or foot moves in the direction of the keeper, until the bird approaches keepers voluntarily; now they can reinforce that with food from the hand.

The keepers cut an old green carpet into a lot of six-inch squares, spread them around the enclosure, and teach each bird to stand on its own green square. The birds quickly progress to standing on scales to be weighed, and to moving from one cage to another, or even into a shipping crate, following their green squares.

Keepers, targets, cues, food: the birds are experiencing many kinds of reinforcers. The ibis stop being afraid of the keepers. On cage-cleaning day the ibis not only don't flap into the walls in panic, they follow the keepers around to see what's going on and make a nuisance of themselves, getting in the way of the work. They also stop pulling their feathers out and pecking each other. The skin problems clear up. And guess what: they play. One ibis, then two, start picking up leaves that blow into the exhibit, clacking their beaks and tossing leaves about and stealing them from each other. Soon all the ibis are playing keep-away with dead leaves. The keepers bring them some bird toys, designed for parrots, and they play with those, too. Even the most conservative scientists agree that play behavior pretty definitely indicates lack of stress.

New birds have been added to the flock and have quickly picked up the customs of the group, right down to standing on their own green square to earn treats. The possibility of captive breeding and healthy, normal, parent-raised chicks, suitable for releasing in the wild, is now a realistic goal. Furthermore the daily training is fun to watch: people often come to the exhibit on purpose at training time, to see these once gloomy birds coming to their keepers on cue, going to their green squares, playing with bird toys, and visibly enjoying themselves.

Erasing Fears with Targeting

Targets, such as the green squares of the ibis, are a highly useful additional tool for shaping. Zookeepers use targets a lot. Suppose you need to move a lion from one cage to another. Instead of baiting him with food (which the lion might ignore) or threatening him (which he might resist) or actually using force (driving big animals with a fire hose is not unheard of), you teach the lion, through the bars, to put his nose on a target, perhaps the padded end of a stick. Then you take the target into the adjoining cage, offer it again, and presto, the lion goes calmly into the next cage to touch his target and make you deliver a treat.

Targets can also be used to teach animals to stand still. At the Dallas Zoo, I visit the zoo's excellent rhinoceros collection. Rhinos are particularly hard to immobilize, being both strong and timid, apt to charge anyone or anything they perceive as a threat. Yet like any animal they need routine medical care, and like elephants they especially need foot care. The keeper introduces me to her favorite rhino, a half-grown male who was born at the zoo. He has learned to stand sideways to the fence around his paddock, pressing his nose against the end of a padded pole, while the keepers draw blood, give shots, or trim his horny feet through the railings.

The keeper shows me some of the rhino's husbandry behaviors and lets me personally move him about with the target pole and clicker. The reinforcer is bits of banana, which he takes from my hand with gentleness and skill. For this young rhino, however, the big reward at the end of a session is not food but a game with the keeper. The keeper leaves the target, runs the length of her side of the paddock fence, and stops. Now *she* is the target. The rhino takes off at a run down his side, screeching to a halt just as he gets abreast of the keeper. Then she turns and runs up the fence. He chases her back, tail in the air and little eyes sparkling. Of *course* this is what young rhinos do! They play Charge!

Targeting is handy with dogs. Suppose you have a dog that is afraid of strangers and shrinks away or even growls or barks if people try to pet him. It's not uncommon, especially if, like that puppy on its back in the apartment lobby, the dog is inexperienced. You can gradually desensitize the dog to people, which takes a long time and involves a lot of cooperation from others; or you can turn your own hand into a target and teach the dog that he gets clicked for nosing your fist. Then get a friend to hold out a fist to the dog. The outstretched hand is now a cue, a green light for a click and a treat. The dog's internal state switches from "Uh-oh" to "Oh, boy!" He controls the situation, he chooses to bump hands, and he wins, every time. Outstretched hands, and by extension the people behind them, become a good thing, and within a few more experiences the fear disappears.

The Bad Loaders: A Targeting Experiment

The first published scientific paper specifically about clicker training described the use of targets to overcome an all-too-common fear-related problem in the horse world: the horse that refuses to get into a horse trailer. At the University of North Texas, under the guidance of Jésus Rosales-Ruiz, Ph.D., a professor in the behavior-analysis department, graduate student Dawnery Ferguson made the "bad loader" the topic of her master's thesis research.

If you've ever watched people trying to get a frightened and unwilling horse into a trailer, you know it can be quite a scene. To quote the authors, "The combination of a horse that fights loading and an owner who uses physical force can produce a very dangerous situation. Injuries to the trainer can include rope burns, lost fingers, broken bones, or bruises and bleeding. Injuries to the animal can include lacerations to the head from banging into the trailer, scrapes and cuts on the legs, broken legs from falling, or even a broken back if the animal falls backwards while rearing."

A bad loader becomes more or less useless. You can't truck it to a horse show or a rodeo or a trail ride. Because you can't get it onto a trailer, you can't even easily sell it. In North Texas, Ferguson quickly located five pedigreed quarterhorse mares that had been turned out to pasture to be broodmares because they were such bad loaders. These mares were the subject of the experiment.

The ultimate goal was to be able to walk each mare up to the trailer, throw the lead rope over her back, tell her to get in, and stand back while she loaded herself. Ferguson and her helpers started by showing that before training started, none of the horses would go in the trailer when told to do so. Indeed, when led up to a trailer, all five mares put on quite a display, struggling against the lead line, rearing, trying to whirl, and so on. These events were dispassionately recorded.

Then, out in the pasture in a series of five-minute sessions, Ferguson clicker-trains each mare to go to and touch a target, a red pot holder on a string. She adds a verbal cue, "Touch," so the mares learn to wait to be told before they go to the target. Every click, behavior, treat, and cue is recorded and videotaped.

The experimenters now borrow a small, dark, step-up (rather than ramped) horse trailer: the scariest kind. They now use successive approximation, changing the environment in small steps. They hang the pot holder on the side of the trailer, then at the opening, then just inside, then all the way in, clicking the horses for moving forward and touching the target in each new circumstance.

Well, of course it works. Even the most resistant mare takes only twenty-five five-minute sessions—a total of about two hours of work—to reach the goal. Now Ferguson can walk each mare up to the trailer, throw the lead rope over her back, tell her to get in, and stand back while the mare loads herself.

No punishment has been used. The students have done nothing to decrease the bad behaviors seen in the beginning; those reactions have disappeared anyway. The effect is permanent and it has "generalized"; that is, these horses are equally willing to get aboard other trailers and to do it for other trainers, including their owner. I'd like to have seen the owner's face the first time he saw that.

Furthermore, the whole demeanor of the mares changed. These horses that once fled to the far side of the field when they saw a person with a halter now come up to the gate and put their heads in the halters voluntarily. They take an interest in people and follow them around. They are friendly. For these horses, the universe now looks different. People, once a cause of pain and fear, are now a good source of predictable pleasant events. Instead of avoiding being caught and handled, the horses are curious, interested, and hopeful; they want to be with people now and perhaps learn new ways to get people to produce food and other benefits. They will never go back to seeing even the horse trailer the way they used to see it. Once a terrifying object, it's now just a familiar path to success and reinforcement.

Using Cues when Clicks Don't Work

I am teaching an experimental clicker class to a group of dog-training instructors. I have been blathering on for weeks about the value of using the cue, in lieu of the click, as a reinforcer, since that's such a crucial part of building behavior chains. I finally have to notice that they are not getting it. So I think up an exercise that might demonstrate the concept through personal experience.

We're working in a school gymnasium that has all kinds of junk in the storeroom. Before class I put together a set of obstacles that are all somewhat unnerving, such as a noisy, crumpled plastic tarp to walk over, a sheet over a broomstick making an opaque curtain between two chairs, and a yard-square piece of plywood that wobbles a little when you stand on it (I duct-taped a bar of soap to the middle of the underneath side). Before we begin, I ask everyone to show the class their dog's favorite trick and the cue for that trick. The golden does a nice bow. The border collie barks on cue. The Doberman spins. They all have something they do easily and well on cue.

The next task is to pick an obstacle and try to lure their dog on or over it with food. The dogs are off leash and free to move as they see fit. Each trainer sits his or her dog on one side of an obstacle and then holds out food and tries to coax the dog across. Every dog immediately runs around the obstacle to get the food rather than going across it.

Now I ask the class to use the clicker and treats to shape crossing the obstacle. In four or five clicks and treats the collie has two paws on the wobbly board but springs off with relief when it hears the click. The golden is shoving his nose against the hanging sheet but isn't pushing all the way through yet. The others are also attempting the start of their scary tasks but are still reluctant.

Now comes the final step: we will use the *cue* for that favorite behavior instead of the click. To get the dog to step farther onto the wobbly board, or to push harder against the visual barrier of the sheet, the trainers will mark progress by giving the cue for their favorite trick, exactly at the same instant that they would normally have clicked. Then of course the dog will do the trick that's been cued, and the trainer can click and treat that behavior.

Each dog tries its obstacle crossing and gets a favorite cue instead of a click. Once. Twice. Then, to my vast delight and satisfaction, I hear cries of surprise all around the room. All the animals have forgotten their fear and conquered the obstacle completely. To get a legal chance to bark, the collie has jumped on the wobbly board with all four feet and is now barking, tail flagging gaily, though wobbling in all directions. The golden has dashed through the curtain and is bowing on the other side. The Doberman has negotiated the tarpaulin and is now doing its spin. The Irish terrier is sitting up with its front paws in the air, on top of a once formidable pile of rope. In a fearful situation, it seems, clicks trump food—and cues, amazingly, trump clicks.

So what happened? In this fearful circumstance, just getting a treat is not much fun. When the trainers tried to lure the animal by holding out food, every dog weighed that primary reinforcer against its present circumstance: which would I rather do, eat a piece of a hot dog or stay away from this scary thing? "Stay away" will always win; it ran around the obstacle instead of crossing it.

Getting a well-loved cue, however, is a different matter. It is reinforcing in itself, and it has a history as a green light to positive events. The dog does the behavior the cue indicates, gets the click, and takes the treat. It discovers that the thing it feared was not that bad. Now it's ready to deal with the scary thing again, any time, with no fear.

Partly this is a textbook illustration of something called the Premack principle. Working with chimpanzees, psychologist David Premack demonstrated that an animal will do behavior it doesn't enjoy in order to get a chance to do a behavior it likes better. Do your homework and you can watch TV.

I think, however, that in this case, by using the cues that are also conditioned reinforcers, we are also cashing in on the animal's reinforcement history. These cues for simple tricks—bow, spin, sit up pretty, speak—have not only been reinforced many times, but have probably produced many happy outcomes, from the laughter of children to a rare taste of the Thanksgiving turkey. That history somehow enables the cue-behavior combination to overcome the fear.

It makes me think of a human example you may have experienced yourself. You are invited to a party at the house of someone you don't know well. When you get there, the house is full of attractive-looking people you don't know, either. They all seem to know each other, though, and are having a great time, laughing and talking. You may feel a strong impulse to turn around and leave. Then your hostess rushes up and asks if you would please pass the canapés or see who needs some more wine. Sure. Doing this job you know how to do, you are now part of the party; the fear dwindles, and by and by you can meet people and start making new friends.

Jésus Rosales-Ruiz calls me from Texas with a new example of the powerfully reinforcing effect of a cue in a fearful situation. His graduate student Jennifer Muller has come up with another research project involving four timid horses and a horse trailer.This time, instead of using targets and successive approximation, the student, out in the pasture, has used the clicker and grain to teach each horse one new behavior and its cue. The behavior consists of walking ten steps forward in a straight line. The cue is a pointed arm and "Go."

Everyone finds the results oddly amusing. You can line a horse up facing a pair of trees that are a few feet apart, give it the "Go" cue, and the horse will calmly walk through the gap between the trees. You can send it through a gate or into a stall. But how about trailers?

On the day appointed for the first testing, the experimenter leads the first horse up to the back of the trailer, throws the rope over its back, points ahead, and says "Go." And the horse calmly walks ten steps forward straight into the trailer on its own, on the first try. The next three horses also receive the "Go" cue and walk calmly into what used to look to them like the gates of hell, with no fear at all.

➤ **Watch the "Touch the Goblin Horse" video in chapter 7 at www.reachingtheanimalmind.com.**

Fear of Failure: When the Cue *Doesn't* Work

There's an odd fear that happens during clicker training, especially if you have a traditional-training background: a fear that affects the teacher, not the taught. It's a feeling of disaster when a cue doesn't work.

The cue is not a command. It permits the behavior to happen; it doesn't make the behavior happen. People often have a hard time accepting that. With commands, the traditional trainer has a backup plan. If your command doesn't get results, you can *make* the animal do the behavior with the leash or the spur or the cattle prod or the elephant hook or simply by displaying your own dominant personality.

Experienced trainers who are starting clicker training bring that traditional baggage along. They may gladly learn to click, and to shape behavior, and to use targets, and to teach new cues. That's all fun. But they still equate the cue with a command. Sooner or later they give a cue that the animal should have down pat, and this time the learner doesn't do the behavior. The trainer panics: *now* what do I do?

You used to have a good way to fix this problem: use force. Now you're not supposed to do that, and you don't see a way out. Damn! Actually, this is an extinction experience; something you used to rely on now doesn't work. The natural and understandable tendency is (a) to get angry, (b) to blame the animal, and (c) to fall back on the old system of physical "correction."

Dolphin trainers know that if you give a cue and you get no response, it's not the animal's problem, it's yours. We've also learned that it really doesn't matter why the animal didn't respond; there are a jillion possible reasons, but you don't have to worry about that, because you can fix most cue failures by briefly repeating the training of the cue the way you established it in the beginning. At Sea Life Park I even gave the process a name: going back to kindergarten.

Knowing the causes of cuing problems, however, might help you avoid them in the future, and thus avoid having to suffer an unpleasant extinction-induced anger experience. Here are the main reasons why an animal (or child or friend or employee) doesn't respond to a cue you think it should know:

- It doesn't really know how to do the behavior.
- You haven't really trained that cue yet.
- The animal doesn't recognize the cue because there's something different about it (for example, you signaled with your left hand when you usually use your right).
- The animal thinks something else is the cue. (A friend going to an obedience trial was especially happy about her dog's rock-solid recall: sit the dog, turn, leave him, turn back, and call "Come"—and he came at a gallop every time. What she didn't know was that when she called, she tossed her head a little and that flipped her long blond ponytail sideways. For the actual competition, she put on her good clothes and did her hair up on top of her head. No ponytail. No recall. No passing score. The dog thought the ponytail flick was the cue.)
- The animal doesn't perceive the cue at all (a hellish problem back at Sea Life Park, where, in the early days, the underwater speakers often conked out, but we didn't know that).
- You have trained the cue in one environment and now you are in another, and you didn't prepare the animal for that possibility (from the beginning, all behaviors and cues should be taught in changing circumstances, so the cues become one thing that doesn't change from place to place).
- You are messing up your cue by adding extras. You tell your dog "Down." That didn't work, so you repeat it, say it louder, bend over, put your hand on the floor, etc. None of this makes the cue more meaningful; the engineering term for all these efforts is *noise.* Finally, however, the dog takes a stab at the behavior. That reinforces your activities. Now, each time you ask for a

"Down" and you don't get it, you add stuff to the cue again, trying to "make" the dog do the behavior. The dog is no longer sure which addition is the important one, so his response becomes erratic. Meanwhile the "Down" cue is messy, loaded with junk. The cure? Get a friend or a video camera to show you just how much unnecessary behavior you yourself are doing. Go back to the clean, simple, original cue, and reinforce responses to that, and only that. The dog will bound in circles with joy and relief.

- The least likely (but most often chosen) reason: there really is something wrong with the animal, and it's not that he's stubborn, or stupid, or trying to make you look bad. The dog won't pick up the dumbbell because he has a sore in his mouth. He can't sit quickly because his hips hurt. Get him checked out.

All of these trainer errors are "beginner" problems, leading to punishment, and causing unnecessary fear and stress in animal and trainer alike. With a little more experience you will routinely build clean cues and use them to mean the same thing at all places and all times, so these problems won't arise. You can still modify your cues, dwindling a hand signal down to the move of one finger, or transferring a gesture to a word. You can broaden them, so it no longer matters which hand you use. You just have to do it knowingly. The end result is that everyone understands the system. The person and the animal develop a rich mutual vocabulary that they both can trust.

The Poisoned Cue

Cues can be wonderfully powerful, but it's a power that's easy to sabotage. Switching back to correction is the fastest way to do that. Up until now the cue has been good news. Hear the word *sit,* sit, get a treat. Then, however, the dog does not sit, and you respond with punishment. Do that two or three times, and the meaning of the cue changes.

The outcome is in doubt. "Sit" used to be a promise; now it's also a threat.

How does the dog feel about that? Still banking on reward or fearing the pain? Look at the dog; you'll see a little of both. The trainer says "Sit!" and the dog sits, but dubiously, slowly, head low, with anxiety written all over its face. You still get the behavior, but you get fear and avoidance, too. You have poisoned your cue.

As I became aware of this phenomenon, I realized I no longer enjoyed watching certain dog competitions, partly because of the visible abundance of poisoned cues. In 2002 I published some thoughts on the poisoned cue in a British dog magazine. I also bounced the idea off Jésus Rosales-Ruiz, the behavior analyst who first became seriously interested in both basic and applied research into clicker training.

Jésus and his graduate students started exploring the poisoned cue experimentally. They learned that the poisoned cue is a real phenomenon; they could re-create it at will, using the students' own dogs. Furthermore, they found that the anxiety-related behavior a poisoned cue generates becomes a permanent part of the cue response, even if you then use only positive reinforcement for hundreds of trials.

Is this ambiguous cue still a conditioned reinforcer? Can you still use it to reinforce other behaviors or to link behaviors together in a chain? Or not? The poisoned-cue concept raises a lot of new questions.

The easy solution to the problem of a poisoned cue is to give the behavior a new cue. The behavior itself hasn't changed, and the new cue will carry none of the freight of the one that accidentally got tainted. Replacing cues can be a powerful tool for rehabilitating the deteriorating performance of agility or obedience dogs, dressage horses, and other animals used in competitive sports, or of pet or shelter dogs who have learned that their name is bad news and that the words *Come here* mean "run the other way." Pragmatically, though, a trainer is wise to avoid poisoning cues gratuitously, and to get rid of poisoned cues if you have some. A poisoned cue is forever a source of fear; and fear is the enemy of good training.

Shaping an Absence

Sometimes the simplest way of getting rid of fear is to reinforce moments when it eases. You can't always do it with words, reassurance, and encouragement; in fact, whether in people or in animals, too much sympathy can sometimes make fearful behavior worse. "Oh, good, she loves me when I'm quaking from head to foot, I'll do that some more." If instead you mark and reinforce moments when signs of fear diminish, you help the fear abate.

I am sometimes called in as a consultant by organizations that work with children and adults with autism. One day at a school I'm a consultant to, one of the teachers, Steve, comes to me with a problem. He's been working with a new arrival, Timmy, an appealing little boy of about seven. Timmy has receptive language, meaning that on the whole he seems to understand what's said to him; but he never talks. Steve's been using clicks and "edibles," favorite food treats, to teach Timmy various skills, such as matching colors, and Timmy is doing great.

Today, however, the barber has come to the school. Timmy is scheduled for a haircut. His previous haircut resulted in a spectacular meltdown. Could the clicker help Tim endure another haircut without that happening again?

"Let's go see," I say. The three of us go downstairs to the barber chair. Tim gets in the chair when told to. The barber puts a wrap around him, and he accepts that; but as soon as the comb and scissors come near his hair, his forehead wrinkles up in anxiety. The barber clips a little, then moves away. Tim's forehead smoothes out. Aha! A visible sign of relief. I tell Steve, "Try clicking when Timmy's forehead clears."

As the barber's comb and scissors move around, starting and stopping, Tim's brow alternately wrinkles and clears. Each time the wrinkles go away, Steve clicks and pops a little piece of potato chip (a favorite treat) into Tim's mouth. Tim's moments of wrinkled brow become shorter. His periods of calm become longer.

The barber finishes with the comb and the scissors and puts them away; we've had no meltdown! Then the barber picks up the clippers for the final trimming of the back of the neck. *Bzzzzz* comes the sound.

Timmy's whole face crumples up in fear. Steve instantly waves the barber away and says, "No clippers this time, thanks." The clippers stop. Tim's face relaxes. Steve cheers, lifts him down from the chair, and gives him a quick hug and a whole potato chip. Does Timmy smile? Almost. Almost. Steve is grinning from ear to ear.

The Cost of Fear

Fear is a part of life in general, I suppose. Certainly it has evolutionary value; we are right to avoid what we fear. It's probably useful that all of us, no doubt down to hermit crabs and below, can apparently learn to recognize what we should be afraid of, in a single try. But I see no good reason why fear should be an accepted, overlooked, and unprevented part of so many of our social institutions and processes. Fear is the enemy of learning. It's the negator of joy, the preventer of play, the inhibitor of trust and love. Fear just gets in the way, slows things down, and causes unnecessary pain. One of the blessings of reinforcement-based technology is that at least as far as animals and children go, we now have a realistic way to keep them and take care of them and teach them without automatically using fear.

What makes that possible is the ability to take the viewpoint of an ethologist—reading, understanding, and respecting the innate signals, from a dog's sad eyes to a little boy's worried forehead—and combine that with the problem-solving skills of an operant trainer, to set up a different and happier circumstance and outcome.

Chapter 8

Conversations

What Animals Can Say

We're used to pets telling us what they want; in fact, deliberately or by accident, we teach them to do so by giving in when they bark, mew, paw or claw us, begging, like babies, for what they want. I want food. I want you to pet me *now.* Pet me *more.* Or, of course, their actions can also tell us "Stop that" and "Leave me alone." All of these, however, are immediate expressions of internal states. What if it's something more complex? One of the things I love about clicker training in all its variations is that it lets us gather information from our learners about much more subtle matters, such as the animal's preferences and even opinions.

You can, for example, give an animal options. My friend Pat raises and clicker-trains horses. She often rides them in the woods around her house. One trail divides in two about a mile from home; however, both sides of the fork eventually lead back to the barn. Sometimes, at that fork, Pat tells the horse to go left, and sometimes to go right. Sometimes she drops the reins and says, "Pony's choice."

The horse pauses, then decides, sometimes choosing one path and sometimes the other. This exercise has no particular point; it's just fun for both of them. Some practical benefits have, however, arisen. When Pat finds herself in a difficult spot in the woods, facing perhaps a mud-hole or a rushing stream, "Pony's choice" lets her horse select the safest footing or path for both of them, something horses can do quite well.

A Conversation with an Elephant

In 1979, long before the current wide acceptance of reinforcement-based training in zoos, Ted Reed, the director of the National Zoo in Washington, D.C., read my book *Lads Before the Wind* and hired me as a consultant, to teach operant conditioning to a group of keepers.

For the better part of a year I traveled to the zoo once a month to give classes and to see what people were accomplishing. The participating keepers were working with a lot of interesting species, from oddities such as hyenas and binturongs to crowd-pleasers such as pandas and orangutans.

I asked for volunteer participants only, so I could help people who wanted to learn, without having to waste everyone's time dealing with resisters. The zoo director, however, decreed that the three elephant keepers had to attend the class whether they wanted to or not.

The elephants were still managed by the traditional methods of social dominance and the pain-inducing elephant hook. The two younger elephant keepers found reasons not to attend my class. However, Jim, a shy, elderly man and a longtime elephant keeper, came often, sitting quietly in the back of the room.

Early one morning before the zoo was open to the public, Jim stopped me on a zoo path and said that he was on duty alone at the elephant house that day. If I had time, he'd like to show me what he'd trained his favorite elephant to do. You bet, Jim.

We go to the elephant house. Jim has persuaded their big African female to lie down on her side in return for a kind word and a mango. I admire the accomplishment. Jim then suggests that since no one is around, maybe I'd like to work with the zoo's half-grown youngster, a female Indian elephant named Shanthi. Yes, please! Jim gives me a bucket of cut-up carrots, apples, and sweet potatoes, and a couple of toys: a big plastic baseball bat and a Frisbee. We go to the front of Shanthi's cage.

Clickers have not yet appeared on the training scene; my zookeeper students are all using the dolphin trainer's whistle. I explain the whistle to Shanthi by giving her a toot and a treat. I toss the bat in the cage and ask her verbally to bring it back. She does. Toot, treat. We do that again several times. Then she begins dropping it just a little farther away each time, making me reach through the bars more and more. "Dolphins play that game, too," I tell her, confiscating the bat.

I give her the Frisbee instead. Shanthi rattles it down the bars like a boy with a stick going along a fence. "Elephants like to make noise," Jim says, so I toot the behavior. Now Shanthi, displaying a nice talent for creative variation, shuffles the Frisbee on the floor with her foot, making a sound like maracas. I whistle and hold out a piece of carrot.

Shanthi gropes gently in my hand with the tip of her trunk, as if she can't quite figure out how to pick up that piece of carrot. Meanwhile, with her near eye, she is peering into the bucket. The message is clear: "What else have you got in there?"

I drop the carrot back in the bucket and hand her a piece of apple. This? Nope, she just fiddles with that, too. How about sweet potato? Yes! That she takes. From then on, I obediently sort out the sweet potatoes and just give her those. What a trainable person I am!

She tries a more traditional training method, too. She makes a half-hearted move with the Frisbee. I choose *not* to mark the behavior and remain still and silent. Shanthi flicks her trunk through the bars and raps me sharply on the arm.

Jim and I yell at her simultaneously. Okay, she says, and doesn't try that again. The possibility of course remains—in her mind, I suppose, and certainly in mine. I am loving working with Shanthi through the bars. I wouldn't dream of going in the cage.

Having found me so obliging, however, about the sweet potatoes, Shanthi then carries our conversation to a new level. She fixes me with a smiling, questioning eye, puts the tip of her trunk through the bars on the side of her cage, and begins feeling around. What is she doing? Jim and I go around the corner to see. Shanthi, with her clever eye looking encouragingly at me, is manipulating the padlock on the keeper's door into her cage. She is suggesting, since I am so biddable, that I open that door and let her out.

Though Jim and I both chuckle, this particular communication makes me sad. It seems like a good time to stop. I give Shanthi a double handful of treats. Jim opens a different door that lets Shanthi into her yard. In my final glimpse of her she is running, tail up and ears fanned out to the sides like wings, chasing a bunch of surprised pigeons into the air.

Elephants, as Shanthi has brattily demonstrated to me, are interesting souls. If I had elephants, I would give them mirrors and also hats; maybe like apes they would enjoy playing dress-up. And I'd give them noisemakers—drums, kazoos, and chimes, elephant-proof percussion instruments. You could have jam sessions. Keepers could play, too. What good would all of this be? I don't know; but in one brief encounter Shanthi told me that young elephants, at least, need more fun than they usually get.

Animals Teaching People

Some years later, as positive training has spread in the zoo world, I'm visiting another zoo, where clicker training has recently been established in a group of about fifteen baboons. A keeper demonstrates for me. She sits down by the bars, opens her kit of equipment and treats, and by name calls over a young female baboon. Through the bars the keeper cues several husbandry behaviors, trained in anticipation of medical care, such as opening the mouth for tooth inspection. Then the keeper brings out a needle-less hypodermic syringe to practice giving a shot.

Seeing the syringe come up, the baboon positions herself sidewise against the bars. The keeper aims the syringe for her hip. The baboon immediately backs up along the bars. The keeper tries for the hip again, and the baboon backs up farther, bringing her forequarters level with the syringe. The keeper laughs. "Oh, wait, I see. I've never actually worked with her personally before. She's explaining to me that she gets her shots in her shoulder, not her hip!"

Neither the animal nor the person is the least bit surprised by this exchange across the barricades of species and language; they are quite accustomed to it. The baboon is directing the person, the person understands and obliges. The clicker training alone has made it possible; these two don't have any past personal experience together at all. I find this downright dazzling.

It's not just primates that can explain things to people. Alexandra Kurland reports this little discussion with a horse. It is a summer evening, just as it is getting dark. One of Alex's students is working with his young horse in an outdoor paddock. Standing next to the horse on the ground, the trainer is shaping the behavior of stepping sideways. To give the animal the freedom to move easily, the owner has removed the lead rope and tossed it on the ground, leaving the horse wearing nothing but a halter.

A coyote howls from a nearby hill and another answers. This makes the horse nervous and fretful; but the trainer wants to finish the behavior they are working on and asks for more moves. Again the coyotes sound off, and now a third one joins in from a hill on the other side of the paddock. This is really unsettling.

A traditional horse trainer would know what comes next: the horse completely freaks out and someone gets hurt. But that's not what happens. Instead, the horse bends down its head, picks up the lead rope in its teeth, and shoves the rope into the trainer's hand. "Can we go home *now*?" Click: yes, indeed, we can.

Asking Questions

A dog trainer reports this communication. She is shaping her children's guinea pig to stand with its front legs on a box, like a circus pony. The guinea pig has put one paw on the box, several times, and been clicked for that. The trainer stops clicking now, waiting for the second paw. As the little guinea pig tentatively extends a second paw, it raises its head, turns, and looks full-face into the trainer's eyes: "Is this it?" It's only a guinea pig; but it asked the person a question. Clicker-trained dogs do that occasionally, but a guinea pig? Wow! The owner answers with a click, and the guinea pig puts two paws on the box and does so with confidence, even zest, from then on.

An Audience for a Cat

Cats don't generally need training, since they already come hardwired with behaviors we like, such as cleanliness and purring. Sometimes, however, cats come up with things you'd rather they didn't do, and then training some alternative comes in handy. When my boys went to college, I moved to New York with my daughter, Gale, who was then still in high school. To brighten up the apartment we acquired a Burmese kitten, Tosca.

Tosca develops a game of waiting on top of the bookcase for a person to walk by, then leaping down onto the person's back like a leopard attacking an antelope. All she wants is to ride around on your shoulder and see the apartment from a new perspective, but the behavior is startling to me and appalling to visitors, especially if they don't like cats. Gale and I teach her to sit up and raise her paws in the air if she wants a ride. Now and then she asks, and one of us is sure to oblige. She still spends time on top of the bookcases, but the leopard leap disappears.

This one shaping experience expands Tosca's ability both to problem-solve and to communicate. One winter Tosca embarks on a personal project: circumnavigation of Gale's bedroom without touching the floor. Tosca can make it from the desk on the west side of the room to the worktable on the north, to the bed on the east, and to the tall bookcase on the south or living-room end. The one place that defies her is the southwest corner. Two doors are here, back to back, one opening on the living room, the other to the bedroom closet. From the bookcase across the two doorways to the desk is too long a jump even for this athletic cat.

The living-room door, nearest the bookcase, is usually standing half-open. Tosca tries jumping from the bookcase to the top of this door. To land without falling she has to jump, turn in the air, then come straight down on the narrow top edge of the door with all four feet in a line. If she is the least bit crooked, the door swings one way or the other and dumps her. It takes practice; from my room, where I am writing, I sometimes hear a thump as Tosca misses the jump and lands on the rug.

One day while I am writing and Gale is in school, I hear Tosca yowling in a most peculiar way. I go into Gale's room to see what's going on. Tosca has mastered the leap from bookcase to living-room-door top, and she is balanced on the top. I've seen that before. Okay, Tosca, what is it?

Tosca blazes her eyes at me, making sure I am watching. Then she springs into the air and jumps off the top of that door to the top of the half-open closet door. She lands again with all four feet in a line, perfectly balanced. From there of course I can see she will easily be able to get to the desk on the west wall and thus complete her above-the-ground circumnavigation.

In the jump from door top to door top, neither door has moved an inch: it's the cat's equivalent of a triple axel. "Tosca, that's absolutely amazing!" I cry. Tosca sits down carefully on the top edge of the second door and bursts into a purr they can probably hear in Brooklyn.

Tosca wanted an audience. This all took planning; she never tried to get my attention until she had the stunt perfected. What is even more surprising to me is the level of communication. The little bit of shaping and reinforcement we've done has created more than a bond; it has created a two-way message channel.

A Dialogue

The most memorable conversation I have ever had with an animal (so far, anyway) took place with an Atlantic bottlenose dolphin, *Tursiops truncatus.* It is the species most commonly kept in captivity, but one I had never worked with myself. The dolphin was not one I personally knew, and on first acquaintance, not one I particularly liked, either. Let me introduce you to Josephine.

My old friend Ken Norris has become a professor and researcher at the University of California in Santa Cruz, California. He is doing some dolphin research at the university's marine laboratory. We are coediting a book on open-ocean dolphin research (including a chapter on my spotted-dolphin studies in the tuna nets) for the University of California Press.

One day on the phone Ken mentions that he's having some problems with his research dolphins: they are not yet trained for the sonar experiments he wants to do. Would I come to Santa Cruz and fix the problem? I strike a bargain: if Ken will finish the introduction we need for the research volume, I will at least take a look at the dolphins.

A week later I arrive at the marine lab to find Ken's animals, two big, old female Atlantic bottlenoses, temporarily stranded on the bottom of an empty holding tank, being treated with antibiotics. It seems they are sick, or at least not eating, a little detail Ken has failed to mention. That would certainly be one reason why they're hard to train!

Two research assistants are trying to give a shot to the one named Josephine. Josephine is thrashing her tail and snapping her jaws left and right; she doesn't look all that sick to me. I sit down and visit with the trainer, Michelle, while the tank is being refilled. Michelle thinks they will eat later in the day and invites me to give them a training session.

So, after lunch, we begin. Each dolphin has a "name cue," an underwater sound that means "You come here": a little bell for Josephine and a clicker for Arrow. As the dolphins swim in circles eyeing me suspiciously, I call Josephine with her bell, shaking it underwater. Josephine ignores me, so I put the clicker underwater and call Arrow. She comes over to me. I start asking Arrow to touch a little neck-sized hoop I am holding in the water, giving her clicks and fish (which she doesn't eat) for each touch. Immediately Josephine barges over, making threatening movements at Arrow and issuing a stream of bubbles and air-audible burst-pulse sounds. I am shocked. I tell Michelle I have *never* heard worse dolphin language, not even from the wild spotter-male gangs insulting each other. Michelle shrugs: "She does that all the time." Tsk tsk.

Josephine now swims up to me herself and bumps the hoop with her rostrum. I give her a whistle and a fish, which falls to the bottom.

Nevertheless she bumps the hoop again; she then departs and drives Arrow away to the far side of the tank. Fine. Obviously Jo is not going to let Arrow work, but now Jo is mad enough to want to work herself.

So I play a joke on her. I have Arrow's clicker in my hand; but now I call Jo with that sound. I make it clear that I mean *her* by clicking a big chain of clicks when she happens to come toward me and stopping the sound when she goes by or turns away. She does come over. I stop clicking and put the hoop in the water. She touches it and gets a whistle. Even though she ignores the fish, she repeats the behavior several times. *Good* dolphin.

These training tanks are level with their surroundings, like a swimming pool, not raised to waist height as proper dolphin-training tanks should be. Ken Norris! Where were you when the architects thought that up? To make it easier to reach the dolphins, I lie down on my stomach on the concrete deck, with my arms in the water.

If there's one thing dolphins are good at, it's making waves. Jo immediately swishes past me briskly enough to send a slosh of water over the concrete, effectively soaking my front side. "She got you wet!" Michelle exclaims. Yes. That was no accident, and rude of Josephine; but so what? It isn't a cold day. More important, if I recoil or go away to change clothes, Josephine *wins,* and we can't have that. Josephine apparently recognizes this as a draw. Though I continue to work lying prone on the concrete, she does not swoosh water over the deck again.

I offer the hoop. This time, gently, Josephine touches my hand with her rostrum instead of the hoop. In what I call "trainer metaphor," that is, using words a person in the same situation might use, she might be saying, "Let's pretend I don't understand quite what you want."

I know better, of course, but I'm big about it; I whistle and toss a fish, which sinks to the bottom; Josephine is still not eating. I offer the hoop again. This time Josephine slowly drifts up to me and gently touches not the hoop, not my hand, but the clicker itself. This time I am not so bighearted. I do *not* reinforce that. I can play at being unpredictable, too, madam! Josephine immediately turns her back to me and goes off to sulk in the middle of the tank.

Josephine is an old Navy dolphin. She was captured as a youngster off the coast of Florida. She's been working for Navy scientists and Navy employees and no doubt various visiting experts for many, many years. She's probably been putting up with a few inconsistent trainers, among the many good ones; and she's become a master at making life confusing and miserable for anyone that makes life confusing for her. I'm not really surprised she's been donated to Long Marine Laboratory. In my experience it's not the first time the Navy has fobbed off a crabby, old-lady dolphin on some innocent researcher.

Fine, I say mentally, to her sulking back view, if you won't play with me, I'll go play with the other dolphin. I get up, move to the other side of the tank, and toss a toy to Arrow. She makes a timid pass at it and gets a whistle and a fish. Josephine of course leaves the middle of the tank and bullies Arrow away from me again. Poor Arrow, I'm sure she didn't ask to live in the same tank with Josephine.

I go back to the spot I've chosen as Jo's training station, lie down, and offer the hoop. No need to call her now; Jo comes over briskly, touches the hoop promptly when asked, gets a whistle, and—aha!—takes her reward fish in her mouth, before spitting it out.

We do this successfully two or three more times. Then Josephine tries another familiar dolphin game. She swims briskly up to the hoop and stops dead about a quarter inch from actual contact. Of course she doesn't think about her action in words, but it is a calculated act. "I can *almost* do it, won't you help me a little?"

This is a fine stunt, and often effective. The trainer is of course tempted to move the target toward the animal and complete the contact. I have personally witnessed a dolphin train a researcher to reach farther and farther in this manner, over days, until the researcher leaned so far out over the water that he actually fell in.

But I know a version of that game, too. The next time Josephine swims briskly up and then doesn't *quite* touch the hoop, I wait a beat or two. Then I move the hoop six inches closer to me, away from her. This gesture makes a distinct statement to Josephine: "I know what you're up to. And now you know I know."

Wow! Is she surprised. I suspect that nobody has ever caught her up like that before. She lets out a huge bubble of air (a dolphin startle response) and sinks tail-first two feet or more (a dolphin distress or annoyance-related behavior).

So we continue. I am not really trying to "train" Josephine. I am just using this little behavior—touch the hoop—to explore and develop the parameters of working together. When Josephine leaves me and sulks in the middle, I do not punish her by giving her a time-out; she is giving me a time-out, anyway. I just get out the dip net and clean up the fish she hasn't eaten, making eye contact with her from time to time, so she knows I am not through with her. In fact, I can do that only because she is also keeping an eye on me; she's not really through, either.

Once when she comes back to me after one of these pool-cleaning pauses, I lie down, call her over, and extend the hoop with one hand while with the other I hold an extra-big and especially delicious herring in the middle of the hoop. Now, by clicking the clicker right next to the herring, I invite Jo to touch *that* instead of the hoop.

Asking a dolphin who won't eat a fish to touch a fish on cue? What a dirty trick! Josephine echolocates loudly on the herring—*brrrrt,* I can hear the pulses in the air. She swings her head back and forth to pick up the returning echoes, then does it again. When she has to believe her senses, that I am *training* her to touch a fish, she pulls away and circles the tank rapidly. As she zooms by me, she raps the hoop sharply with her rostrum, hard enough to make my hand sting a little. Just as clear a statement of opinion as you could possibly wish. She is saying, right back at me, "I know what you're up to. And now you know I know!"

I end the session. We will have one more session tomorrow. Jo has progressed from ignoring food to holding a fish in her mouth several times. We both certainly have a lot to think about. That's progress. I'm happy.

Michelle now gives the animals their evening treat, a highly preferred mackerel that also contains, tucked in the body cavity, essential antibiotics and other medications. Josephine not only performs a nice high jump in response to Michelle's jump cue, but wolfs down two mackerel, the first vigorous eating she has done all day.

Worthy Adversaries

Dolphins' eyes look out to each side, like horses'. They usually make social eye contact with each other, and with people, by looking with one eye or the other. Dolphins do, however, have binocular vision straight down; that is, they can see with both eyes at once only in that direction (handy, I daresay, for judging the depth of a predator below). The next day when I come into the training area and take up my chosen station at tankside, Josephine does something I've never seen before in my life: she stands up on her tail, belly forward, looking around her own jaws and making intense eye contact with both of her eyes meeting mine, a startling experience.

Josephine deserves some kind of social response for that and she won't let me touch her, so I greet her verbally. Usually I avoid that with dolphins. You may think you are encouraging the animal with chit-chat, or pleasing it, when what you are doing is often quite meaningless. This time, smiles and pleasant words are all I have with which to respond to her own remarkable greeting.

Again we start off with coming when called and touching a target, the hoop. Michelle, working with Arrow across the tank, gives Arrow a fish. Josephine barges over, drives Arrow away, and eats the fish herself. Hmm. Her appetite is improving, though I cannot say the same for her manners. Josephine begins gulping down the little herring and capelin I give her for touching the hoop. Hurray. The trading post is open and we are in business: I have fish and some ideas for you. What do you have for me?

I uncover a couple of other common trained behaviors and cues Josephine already knows: waving a pectoral fin in response to my hand wave, and resting her chin in my cupped hand. She also responds nicely to my jump cues. Each behavior earns a whistle and a fish.

Once I give her three little capelin, instead of just one. Surprise! She positively *counts* them, aiming her rostrum at one, the next, the other, back and forth. Then she eats them. The next time I surprise her with multiple fish, she gobbles them all instantly. Once, just to keep providing her with novel experiences, I give her a single especially small fish, minnow-sized. She mangles it, then goes by at speed and throws it into the air straight at me: "Here's what I think of that fish; take it back!" How funny! What a great animal!

After another of these bickering exchanges, Josephine breezes past me, a yard away, and just lifts her large tail from the water and sails it past my nose. She doesn't slap the water in front of me and get me wet again; she certainly doesn't hit me with her tail, though she could. She just glides by. "See what I could do if I wanted to?" I know, Josephine.

Once when I give her the jump cue, she takes off, goes through all the motions, but doesn't actually jump. That can fool a trainer who whistles too early, but it doesn't fool me. No whistle, no fish. I give her the jump cue again. This time she takes off with a speed-building rush that accidentally on purpose makes a huge splash. She not only soaks me from head to toe, Michelle and a nearby volunteer are dripping wet, too. Meanwhile Jo is in midair showing off a splendid leap, and I give her a whistle for that. She completes the jump, then stops and cocks an eye at me: "Oh, what a shame, you're all wet; but I was doing what you told me to do, wasn't I?" Yes, you were, and you got your whistle, and here's a nice fish.

With the animals eating and working again, my job is done. I will not be back. I'd been moved that Jo had so obviously been excited to see me when I arrived that morning. Now I feel sorry for her. She's going to feel as if the circus left town.

Josephine's Golden Years

Though our encounters might have seemed adversarial, Jo and I were, in fact, playing. She was playing dolphin jokes on me, and I was playing trainer jokes on her. When, for example, she rapped the hoop after I'd told her I'd pay her (with a fish) for touching a fish, she wasn't really mad. Had she been truly aggressive, she could have struck me instead of the hoop and easily broken my arm. And my messages to her were not meant unkindly. I was conveying that while I knew she'd been disappointed and confused in the past, I wouldn't do that to her; and I wouldn't let her do that to me, either. Let's be colleagues instead.

The main problem here, aside from logistical difficulties such as the tank design, was that Josephine and Arrow were the wrong animals. Young dolphins enjoy a puzzle and will willingly work at complex research tasks. Josephine, besides her presumed long history with many easily conned trainers, was too old. In the Florida waters where both animals were originally captured, Josephine would now be a senior female in a band of females and calves. There her dominance would be appropriate for keeping the peace and driving off pushy males.

My recommendation was that these two animals should either be retired or released, and the marine laboratory should get some young dolphins instead. That is what happened. Ken got some other dolphins to finish his work. Arrow, under the provisions of the Marine Mammal Protection Act, was marked with an identifying sign on both sides of her dorsal fin and released into her natal waters. During my term on the Marine Mammal Commission, I was able to make sure that harmless and permanent freeze-branding identification became a condition for all dolphin release permits. Thus we know, from subsequent sightings, that Arrow became a permanent member of a band of female dolphins.

Josephine was precluded from release by a chronic kidney problem that would require lifelong medication. She was relocated at the Dolphin Research Center in the Florida Keys. She became an important member of the center's female-calf band. She was allowed to choose her companions and her dwelling place. She preferred one of the medium-sized enclosures and had no interest in going back into the ocean; she didn't even like going into the facility's large fenced lagoon. She was a whiz at helping newly arrived dolphins get used to their new surroundings. She also made herself useful by introducing junior trainers to some of the humbling aspects of working with dolphins.

She lived for many more years. I visited her once with my grandson Max Leabo, then thirteen years old. I don't know if Josephine remembered me, though she let me stroke her. She took a definite interest in Max, however, soliciting his attention and making eye contact (with one eye, from the side, in the normal dolphin manner). When he sat down on the dock beside her, she actually played with him, spitting water and fetching toys, in a gracious and even grandmotherly way.

Chapter 9

Questions

As clicker training grows, and especially as ClickerExpo brings more and more newcomers into contact with experienced operant trainers, questions arise. Not new questions; the same questions, over and over, but from new people. Here are some that may already be troubling you.

Why Can't I Just Use My Voice?

Unless your learner is deaf, or lives underwater like a dolphin or a fish, you can certainly use your voice for cues. As long as you standardize the cue for each particular behavior, many species, including all of our domestic animals, can get pretty good at recognizing verbal cues. And if you eventually need dozens or hundreds of cues, well, fortunately you have an ample variety of words.

So why can't we just use our voice as a click, too? That's a good question; we clicker trainers hear that one often. "Why do I have to click? Why can't I just say *good,* or *yes,* to mark the behavior I like?" Well, you can. My pony children did wonders with "Good pony." Of course, they were scrupulous about always using that same word or phrase, and no other, as a marker. They were scrupulous about timing the phrase to occur during the action they were looking for, not after it stopped. And they were scrupulous about never using that word or phrase in casual conversation or for other purposes, at least never around the ponies. The marker was the marker, not to be confused with anything else.

The pony children were young, they had no previous experience, and they just accepted the new rules and followed them. Most adults find it difficult to be that disciplined about their words. It's hard to go all day without saying your chosen word—*good* or *yes* or *okay*—by accident; and each time your dog or pony hears that sound without results, you weaken the word's value as a marker.

Then there's the question of timing. One advantage of using an artificial marker is the precision that it teaches *you.* If you are not already skilled at using a marker to shape behavior, your timing will be off when you use your chosen word. I can take four strides across my living room in the time it takes most people to say "Good girl." Even if you use a short word, you still have a handicap when it comes to marking a brief event.

Find a friend to bounce a ball on the floor next to you. Pick up a clicker and try to click at the instant the ball hits the floor. (You don't have to use a clicker; you can tap a spoon on a tabletop, instead.) It's harder than it looks; sometimes you will click or tap after the bounce, not on it. However, you will instantly *know* when you were late, and on subsequent bounces you'll get more accurate.

You won't get that feedback from your own voice. Try to say "Yes!" every time the bouncing ball hits the floor. Your friend bouncing the ball will know when you were late or early, but you won't. It seems as if when you hear an outside sound, your brain takes a clear snapshot of what else is going on at that very instant. But when you hear your own voice, even if the words came after the event you were watching, the brain quickly covers for you: "Oh, yes, your timing was great!" If your word was late, you can't distinguish that error and you can't self correct. Furthermore, if someone *else* corrects you, you'll be annoyed. Pick up a clicker and you circumvent that whole mess.

The Neutral Stimulus

Probably the biggest drawback of using the human voice as that universal marker, the click, is that it already has too much meaning. Ideally, like Pavlov's bell, the marker should start out as an unconditioned or neutral stimulus, one that means absolutely nothing until you turn it into a conditioned reinforcer. And if there's anything on the planet Earth that is *not* a neutral stimulus for most people and animals, it's the human voice.

The human voice is *designed* to convey many messages at once. Even a single word—*hello,* on the telephone, for example—identifies the speaker's sex, approximate age, identity, and something about his or her current mood. You use the voice for good things and you use it for bad things. You say "Yes!" but you are tired or impatient or not really pleased. Your voice gives you away. We listeners know what you really mean. You can never really clean out that subtext; and, at the very least, it must distract the animal by always posing a question. What does this "Yes" actually mean this time?

But let's suppose you had perfect timing, knew just how to use your marker, you gave your "Yes" in exactly the same tone every single time: wouldn't it really be just as good a marker as a click?

Voice vs. Clicker: A Test

Lindsay Wood, an experienced clicker trainer and a graduate student in the psychology department of Hunter College, set up a simple experimental protocol to look at the difference, if any, of using a click versus a word. At a nearby animal shelter she selected twenty young, friendly dogs, all newly arrived and all similarly untrained (for example, none of them responded to standard commands such as come, sit, and down). Taking one dog at a time into a quiet room, she sat in a chair and shaped this behavior: go over there and bump that standing target with your nose. For half the dogs she used clicks and treats to shape the behavior. For the other half, she used the word *yes* and treats. Each training session consisted of ten two-minute intervals. Every session was videotaped so an outside observer could confirm that the timing was correct and other procedures were the same with the two groups of dogs.

A few dogs didn't complete the program: two got sick, one was adopted midcourse, and one never got over being afraid in the new room and wouldn't participate. The remaining dogs all achieved the goal: they would bump the target, come back for their treat, then go right to the target and bump it again, as long as the session continued.

There was a big difference in how fast things went. The dogs getting the click completed the training in an average total time of thirty-six minutes. The dogs getting the verbal marker took an average total time of fifty-nine minutes. The average total number of reinforcements for clicker dogs was 83; for verbally reinforced dogs, 126. Clicker was certainly quicker.

When the Click Counts Most

Of course this experiment didn't tell us *why* the clicker was quicker. It wasn't intended to solve that mystery. However, Lindsay's protocol teased out another important piece of information about using a marker. The difference in speed of acquisition showed up most strongly while the dog was learning something new.

While the trainer was shaping the behavior of going to the target, clicked dogs got there in an average of seven tries. Dogs hearing "Yes" needed an average of seventeen tries. Learning to bump the target rather than just touch it took an average of five tries with the clicker and an average of nine with "Yes." Once the dog understood the behavior, however, and the trainer was just maintaining an already-learned behavior, there was no difference between the two conditioned reinforcers. "Yes" worked just as well as a click to keep a behavior going. But in capturing and shaping new behavior, the initially neutral and nonsocial stimulus, the click, made a dramatic difference.

What this suggests to me is that the key difference is the clarity of the information. The click says "Right. That's it." At any time in any place with any clicker, and even with a totally unfamiliar person holding it, the click means "Right. That's it." The spoken word, unavoidably, means much more, maybe too much more. Was that word directed at me? How does it compare to other times I've heard it? What's the mood of the speaker? And so on. That fuzziness somehow slows things down.

Clicker trainers are aware of the difference from their own experience. Once the clicker-trained animal catches on to a new behavior and its cue, you can maintain that behavior forever with a pat or a smile, or just a chance to do other good things such as going for a walk. There's no need to have a clicker in your pocket all the time. Where the clicker is really needed, and where you'll go rummaging through every drawer and coat pocket to find one, is when you want to teach something new.

Clicker Using without Clicker Training

I sometimes see people who compete with their dogs in agility, or in the dancing-with-dogs sport called freestyle, who use the clicker a lot, and whose dogs are happy and enthusiastic, yet the dogs don't seem to be clicker-trained. Take one aside and try to shape a new behavior by clicking small moves, and the dog is totally bewildered. Like a conventionally trained dog, it waits to be shown what to do.

These owners seem to develop new behaviors in a more conventional way, by leading or luring the dog through the moves over and over, using lures, praise, and encouragement. They then maintain the behavior, once it's more or less learned, with clicks and treats. As a consequence the dogs see the click as a secondary reinforcer, all right, meaning "Job's done, treat's coming," but they don't see the click as information about their own moves, since it hasn't actually been used that way. They are better off than dogs that are coerced into the behavior and punished for errors, but they aren't really using their brains.

How about Praise?

But isn't praise and a show of affection important? People sometimes flinch at the whole concept of training with a clicker instead of praise: it's a mechanical device, and that's a sort of evil in itself. Clicker training doesn't mean throwing praise and approval out the window. Praise can be a powerful reinforcer, depending on your history with the learner. Praise, however, is a poor marker, taking too long and often coming too late to communicate anything specific about what the learner needs to learn; and that's the information the animal needs.

Terri Arnold, a famous and highly influential dog-obedience expert, once phoned me out of the blue (we had never met) to tell me that she'd been experimenting with the clicker. She found that her obedience-champion dog really *did* respond better to that metallic sound than to her voice. Terri told me her reaction: "How come my dog loves this darned thing more than she loves me!" She was so furious she threw the clicker down on the kitchen floor and stomped it to pieces.

I laughed, as she expected me to. I could see why she'd been mad. It was an example of extinction-induced aggression, the ire we all feel when something we'd always counted on is no longer true. I thought it took a generous spirit to share the story with me at all. Of course the dog still loved Terri; but it learned faster from the clicker because of the clarity of the information.

The difference between marker-based training and everything else is not merely that one avoids punishment and concentrates on the positive. Many trainers now rely on positive methods rather than punishment. The correct use of some kind of nonverbal marker communicates what you want so clearly that it makes all positive training easier, quicker, more efficient, and much faster. How much faster? Somewhere between Lindsay Wood's average of more than 40 percent to what many of us have experienced as 100 percent: a new behavior acquired on a single click.

What gets most of us into the business in the first place, then keeps us there earnestly trying to persuade others to join us, is that this works so well. Being able to communicate so specifically and so directly—and enabling the animal to communicate back equally efficiently (yes, I get it; no, I don't get it)—is too valuable a tool to pass up. In comparison, many a program based on dominance and control seems like one long time-waster. The dividends, of course, beyond greater efficiency, are a richer communication, a closer bond, and much more fun during the process, for learner and teacher both.

But What about Punishment?

If you have always trained or taught animals or students with aversive control, it's really impossible to envision how you could do it without those tools. Trainers in the audience at a clicker seminar or lecture often start a question with the phrase "I don't see how." "I don't see how you could possibly use the clicker for . . ." training gundogs, or guide dogs for the blind, or guard dogs, or elephants, or juvenile delinquents, or whatever challenging organism they work with themselves. All of these questions come down to the same thing: I don't see how you can train without at least sometimes "getting tough"; I don't see how you can train without punishment.

The enthusiastic teacher is tempted to start addressing whatever example was given with stories about conversions. Yes, people *are* training gundogs or guide dogs or guard dogs with a clicker, and here's how they do it! But the more you explain, the more fodder you give the questioner for "Yeah but . . ." ripostes. Each time your questioners prod you into yet another defense, you have reinforced them for yeah-butting again. That is an endless and unproductive path.

The punisher's arguments can also display elitism. "I manage these difficult populations with a skilled use of force. *You,* obviously, don't need that level of skill because your population is average and easy to deal with. Therefore I, with my elite population of learners, wouldn't need your kind of training." That sense of being one of the elite is a pleasure that's often hard to give up.

One day a friend asks me if I'd be willing to give a clicker class to her

West Highland terrier club, and I say yes. I bring along a bag of clickers, a lot of chopped hot dogs, and two clickerwise friends. Soon people are clicking all over the room. Little white dogs are learning to spin, wave, back up, lie down, and bark and be quiet on cue.

Then I notice one woman just sitting in the middle of the room with her own little Westie crouching underneath her chair. "Why don't you try this out with your dog? It's fun!" I say, offering a clicker.

"Oh, that wouldn't work with my dog," she answers firmly.

Perhaps the dog is sick, I think, and can't have treats. "Why not?" I ask politely.

"My dog's from England!"

I've heard the equivalent of the "My dog's from England!" argument from a lot of people now, especially teachers of human beings. That might work for *your* (boring, ordinary) students; it definitely wouldn't work for *my* (exotic, challenging) students. I deal with this resistance by nodding, smiling, and talking to someone else. These people will come around, or they won't. I'll save my strength for the people who are ready to learn.

I Have a Problem . . .

Another class of questioners don't really want new information. "I have this problem with my pet." Almost always the problem is a product of the owner's behavior. These people don't really want to know how to change their own behavior; they just want you to make the problem go away. I try to duck out of these situations, too; if you give in and try to fix the problem they present, you can bet ten more will grow in its place.

At a fund-raising dinner I meet a woman with an interesting job: she is a museum curator. Alas, since I am introduced to her as an animal trainer, she doesn't want to talk about art; she wants to talk about her cat. Her cat gets on the kitchen counters while she is cooking, and nothing she says or does makes it get down.

I suggest she get a tall stool or put up a shelf where the cat can sit and watch the cooking without getting in the way. I should have known better. Some months later we meet by chance at another gathering, and again she wants to talk about her cat. The shelf in the kitchen has worked pretty well to keep the cat hairs out of the gravy, but now the curator has a new problem. The cat is coming into her bedroom at night and knocking things off the bureau.

She tries to ignore it, really she does, but lately the cat has also taken to knocking the pictures crooked (something no doubt particularly annoying to a museum curator). Do I tell her, "By your patience and forbearance you have created a monster?" Do I point out that she is actually reinforcing the escalated behavior by waiting until she can't stand it anymore to do something about it? Do I address the root cause, the cat's high energy level, and talk about ways to keep her lively cat busy in the daytime so it is tired at night? No. She is not asking for real solutions; she is asking me to repair her cat's behavior, as if it were a car. I tell her to close the bedroom door.

The Punishers

One outcome of people's focus on problems is the proliferation of commercial trainers who are superb at suppressing behavior. Pain or terror may well be involved in what they do, but most compulsion-based trainers are deft enough so that even a highly severe "correction" is not obvious. What is obvious is that the problem behavior has gone away. In fact, a lot of behavior has gone away; sometimes the animal is now doing nothing at all.

I once went to a weekend gathering at the home of a wealthy man who had two Labradors, one black, one brown. He told us they were perfectly trained; he had purchased them that way. What did they do? Absolutely nothing. They did not bark at cars in the driveway. They did not greet guests. They did not wag their tails or solicit petting. They went outside only to relieve themselves, and only at specific times of the day when they were told to do so. Otherwise they lay around in the halls (*not* on the good rugs, and certainly not on the furniture) all day and all night. They were ornaments, and not even that ornamental, since their bodies were flaccid and shapeless from years of doing nothing wrong by doing nothing at all. From the standpoint of the man who owned them, they were perfect pets.

Stopping behavior through adroit use of aversives can occasionally be done with great speed, sometimes, like good clicker training, producing results in a single instance. That impresses clients, of course. The difficulty with suppressing behavior, however, is that it doesn't really fix whatever is maintaining the behavior in the first place. Stopping behavior also does nothing to teach new and more suitable behavior. It doesn't make the pet more interesting or fun. And if aversives or punishments are used—and they always are—the hapless owners may be left with unpredictable fallout in the form of fearfulness, stress-related physical problems such as excessive licking, or of course fear-related aggression.

Why Wouldn't You at Least Correct Mistakes? What's Wrong with That?

Okay, so punishment is not a good way to teach behavior. But why, why, why, people still ask, do we refuse to correct mistakes during the training? Surely correction is useful information?

It's not the information that's the problem; it's the reprimand. The information "Nope, that isn't it" is indeed useful feedback and one clicker trainers use all the time. The message "That's not it" is embedded in the use of clickers, conveyed not by the addition of something bad but by the absence of the click. But cuing a behavior, then punishing the animal because it failed to give a response—or because the response wasn't what you had in mind—has the big downside of poisoning your cue; and reprimands for behavior offered voluntarily, in the hope of reward, are even more destructive. By salting a training session with aversive experiences, you risk poisoning the whole process.

I'm visiting an Arabian-horse farm where the trainers use the clicker. They are getting such good results that other trainers are sending them "spoiled" horses for retraining. I'm watching a session with one of these remedial cases, a beautiful Arabian broodmare. Her only job, aside from having foals, is to stand still in the show ring and win ribbons for her beauty.

Arabians are supposed to be spirited. In the show ring an Arabian should hold its head high, with pricked ears and an animated expression. One way to get a horse to look lively and keep its ears pricked is to swish a whip threateningly around its head. With luck, just as the judge gets to your horse, the head is high and the animal looks alert.

This mare, however, has been threatened (and probably actually struck) a few times too often. Now when the whip comes out, she pins her ears back flat to her skull, shoves her muzzle forward as if prepared to bite, and makes an evil face, threatening right back. It works for her! The whip disappears. But it doesn't work for the handler. No judge would give a ribbon to a horse that looks like that! She can no longer be shown, and that definitely affects her value.

The clicker trainer, a young woman in jodhpurs, is working on getting the mare to prick her ears for a click and a treat. She tells me that she captured pricked ears a few times in a previous session, once when another horse was led past, once when a tractor started up; but according to the trainer the behavior isn't "operant" yet, meaning that so far the horse isn't doing it on purpose.

The trainer and the horse are standing in the sunshine facing each other, bucket of carrot slices close by, clicker in hand. The mare gets a click and a treat for free. Then the trainer waits; and the mare goes to work. She knows she can make the trainer click. She knows it has something to do with ears. But what?

She puts one ear forward, then back. No click. She puts the other ear forward and back. No luck. She rotates the openings of her ears around, as if listening in all directions. Then she flops both ears to the sides, like a rabbit. (I'm silently amazed; I didn't know horses could do that!) Then she pricks both ears forward. Click!

Aha! She's got it! Now she does it again and again. Prick, click, carrot. Prick, click, carrot. In a few more clicks the handler adds a cue—a finger pointing straight up. Now the mare can point her ears forward and keep them there as long as the trainer's finger is up. The mare and the trainer are both looking delightfully pleased. That's a look you could take to the bank!

But what if the handler had actually corrected each error, even just verbally? What if she had said "No" to ears moving separately, to swiveled ears, flopped ears, and so on? That correction from the trainer, even if totally absent of physical abuse of any kind, is nevertheless aversive. That can halt the learning altogether.

You have been encouraging the animal to take chances and explore. She's getting her own information about what works and what doesn't; she doesn't need extra input from you. But now when she innocently tries something you don't want, you "correct" her. Uh-oh. That ends the happy exploration. Instead of trying to learn new things, she will now do nothing, to stay out of trouble.

But That Wasn't So Bad...

The aversive you step in with doesn't need to be severe, at least not from your standpoint, to have that effect. You may grade your punishments from mild to drastic; punishers often do. I've seen a dance teacher bring a little ballerina to tears with verbal corrections, then reprimand her for crying. "Why are you so upset, that was nothing, I could get much tougher if I wanted to!" However, just like reinforcers, what's painful and what's not can only be judged by the recipient.

I am watching a trainer working with a big and bouncy shelter dog. She has been using the clicker for sitting and for standing quietly. Now the dog jumps up on her and tries to lick her face, and she responds by turning her back to him. To her, that is a gentle correction, but the dog cowers as if she'd lashed him with a whip. This social rejection, just when things seemed to have been going so well, is a devastating blow. It can take a long time to undo that loss of traction.

ıt in crates, all of which at least initially might be aversive to the gs. These arguments that clicker training involves aversives are gen-lly put forth, I think, to justify the arguer's inclination to keep using or her own favorite corrections.

The flaw in the assumptions is this: while all punishment is aver-e, not all aversives are punishment. Life is full of aversive events. It ns. You stub your toe. The computer locks up. The train leaves with-t you. These things happen to all of us, and to our pets. Even the st caregiver cannot spare an animal or a child from all of life's little ersives. What we try to avoid is deliberate use of aversives to train navior.

It is work, it's true, to figure out how you might resolve a challenge developing new behavior. It sometimes takes a long time to clicker-in a dog, step by step, to be calm and confident around strange dogs the street instead of attacking them on sight; but it can be done. It is rk, it's true, to make a step-by-step plan, schedule some clicker ses-ns, and teach your Rottweiler to accept your son's white rat as a new usemate instead of a new chew toy; but it can be done.

These questions are of vital importance to each new questioner. y time a new technology comes along, the people who were success-ly using the old technology are going to be in an extinction curve; y're going to protest and feel anxious and even become aggressive mselves. All of these emotions, however, arise from lack of knowl-ge. As soon as people stop fretting and actually start using the tools, questions go away. So the real way to answer all of these questions ust to keep spreading the technology.

New Questions

ave been fortunate, in these years of teaching science-based train-, to animal trainers, in having some pretty reliable advisers when estions, in the basic sciences of ethology and behaviorism, come up t I can't answer myself. Erich Klinghammer has constituted a direct eline to Lorenz's views of behavior. I am also close friends with

So Does Clicker Training Mean You Can Ne

No.

Of course you can reprimand in daily life. Animal
that mother dolphin in the tuna vessel's backdown ch
her baby into the air when it was dashing playfully ab
net. If I'm getting ready for company and one of my d
interest in the cheese and crackers on the coffee table,
expect the dog to leave the cheese alone—as long as I
way. What I *can't* do is kid myself that my power extend
I'm not around.

Being "positive" is not the same as being permissive
to things kids want to do that are unsafe or impracti
able. You can exercise your own intentions and prefe
arrange life without having to please everyone all of
case most of the daily events that people tend to want t
ishment are actually not training problems anyway, b
problems. The baby is about to stick a bobby pin into
Saying no is not the answer. Until the baby is older, y
cover the light sockets and keep small objects out of t
The puppy is peeing on the rug? Confine the puppy to
laundry room, or to a crate and a play area, when you
take it outside. Managing the environment is the sen
to punishment, especially when the goal is a behavi
hasn't learned to do yet.

Clicker Training Is Not Really All Pos Anyway, Isn't That True?

Some doubters argue that clicker training is by no me
sives. During clicker training, some of the dog's efforts
isn't that aversive? Clicker sessions end; that's aversiv
ers say. The chance to earn treats is over, and the dogs
point out that clicker-trained dogs wear leashes and

Skinner's daughters, artist Deborah and Professor Julie Skinner Vargas, and Professor Ernie Vargas. The Vargases are erudite and insightful behaviorists. When I'm stuck, I can just call them. Now, however, the thousands of modern trainers all over the world are raising new questions, questions that cannot be answered by either ethology or behaviorism.

First: how come our clicker-trained animals learn so fast? Learning is supposed to take many repetitions; but we are all accustomed to capturing new behavior in just a few clicks.

Second: how come animals remember their clicker behaviors so well? Learning is supposed to fade over time. Traditional dog and horse trainers put in a lot of effort polishing, retraining, and repairing what their animals have previously been taught. But clicker-trained behaviors remain in the animal's memory apparently forever. Why? And how?

Third: how come the clicker often seems to be more powerful, more reinforcing, than the treat it stands for? After all, a one-inch piece of banana is not a significant item of diet to a rhino; one-eighth of a hot dog is hardly vital to a ninety-pound mastiff; and yet both animals will happily work for click after click after click, backed up only by these trivial reinforcers. Sometimes, in fact, the "primary" reinforcer isn't even desired. Many of us have experiences of animals, such as the dolphin Josephine, refusing the food, but still offering behavior (however contrarian). Dogs on the veterinary table, too scared to even think of eating, can nevertheless be shaped with clicks alone to touch a target—the vet tech's hand, say—and thus stand still even during painful treatments. It seems as if the click somehow becomes the important reinforcer, and the backup food is the token! What is *that* all about?

Why Is the Click So Much Fun?

And finally, why is the clicker so much fun? Debi Davis, a leading figure in the clicker training of service dogs for people with limited mobility, has a papillon for her own service dog. These tiny dogs, not much good for pulling a wheelchair, are perfect for jumping down from your lap and retrieving your glasses or the pencil or car keys that just fell on the floor. Many clicker-trained dogs brighten up or wag their tails at the sight of a clicker. Debi's papillon went a step further. At clicker classes the little dog took to sneaking around under the chairs, poking into people's bags, and bringing back clickers. "Here, Mom, can't have too many of these!"

Clicker Thrills

In teaching people to clicker-train we often have them train each other, using the clicker to shape, without words, some simple behavior such as writing on the blackboard or switching on a light. If you are the "animal" in this shaping game, you try various things. Finally you get a click. Hurray, you're on the right track! You feel the elation not just in your thoughts, but in the pit of your stomach. Animals apparently get that zingy feeling, too, and they show it, not just initially in the "lightbulb moment" when they first catch on, but at other moments of success, by prancing, barking, or running around in circles.

That elation has nothing to do with the primary reinforcer. Learning in this fashion provides primary reinforcement, of course; but it also seems to be just plain fun. Neither ethology nor behaviorism explains why these effects are almost commonplace with an abstract marker such as the clicker, but are rare—indeed, face it, pretty much unheard of—without it. So what's going on here, anyway? And where do we go to find out?

Chapter 10

Answers

The Amygdala Involvement

Barbara Schoening, a German veterinary physiologist and clicker trainer, tracks me down at a conference with the start of an explanation. Barbara mentions the amygdala, two clumps of tissue in the primitive part of the brain sometimes called the "reptile brain," which developed early in evolution, before there were any mammals like us. We share this old, interior, basic part of the brain with, for example, turtles and lizards, and it's pretty crucial for things like breathing and walking. On top of that old system, we mammals have a new part of the brain, the cortex, which is where our conscious thinking happens.

The amygdala has several functions, some no doubt still unknown; but it's generally thought of at present as the fear center, a sort of automatic alarm system that responds to possible signs of danger instantaneously and without any previous conditioning. Hear a loud crash behind you and you will jump out of the way before you even turn to see what it was; your amygdala makes that happen. The clicker, Dr. Schoening says, is the kind of stimulus—short, sharp, sudden, unusual—that is known to be processed by the amygdala. Maybe that has something to do with its unusual effects.

I have a memorable personal experience of this effect. I'm touring the Brookfield Zoo in Chicago with the zoo's director, George Rabb. He takes me to the reptile building, currently under construction and closed to the public. We walk along a line of glass-fronted exhibits, each containing a snake or two. In the middle of the row Rabb asks me to stop for a moment. He walks past the next exhibit himself and then invites me to catch up with him. As I pass, bang! Two big cobras strike the glass right next to my shoulder. Of course I jump a mile, giving Dr. Rabb a good chuckle.

The snakes know Rabb, but I'm a stranger. In snake and person alike, the old reptilian brain we share triggers instant protective action. It is this powerful, primitive system that Schoening proposes as the pathway for our little clicker. No wonder the results might be different from using traditional training!

So, does the click go through the amygdala? How do we find that out? My initial pragmatic approach is to look for a brain researcher with some wired-up rats who would clicker-train an animal—or let one of us do that—then track where that click goes, inside the brain. This does not prove easy to do. I manage to meet and talk to a few scientists who have just such rats in their lab. These animals have been surgically fitted with a painless, permanent metal skullcap through which wires from specific locations inside the brain can be connected to a computer. The researchers I locate, however, are baffled by my questions and totally uninterested in using their expensive and delicate research animals for casual experiments suggested by outsiders.

Clicks and Dopamine

I am not the only clicker trainer being drawn toward new developments in neuroscience. Many others are circling around this mountain of mysterious information and sending me what they've found. Pretty soon I have a laundry basket full of books, reprints, Web articles, tear sheets, and e-mail notes, all related to some aspect of brain research that someone, somewhere, is pretty sure has something to do with the clicker.

One candidate for involvement is the brain chemical dopamine. Neuroscientists studying addiction report that their cocaine-using rats experience a cascade of dopamine, which has been associated with pleasure, when a prolonged session of lever-pressing finally produces a dose of cocaine. But in fact it is not the cocaine delivery that causes the dopamine cascade; it is the sound the machinery makes when the delivery starts: the conditioned reinforcer, the good news. The click.

The dopamine, it seems, is not related to consummatory pleasure (actually eating the food, drinking the water, or taking in the addictive drug), but to the happy anticipation of knowing you are about to get what you want. That seems useful to know. Perhaps our little click affects the brain chemistry not only in a way that words do not but, more important, in ways that the basic primary reinforcers such as food treats do not.

That does not explain the rapid learning or the long-term retention. I need to know more. Then I run across a newspaper article on neuroscience and fear, which directly discusses the role of the amygdala. I am particularly interested in the descriptions of work by a neuroscientist named Joseph LeDoux.

The Conditioned Fear Stimulus: A "Devil's Click"

Some neuroscientists think that only humans have genuine emotions, since only humans are able to report verbally on the nature of the feelings (what hubris!). Others think that emotion, so subjective and interior a process, is an unsuitable topic for investigation. (They aren't alone; many ethologists and behaviorists think so, too.)

LeDoux, however, like Darwin and Lorenz, thinks that animals obviously experience emotions, since they often visibly display species-specific signals reflecting their internal state of affect or emotional condition. If so, real pathways exist in the brain, and emotion should be a valid area to study. But what emotion? Some possible emotions—joy, sorrow, jealousy—are hard to demonstrate in an experimental animal. An obvious and unequivocal emotion is fear.

Fear is easily created. You present some kind of neutral stimulus such as a light or a sound, pair it a few times with something dangerous and unpleasant such as an electric shock, and bingo. The next time you present your learner with the previously insignificant stimulus, that organism, whether rat, rabbit, or graduate student, will experience and exhibit fear. That fear will give you predictable and measurable side effects such as a racing heart, increased respiration rate, and (in the case of humans) sweating. Meanwhile your once insignificant sound or light has become a conditioned fear stimulus; you can provoke the fear without the ensuing shock, any time you want.

It's not hard to establish a conditioned fear stimulus, and many traditional animal trainers use one intuitively. It might be a word—*Ach!*—or a mouth sound, such as a hiss, or even just a facial expression. It is a conditioned punisher meaning "Something bad is coming."

Instead of strengthening behavior, it stops behavior. If the dog is doing something wrong, you give your secondary punisher, your "Devil's click." If the dog stops, fine; you do nothing. If the dog keeps on with the behavior, wham! You yank that leash, and hard. It's a powerful tool for making a bad behavior stop on the spot, greatly impressing onlookers; but it's not particularly efficient for teaching the animal to do something better instead, and there's no guarantee that the behavior will not resurface if the trainer is no longer around.

At the Center for Neural Science at New York University, LeDoux and a sizable team of students and associates have been studying the conditioned fear response and its neural pathways in the brain. The work is of immense value in understanding and treating human fear-related problems such as anxiety, panic attacks, and post-traumatic stress disorder.

By pairing a light, say, with electric shock, they found that the resulting conditioned fear stimulus, once learned, bypasses the cortex, the thinking, more modern part of the mammalian brain. Instead it travels immediately to the amygdala, and from there to other primitive parts of the brain governing memory and emotion. This shortcut to the alerting system in the old part of the brain produces some unusual effects. Like the click, a conditioned fear stimulus can be learned in one or two tries. Like the click, the memory is permanently retained. Like the click, the conditioned fear stimulus instantly produces a flood of emotion.

Finding Joe LeDoux

I now think that the click is in fact a conditioned "joy" stimulus, and that it might travel the same path as LeDoux's conditioned fear stimulus. Is that true? I have already discovered that it is useless to ask neuroscientists questions that lie outside their specialty. The dopamine guys know the dopamine guys, but they don't know the cognitive-processing guys. A question about the amygdala draws blank stares in hippocampus circles and vice versa. The simplest way to find out seems to be to ask LeDoux. I craft a careful letter asking for an appointment. Dr. LeDoux responds politely, telling me to call him after the Christmas holidays. In January I call again. He is busy with students and suggests I try in June.

In June, after phoning again without results, I decide to change tactics. I'm in New York anyway, to see my agent and my editor. I grab my laptop with its illustrative video clips, sweet-talk my way past the New York University security desk, and show up at LeDoux's office door.

A graduate assistant springs up from a desk in the anteroom. "No visitors! He's writing a grant proposal!" he cries, barring the interior door, presumably LeDoux's office, with outspread arms. Wow, that's fealty all right!

"I have one question about the amygdala," I say politely.

"Come back Wednesday!"

No. I know this tactic. I'll wait right here.

Now a third person standing nearby introduces himself: Chris Cain, a postdoctoral research fellow at the center. "I think I could answer your question. Would I do?"

You bet!

We go to a communal workspace down the hall and sit down. I pull out a clicker and start to explain clicker training. He's heard of clicker training. He wants to discuss his brother-in-law's Labrador retriever. Dodging that topic, I ask my question: does the click go through the amygdala, and is that why the learning is the way it is?

"It's a conditioned reinforcer," he says.

Hmm, I've never heard that term from a neuroscientist before. "It's also an event marker," I say, launching into an explanation of that crucial function.

"But it's a conditioned reinforcer," he repeats.

"Yes, of course, that, too."

"But *all* conditioned reinforcers go through the amygdala."

What? They do? I'm astonished. If that's true, there's no need to clicker-train a wired-up rat. We can take it as a given that the click takes the old, efficient low road of the amygdala. Wow! That was worth the trip right there.

Now he gives me an even more important piece of information. "You need to talk to the people who are studying conditioned positive reinforcers and the amygdala: the Cambridge Group."

For roughly thirty years, first at Cambridge University in England and now at Johns Hopkins University in Maryland, a sizable cluster of neuroscientists have been using wired-up rats and a wide variety of conditioned reinforcers to study appetitive behaviors such as addiction and obesity. Primary and secondary reinforcers are a means to an end with them, not their main focus, but they do know a whole lot about how reinforcers work in the brain. This kindly man swivels around in his chair, gets on the nearest computer, and finds a name, Peter Holland, at Johns Hopkins University in Maryland.

Dr. Cain walks me to the elevator. Pressing a clicker into his hand for his brother-in-law, I pour out my gratitude. I have seen no way around contacting LeDoux, and yet it has been so difficult that I was beginning to feel like a stalker. Cain assures me that Holland will be more accessible. Cain reveres LeDoux, everyone in the lab loves him, but they all know how short his time is.

Clarity at Last

Sometimes cross-fertilization between two disciplines produces instant results. In talking with Peter Holland at Johns Hopkins, I discover that this band of neuroscientists have had answers for a long time to things they didn't know were other people's problems; and that includes the questions we clicker trainers have been asking, and some more besides.

This whole area of research, focusing as it does on things animals *want,* not on things they avoid, is based on positive reinforcement. That's convenient; we are already playing the same game. Furthermore, Dr. Holland is a scientific polyglot. He is of course a neuroscientist, fluent in brain terminology, but he is also completely familiar with the Skinnerian reinforcement jargon. He's highly interested in ethology and, more or less for fun, I gather, teaches an undergraduate course in animal behavior. That means we share yet another vocabulary. Finally, he is aware of clicker training and to my astonishment mentions some of my own publications. So, the first question again, does the click go through the amygdala?

Yes, indeed it does. All secondary reinforcers go through the amygdala, not exactly where the fear stimuli go, but through other parts of those structures, bypassing the cortex, the more modern part of the brain. From there, as with LeDoux's conditioned fear stimuli, the message of the conditioned reinforcer goes directly to areas governing emotion and memory. Holland and his colleagues might use a light or a tone or a physical object such as a block of wood or even another rat as the secondary reinforcer; but the news always takes the same path, straight through the amygdala to sites for memory and emotion. And that is important for us. Maybe our markers really are different from other kinds of learned information.

I ask about some of the other odd effects we have noticed, such as speed of learning. We're used to seeing the animal catch on to new behavior in five or six clicks, or even much less. Is that real? Do these guys see it, too?

Even though these neuroscientists are dealing largely with classical conditioning, not with operant conditioning as we do, they get rapid learning, too. In fact, they expect it. If it takes a student more than half a dozen presentations to teach a rat new information, then the professor knows that something's wrong, either with the student's setup or with the procedure.

What about long retention? Yes, that happens for them, too. Unless you deliberately decondition the response or teach some conflicting response (poisoning your click, as it were), whatever the animal has learned via conditioned reinforcers is remembered, apparently indefinitely.

And, finally, what about emotion? To us that click, our conditioned, secondary reinforcer, produces a sometimes dramatic surge of emotion, a sense of elation or joy. In animals and people, too. Holland prefers a more neutral term, *excitement,* as evinced in his rats, he says, by heightened respiration, increased activity, head turning, increased hormonal output, and so on.

I'm happy. LeDoux's constellation of fear symptoms is produced by a conditioned fear stimulus passing through the amygdala, creating instant memory and strong emotion. Holland's conditioned positive reinforcers, passing through another part of the amygdala, produce a different constellation of visible symptoms, but also create instant memory and this strong emotion. It's the same process. Yippee.

So Barbara Schoening's surmise is right. The click goes through the amygdala. That explains some of the attributes that make marker-based training, shaping, and our learned system of positive cues so different from teaching via verbal instruction, luring, coercion, and punishment.

Fear of the Click

This confirmation of the amygdala's role also explains to me an occasional problem for the dog owner new to clicker training: the dog that for no known reason seems to be terrified of the clicker.

The flexible piece of steel inside clickers makes a relatively loud snap. For some sound-sensitive dogs that is probably not a neutral stimulus; it's so startling that it triggers the amygdala-based alarm system, and the dog ducks and runs. The owner often responds by pointing the clicker at the dog like a TV remote and clicking some more, simultaneously tossing treats and talking reassuringly. Of course, repeating the click while the dog is already scared turns the sound into a conditioned fear stimulus, generating more fear each time. Now the dog is diving under the bed or peeing in terror. Tossed treats may become conditioned fear stimuli, too.

All the owner has to do is put the clicker away for a while and use a truly neutral stimulus, such as the blink of a flashlight, to teach the dog how to earn treats this new way. Once it discovers that a blink is really, really good news, you can tactfully precede the blink with a soft click (in your pocket or behind your back) and turn the sound into good news, too.

Levels of Reinforcement

We trainers utilize at least three levels of reinforcers. First, the primary reinforcer, something the learner really wants; then, the secondary reinforcer, the signal that the food or whatever is on its way; and finally, the cue, giving information about what to do next, to get the secondary and primary reinforcers to happen. Second- and third-level reinforcers are important to learners because they contain information. *Information* is not a word most behaviorists use, tainted as it is by implications of imaginary, unprovable mental processes; but it's a perfectly good word to engineers, who know that information, or feedback, is necessary even to machines.

Levels of reinforcers are like steps up the ladder. The basic or primary reinforcer—the food, water, or whatever—is crucial. Without the first rung, you can't start up the ladder at all. The next rung up is the marker or secondary reinforcer, carrying the information that good stuff is coming and that you're doing the right thing to get it. The third rung up is the cue, giving information about how to make the lower levels of reinforcement happen.

The cue differs in one key way from the secondary reinforcer or click. The click meaning "You win, and now you get paid" comes after the behavior has occurred. The cue comes before the behavior and identifies specific actions that will lead to the end result. That discriminator function is obvious to the bystander, which is why it's so easy to think of the cue as being like a command, something that "makes" the behavior happen; and so easy to blame the animal if it "disobeys" the cue.

The reinforcing aspects of the cue are more subtle. Sometimes you can spot side effects, called "superstitious behavior," created by a cue reinforcing some other action accidentally, as with the guy who irritably pounds the steering wheel until the traffic light turns green. The more obvious side effect, however, is the innate behavior of the learner: the pricked ears, sparkling eyes, and keen attention of animals waiting for and getting their cues. Just like the click, the cue that has become a conditioned reinforcer goes straight through the amygdala and creates visible excitement.

Dogs that are working for cues don't act like dogs that are working for commands. They are merry and enthusiastic rather than somber and cautious; I have heard traditional trainers complain that these dogs are undignified, that they "act like puppies." Traditionally, I guess, highly trained dogs should *not* give the frivolous impression that they are also having fun!

The Nature of Cues

A cue is only reinforcing if the recipient really knows both what it means and how to do the indicated behavior. If you as a pet owner are just using cues around the house in everyday life, it probably doesn't matter too much if you say "Here, boy" sometimes, and "Come" at other times, as long as the dog comes when you call; or if you ask for "Roll over" and the dog gives you "Spin" instead. But if you need and want accuracy and reliability, you need your cues to be accurate and reliable, too.

A good cue should have the same attributes as a click. It should be short, precise, the same every time, easy to perceive, and different from everything else in the environment. It should always, if responded to correctly, be followed by positive outcomes, never given additional meanings, and never misused by turning it into conditioned fear stimuli, the cue for punishment. We waste a lot of opportunities if we don't use, attend to, and protect the real nature of cues.

An Evil Side of Tertiary Reinforcers: Fatness

There's more than one sort of third-level reinforcer. One can establish a conditioned reinforcer that doesn't just indicate that reinforcement is available, but that identifies in advance just what sort of primary reinforcer awaits. That's why corporations pay so much attention to brand names and logos and package design. They need us to see and recognize those learned reinforcers and go out and buy the product. But the work of Holland and his colleagues suggest that these learned stimuli have an insidious side effect: they can create a desire where none really exists. Good for corporations; not so good for us.

One of the problems the Johns Hopkins neuroscientists have been studying is obesity. Overeating is of course a major factor. But what keeps making that happen? It's not just weakness of will. Something more elemental is going on in the brain. Holland and his pals and students can demonstrate that second- and third-level conditioned reinforcers may be at least one cause.

They choose a rat and offer it a variety of foods. The rat, feeling hungry, goes to the feeder, chooses a food, and eats. The investigators identify two kinds of food that this particular rat likes best: the rat versions of, let us say, pizza and ice cream. Now they pair new conditioned reinforcers with each kind of food. These conditioned reinforcers explain to the rat not just that food is coming, but what kind of food: "When you see the blue light, you are going to get pizza! When you see the yellow light, you are going to get ice cream!"

Now they put the rat in a place where both kinds of food are freely available twenty-four hours a day. Pizza over here, ice cream over there. No clicks, no cues, just help yourself. The rat can eat his favorite foods until he's full, anytime he wants; and he does so.

Now, when the rat is full, the experimenter turns on the blue light. Ah! Pizza! thinks the rat, and although he's not hungry, he goes over to the pizza place and has some pizza. Give him the yellow light and he goes over to the ice cream place and helps himself to ice cream. The lights trigger the behavior of going to *and eating* specific food even if the rat's body is not at all interested. Under this circumstance the rat may eat as much extra food as he would eat if he were really quite hungry; and he was full when he started. Does he become obese? Yes, indeed, he does.

Now just think how often during the day we are all blasted with learned cues involving food. On the TV; in every magazine and newspaper; on the train, on the bus, walking around town. Oh, boy! Put on your sunglasses when you go past those Golden Arches! It's not the Big Macs that will do you in; it's the abundance of cues that bring you through the door even if you're not really hungry that do the harm.

One More Reason Why Quitting Is Hard . . .

Secondary and tertiary reinforcers are wonderfully powerful, in all species and at all levels; but it's not just the reinforcing aspects of food, drugs, and their associated conditioned reinforcers that make quitting habits and addictions so difficult. Joe LeDoux, the authority on conditioned fear stimuli, points out what I'd call a simple wiring problem: messages from the amygdala tend to be one-way traffic. Connections from the amygdala up to the cortex, the thinking part of the brain, are better developed than connections from the cortex back down to the amygdala. Once an emotion or a craving is turned on by a conditioned reinforcer, it's easy for the thinking brain to pick up the news but actually mechanically difficult to signal back, "Turn it off, pal." I know how difficult it was to finally quit smoking after years of trying. It's kind of comforting to think, well, it wasn't just me; perhaps the nervous system really isn't set up for dealing with that kind of problem.

More to Come . . .

Is there a fourth level of conditioned reinforcer? Oh, I bet there is, and probably more. Kay Laurence talks about using your eyes to tell your dog when you are available for giving cues and when you are not; that is, when the trading post is open and when it is closed. First you would make a habit of preceding verbal or manual cues with eye contact. Then, by deliberately *not* making eye contact, you can prevent your dog from eagerly throwing behaviors at you ("Look, I'm bowing, I'm spinning, click me!") while you are on the phone or standing in line at the post office. Borrowing from the geologists, who commonly use these sequential terms, I'd call that a quaternary reinforcer, a conditioned reinforcer four rungs up the ladder, but good information for the animal just the same.

Science and Fun

Holland and his associates indeed have some answers for us, and good ones, too, about how and why the click works the way it does. They have answers I didn't even anticipate about why and how cues are so powerful. However, emotion itself is not part of their investigation. They agree that animals are excited by the arrival of information, whether from a marker or a cue, but the question of why that should be so is not in their department. That leaves me still hunting for an answer to one more question: how come this whole business seems to be so much *fun*?

Laughing Rats

Jaak Panksepp, another distinguished neuroscientist and the author of a popular book about emotion and the brain, is interested in the positive emotions, including having fun. He is somewhat notorious for his papers on laughter in rats. He noticed in his laboratory that young rats like to roughhouse with each other. If you use your hand as a playmate, as you might with a kitten, a young rat will wrestle and play with you, too, and even chase your moving hand around, hoping for a game.

Panksepp wondered if the rats might be making high-frequency sounds during their games. He purchased a bat-finder, an instrument that brings high sounds down into human hearing range. Sure enough, roughhousing rats chirp and chatter when they play. Panksepp identifies that as laughter. His fellow scientists deplore the word but accept the facts: rats can play and have fun.

➤ **Watch the "Laughing Rats" video in chapter 10 at www.reachingtheanimalmind.com.**

The SEEKING Circuit

One of Panksepp's primary interests is the hypothalamus, another part of the primitive brain that is associated with basic emotions. Researchers have found that stimulation to particular parts of the hypothalamus apparently causes pleasure. Rats will press a lever over and over to get that stimulation as long as it is available. If you don't stop the experiment, the rat will continue working until it actually collapses from exhaustion.

Scientists initially assumed that the stimulation must be incredibly pleasurable. Panksepp disagrees. Looking not just at the data but at the actual rats as they are pressing the lever, they don't look to him like rats enjoying some nice sensation, but like rats on a hunt. They are excited, eager, even frantic, digging at the lever as if they are trying to get at something underneath or behind it. It is as if the stimulus in the hypothalamus says "Search!" and, when they search, says "Search!" again.

Given stimulation in the same area of the hypothalamus, human medical subjects report a sense of excitement, a sort of restless eagerness, quite enjoyable really, although agitating. It seems as if something really marvelous is about to happen, if you can just figure out what it is. Panksepp identifies this phenomenon as being part of a system he calls the SEEKING circuit (this formal scientific term is spelled with capital letters).

The SEEKING circuit is a set of connections in the more primitive areas of the brain that initiates and maintains searching behavior. The SEEKING circuit, Panksepp says, sends small animals out of the nest in the morning "looking for worldly goods." The SEEKING circuit, he says, also makes him a neuroscientist.

From an evolutionary standpoint the SEEKING circuit is probably just as important as the amygdala's automated alarm system. What good does it do you to escape being eaten if you can't also find your own breakfast? Every organism needs a system that promotes investigating and utilizing the environment.

I see some connections here. According to Panksepp, it's easiest to keep an animal in the SEEKING state and at high levels of excitement when small reinforcers occur at frequent but irregular intervals. Doesn't that sound a lot like clicker training? Would Panksepp agree? I write to Panksepp, asking for an appointment and offering to bring some clicker-training video clips to show his students.

Visiting Panksepp

A few weeks later I am climbing off a plane at the tiny Pullman airport in eastern Washington. Panksepp is at Washington State University, on the Washington-Idaho border. This is Palouse country, home of the Palouse Indians and the Appaloosa horse. It's a lush, rolling landscape of wooded hills, wheat fields, apple orchards, brooks, little rivers, and horse-dotted pastures, now, in the early spring, absolutely teeming with birds.

Jaak Panksepp, bouncing on his toes, is waving through the airport fence. Born in Estonia and reared in the United States, he has a slight European accent and a lot of energy. He's lined up a busy two days for me. I give graduate seminars on clicker training in two different departments, with Panksepp supplying commentary and a stream of questions from the front row both times. I meet with researchers and students all over the university to discuss training problems ranging from teaching chickens to jump to drawing blood from hibernating but wakeful grizzly bears.

There are students with questions at every meal, a fine party in my honor at the Panksepps' house, and a major public lecture to give at the veterinary college (good thing I brought all those video clips!). Panksepp has no hesitation: of course clicker training is an example of the SEEKING circuit in action, and he says so to every audience. Furthermore, of course, it's fun!

The Importance of Fun

There's a good evolutionary reason for searching for necessary resources, and the occasional success reinforces the process; however, there's more to it than that end goal. The urge to seek and explore needs to function not just when you are in need of food or warmth or shelter, but when you're feeling quite relaxed and happy already. That's when you have the energy and the desire to go exploring, so exploring needs to be reinforcing in itself, or we wouldn't get up and do it for "no good reason." Konrad Lorenz observed that it seemed that every species of animal, given the opportunity, would go exploring. I think the exhilaration of looking for something new and desirable, from a water hole or a berry bush to a new restaurant or a great pair of shoes, is so crucial, whether we actually find good things every time or not, that Mother Nature built in another reinforcer for SEEKING behavior: it's fun.

We hunters and gatherers are totally familiar with this experience. Of all the larger mammals, none of the others come anywhere near us in our ability to find all kinds of new things to do in new environments. SEEKING-circuit activation is also probably a crucial part of daily life. I get that SEEKING-circuit sense of excitement from window-shopping, traveling, snorkeling, bird-watching, crossword puzzles, computer games, turning on the evening news, and playing

Monopoly with my cutthroat grandsons. We even enjoy the sensation vicariously, by watching sports, going to action movies, and reading novels and comic strips.

Thanks to Panksepp's assurance that clicker training is an example of his SEEKING system in action, we have a scientific rationale for the sense of excitement and fun we all enjoy, learners and teachers alike, as we clicker-train. From the pro golfer using a clicker to straighten out someone's slice to the duffer he's coaching; from a fifth-grader teaching his hamster to give him a high five to the hamster that's getting the clicks—the process produces for all of us that ineffable SEEKING-circuit feeling: Hey! This is cool! This is *fun*!

Clicker trainers have a strong gut reaction against punishment; and the more experienced we are, the stronger the feeling. Well, thanks to Panksepp, we have a scientific rationale for why mixing correction and reinforcement is harmful rather than helpful to the learning. It's not just a moral issue; it's common sense. Correction or rebuke switches the learner from the hypothalamus and its SEEKING mode to the amygdala's path of avoidance and fear.

People say, "Oh, the animal quit on me." Or, "This child is just lazy." Or, "She's not paying attention." Or, "He's not really trying." Or, "My dog is so easily distracted." But you did it. The learner is exploring ways to get reinforced, and by introducing punishment you've poisoned the whole process; the SEEKING circuit is no longer in operation. It might be hours before that system switches back on, for you; or it might never do so at all. Your learner will save its fun times, seeking and exploring, for when you are not around.

Respect for the Organism

Panksepp is enthusiastic about clicker training for another reason. He is incensed at what he considers a serious error in science in general: "The animal is regarded as a passive vessel. Stimuli arrive from the outside world, or from the hormones and so on inside, and the rat responds. That's the way people see it. But the rat is *not* a passive vessel. The rat has intentions and preferences. You have to be aware of that." Clicker training, Panksepp says, assumes that the organism is an active individual with contributions to make. "Clicker training creates respect for the organism." That, of course, means treating our own species respectfully, too, especially when we are teaching and learning with each other.

And clicker trainers are aware of that because now we're finding out more and more about how to teach humans all kinds of skills—without scolding, without punishment, without extensive verbal instruction with the clicker.

Chapter 11

People

Coaching with a Click

Theresa McKeon bought a horse at auction. Big mistake. It was a nice-looking horse, but when you got on its back, it had a plan: to get you off, then leave town. Theresa went to the Internet and found out about clicker training for horses. She retrained the horse until it was safe and calm, then sold it. Then she looked at the clicker in her hand and thought, I could use this in my day job.

Theresa is a national-level gymnastics coach. It's serious business. Students who start as wriggly seven-year-olds may in their high school years be competitive enough to win not just trophies but full four-year college scholarships. It's an investment of time, money, and dedication. It's also an investment in guts, not just because gymnastics is scary and dangerous, but because it involves a lot of getting yelled at.

Here's the thing: words are not a good way to convey specific information about moving the body. Teaching a handstand, the coach might say, "Keep your legs straight up." But when you're upside down, you can't really see where your legs are, and the scolding "No, no, no, you're over too far, straighten *up*" doesn't necessarily help. What is "too far"? Where is *up,* exactly? The best you can hope for is that after more tries you'll hear a grudging "That's better," and the coach will find some other prey.

A coach with a clicker can do things differently. Theresa has been e-mailing me about her work. She lives in North Carolina. I pay a visit. We drive to the professional gymnasium where Theresa works. In this huge space, high-ceilinged like an airplane hangar, perhaps ten coaching sessions are going on simultaneously. Along the back wall teenagers are running and springing into the air in dolphinlike flips and spins. At the far end a man with a bullhorn is directing fifty high school cheerleaders in a group formation. At the balance beams, the high bars, the floor mats, everywhere in this huge space, loud instructions and reprimands ricochet in all directions. What a racket! Only around Theresa is it quiet.

The Language of the Click

Theresa lines up a class of those wriggly seven- and eight-year-olds. She asks them, one by one, for a handstand. They've already learned how to step forward, put their hands on the floor, stiffen their arms and shoulders, and turn themselves upside down; but they're still pretty wobbly. Theresa now tells them she will click for "Toes at twelve o'clock." The first child stands on her hands. Just as her wavering legs pass through the top of the arc, Theresa clicks. Oh! That? That's twelve o'clock? The child may be surprised; she thought she was straight when her toes were somewhere else. But now she knows exactly what she felt like at the instant of the click. She can re-create that feeling. When Theresa asks her to do it again, she goes to a perfect vertical at once, earning another click. Each child takes her turn. In a couple of rounds all eight pairs of toes are straight up.

Theresa changes the goal and clicks for "Ankles together"; and each child gets that. Then she clicks for "Toes pointed"; and one by one they get that, too. Now the handstands are straight up, the legs are together, and I can see that pointing the toes has somehow made the knees straighten out, too. Furthermore, with the legs stabilized, everyone's balance has improved. Some kids can stay in the handstand much longer than they ever could before, an experience so gratifying Theresa actually has to instruct them to come back to earth, please. The change is permanent. It took less than ten minutes. And no one got yelled at, not even once.

➤ **Watch the "Handstand" video in chapter 11 at www.reachingtheanimalmind.com.**

Theresa takes me to another part of the gym. A group of advanced sixteen-year-olds have asked her for a little clicker assistance. They are practicing a complex maneuver on the parallel bars. You jump up and grab the first bar, swing up and stand on it, then leap through the air, catch the second bar, swing all the way around it in a full circle in the air, let go again, do a backward somersault in midair, and land on the mat on your feet.

They can all do this maneuver just fine except for the very end. After the somersault, about half the girls are landing off-balance and falling on their fanny. Each girl laughs ruefully as she scrambles to her feet. I notice, too, that each girl glances warily at the coach: Uh-oh, I'm probably in trouble. But Theresa is smiling and silent.

"They need more momentum," she says to me. Turning to the class, she tells them that she is going to click them for straight knees in the flight between the two bars. Straight knees? That's easy. One by one they run, leap for the first bar, swing up and stand on it, then leap for the second bar, their minds on "straight knees" as they take off. Those that have straightened their knees hear a click in midair. When they complete the huge swing around the second bar and let go, do their somersault, and land, to everyone's amazement they land standing on their feet. Thinking about straightening the knees, they are taking off with a bit more of a shove; that provides the extra momentum that lets them land with the weight forward enough to stay upright. Click!

Where's the Primary Reinforcer?

You can't hand out potato chips or candies to people who are flying through the air or standing on their hands. So where is the primary reinforcer in all of this? For the older athletes the information is all the reinforcement they need. For a person who has just ruined a dazzling aerial performance by falling on her rump six times in a row, just landing on her feet is powerfully reinforcing. Younger children are more likely to need backup reinforcers such as stickers or toys. Beads are popular; you get a bead for every ten clicks; save them up and make a bracelet. Or students can earn tokens, then pool their tokens for group rewards such as a pizza party for the whole class. Older students do get occasional tangible reinforcers every now and then, such as "Permission to skip Saturday practice" cards, a highly coveted reinforcer; but mostly, success is the payoff.

Of course, training this way is not something you can do continuously. Tagging sessions are intense, for both teacher and learner, requiring enormous concentration; it's best to keep them brief. Theresa sprinkles brief five- or ten-minute tagging sessions throughout the afternoon, alternating with strengthening exercises, games, endurance sprints, and other activities.

Meanwhile, how do the learners keep track of their tags? The gymnasts sometimes wear little counting devices pinned to their waists, enabling you to slide a bead down for every ten clicks. But even the littlest children are surprisingly good at keeping track mentally. At the end of an afternoon in the gym, I ask one small girl how many clicks she got that day. She beams. "Eighty-seven!"

Theresa exclaims, "Eighty-seven? How often in your life have you been right eighty-seven times in one day?"

The whole class laughs; *never* is the answer to that one!

A New Name for Clicking

Of course, it's not long before a posse of angry parents shows up at Theresa's gym. "This clicker business has got to stop, and right now. Clicker training is for dogs, everybody knows that, and you can't treat our kids like animals!"

Personally, I'm rather pleased to hear that "everybody" knows that clicker training is for dogs. From the standpoint of my company (which president Aaron Clayton has renamed KPCT, Karen Pryor's Clicker Training), that's pretty good market penetration.

For Theresa it's a headache. She announces a parents' meeting for the next day and goes home to think up a solution.

At the meeting the next afternoon she presents a new concept to the parents. "What we are doing at this gym is not 'clicker training.' It's a new technique called TAGteaching, teaching with acoustical guidance. This little soundmaker"—she holds up a clicker and clicks it—"is called a tagger." TAGteaching, Theresa explains, will help their children learn faster and do even better in competition.

"Oh, TAG, that's nice!" the parents all agree. They go home satisfied that their children are getting some new coaching techniques—which they are. Where logical persuasion might fail, semantics wins out. From now on, in training humans, a click is called a tag, the person holding the clicker will be the tagger, and a certified teacher who has learned to use the technology correctly is a TAGteacher.

Peer Tagging

One of the joys of this new system is that the coach no longer has to do all the teaching; the students can click each other. Theresa names it peer tagging. I watch a pair of fourth-graders working on the balance beam. One girl is doing a handstand, then rolling forward until she is upright again. As she comes erect, she throws her arms up and out triumphantly: Ta-da! I've seen that on TV a million times. What I hadn't noticed on TV was that this "Ta-da!" position also includes tossing the head back proudly. Gymnasts call this the chin-flick; these two are working on the chin-flick.

The girl on the ground watches intently, her clicker in her hand. The girl on the beam lands, stands, throws her arms out, and her chin goes up. Click! The click reinforces both girls: the one on the beam, for remembering to do the chin-flick, and the one on the ground, for capturing the move she was so intently hoping to see. Many of the children who are enrolled in gymnastics have been diagnosed with attention deficit disorder. They are busy, busy kids whose ability to concentrate seems next to zero. Now, while peer tagging, they are paying downright fierce attention to just one thing.

➤ **Watch the "Chin-flick" video in chapter 11 at www.reachingtheanimalmind.com.**

Often the child doing the clicking mimes the same lift of the chin or straightening of the legs that she is marking in her partner. Here neuroscience comes into the picture again, with a discovery of something called mirror neurons. When one monkey watches another monkey do something, these mirror neurons become active. Even if the monkey doesn't move, the neurons in its brain respond as if the movement were really happening. Mirror neurons may be at work when an athlete is advised to visualize a perfect movement and can then execute it; or when repeatedly imagining going through a movement seems to strengthen the muscles as if the move had actually been carried out. Perhaps the tag facilitates this subtle learning.

Certainly peer tagging benefits both children; for one thing, I can see that they really do become peers. The mutual reinforcement (Yay, I got a tag! Yay, she did it right!) makes them friends. The little girl who's just learning English, the little girl who's a bit plump, are giggling equals of all the others, not the ignored fringe members of the class as they might otherwise be.

A Contagious Idea

Theresa's colleague Beth Wheeler runs a dance school in Marblehead, Massachusetts. Beth converts her entire school to TAGteaching. To use the new technology with her children, Beth breaks each dance skill down to small elements. Each element is called a "tag point." A tag point is a specific move or position, describable in just a few words, that is something the learner can already do easily.

I visit the dance studio and am treated to the sight of thirty little girls taking turns running down the length of the floor, jumping in the air every other step. None of them jumps particularly high; a few inches at the most. Now Beth divides them into pairs and sets them to tagging each other for a series of tag points, starting with a foot turn. Step, turn the pointed foot; if the foot turns correctly, click, and do it again. Across the room each pair goes, with one child tagging, the other performing. Then they change jobs and cross back. When everyone has accomplished that, Beth demonstrates sweeping the leg forward, with the foot in that turned position, and they all do that. The third tag point is to bend the left knee as you sweep the right leg, and they all click each other for adding that move into the system.

Don't the children get confused, with everyone tagging at the same time? Never. We can almost always tell which click is ours even in a sea of similar sounds. When everyone has acquired the three new tag points, the music starts. Beth calls out, "*Sautez,*" or Jump, just as each knee bends. Thirty little girls cross the room, springing repeatedly amazingly high into the air, like stotting dolphins. A dozen watching parents burst into amazed applause. Learning that combination of tag points has made them all better jumpers, in just a few minutes. The skill is permanent; and learning it was reinforcing.

Joan Orr, a biochemist in Canada with a personal interest in sports training, finds Theresa on the Internet. Orr tries TAG first with some Down syndrome teenagers in a Special Olympics program. The kids love it, learn quickly, and prove to be good at peer tagging each other, too. The biggest training challenge is their regular coaches' traditional criticism-based methodology. Although for these students tagging is visibly more effective than verbal correction, change in the coaching procedures is not going to happen soon.

Golf

Joan Orr moves on to another obvious application: golf. Her retired uncle and aunt are dedicated duffers. Joan meets with her uncle and aunt and their club golf pro and offers to give them all a TAG lesson. Her uncle declines to be a guinea pig, but her aunt is willing and so is the pro; they agree to try it for nine holes.

Of course, the golf pro can see some things the aunt is doing wrong right from the start. Perhaps her feet are too close together, her grip is incorrect, her backswing is angled incorrectly, and so on. He is about to nag her for all of this on every swing; but in TAG, as in clicker training, you may only mark one thing at a time. Joan explains the TAG methodology to the coach by asking him a few questions.

"Can you tell me five problems this client has right now? Good. Which one is the most important? The stance? Fine. What is wrong with it? Everything? Well, what would make it better, and can you say that in five words or less?"

He can. "Feet should be a shoulder's width apart."

"That's your tag point. Now tag only for that, until your learner is doing it right. Then move on."

Okay, says the coach. He starts with the aunt's foot placement. Then they work on the grip. Being a skilled athlete himself, the coach has excellent timing and always makes the sound as the move or position he's looking for takes place. The sound quickly becomes reinforcing; Joan's aunt beams at her repeated successes. When each new tag point has been tagged (that is, clicked) several times, the new move or position becomes incorporated into her swing.

They move from hole to hole, raising criteria and adding new tag points stroke by stroke. Joan gives the coach occasional guidance: "Always start with the words *The tag point is . . .* to set her up to learn the next thing." "You've said 'Turn your head left and lift your right heel.' That's two tag points; break them down and do them separately."

They complete this nine-hole TAG lesson and have another the next day. The coach enjoys a client who's actually doing what he told her to do. Joan's aunt is having fun, too. They knock fourteen strokes off the aunt's golf score.

TAG turned a golf lesson from a long series of repeated failures into a steady succession of little successes. That's more fun for the client, of course, and it's also less frustrating for the coach, since even the least capable student can make *some* progress. Tagging also helps the coach plan ahead, instead of relying on correcting problems as they arise. You need to select tag points, decide what you're going to tag first, and be ready to break the behavior down into even smaller units if the tag point you've chosen isn't getting results. The methodology is great for beginners, but it also enables coaches to sharpen the game of advanced players, selecting and modifying small but crucial elements of their game with just a few tags from your handy tagging device, the clicker.

➤ **Watch the "Coach Doing the Happy Ferret Dance" video in chapter 11 at www.reachingtheanimalmind.com.**

The Fosbury Flop

Joan Orr's local high school is big on track. The coach tells her that one of the hardest things to teach is a maneuver called the Fosbury flop, a method of going over the high jump upside down. It might take a year or more to teach an athlete to accomplish the Fosbury flop correctly.

Joan Orr goes to the Internet and downloads a slow-motion video of an Olympic gold-medal winner doing the Fosbury flop. She picks out some likely tag points: a leg lift at the beginning, the arch of the back, a throw of the arms, and the kick of the legs in midair. She rigs up a jump in her backyard consisting of an elastic string stretched between two lawn chairs, with a mattress to land on. She practices with one of her daughters, then corrals a nine-year-old neighbor for a videotaped test.

Joan tags each point until the child can do all of the moves correctly and in sequence. In fifteen minutes the girl goes from a tumble onto the mattress and a sheepish, giggling "I *can't,*" to arcing through the air upside down, a yard or more above the waist-high string, in a perfect Fosbury flop. The resulting video clip, a particular favorite in the TAG world, summarizes the training in two minutes and shows the soaring result in slow motion to the theme song from *Chariots of Fire.*

➤ **Watch the "High Jump" video in chapter 11 at www.reachingtheanimalmind.com.**

TAGteaching and Clicker Training

Although TAGteaching and clicker training are similar in that they eliminate correction, utilize the marker to establish new behavior, and convey information about the behavior to do in specific ways, there are differences. TAGteachers don't use much shaping. Shaping is *such* a big part of teaching animals without force. It often takes time. It's easy to go down the wrong path by accident. For the learner, successful improvement involves guesswork and trial and error; think of that Arabian mare trying to figure out what to do with her ears.

Except in teaching learners with developmental deficits who lack verbal skills, a TAGteacher can use words instead of shaping. He or she may have to break an end-goal behavior down into several components and click each one separately: toes at twelve o'clock, ankles together, toes pointed; but each component or criterion is something the learner can already do, and the cues, or tag points, are all words that the learner already understands. There's no need for trial and error. This saves a lot of time.

Another major difference is that a TAGteacher doesn't have to establish artificial cues for behavior: the "beep-beep-beep" telling dolphins to spin, the word *whoa* telling ponies to stop, the German shepherd's blue bowl meaning "sit." The tag points *are* the cues. The tag point is what you do now to get a conditioned reinforcer, the tag or click. Although the actual tag point will change frequently, the words *The tag point is . . .* are always the same. That phrase becomes the constant element. Interestingly, and appropriately from the neuroscience standpoint, those words *The tag point is . . .*, become a tertiary conditioned reinforcer just like the cue. It comes before the behavior, and is two steps away from the end reward. The tag point leads to the tag and the tag leads to the primary reinforcer, whether it's a bead for your bracelet or the knowledge that you've at last done the backflip just right.

Theresa McKeon observes a diagnostic physical reaction in her students as they hear those words *The tag point is . . .* Their eyes brighten, their breath quickens, they focus intently on the teacher: they evince, in Holland's term, excitement; in mine, elation. That's the sign that a conditioned reinforcer is taking effect.

The TAGteaching approach, in effect, can turn coaching and learning into a SEEKING-circuit experience: fun. It's not just the eventual accomplishments that are fun—winning the game, say, or the competition; it's not just the increased rate of reinforcement that makes this a positive experience. As clicker training does for animals, TAGteaching does for people: it engages just that part of the brain that we all love to use and get to use far too little: our inner happy explorer, our SEEKING circuit.

Tag Language

The words of the tag point itself must be exact. It must ask for what you want, not for what you don't want: "Look at the window" is a tag point; "Stop looking down" is not. The tag point may not contain the word *and* as in "The tag point is clap your hands and look to the left." The learner might be able to *do* the two things simultaneously, but you must tag them one at a time.

The tag point must describe a precise, observable, measurable act. "Raise your foot higher" is not a tag point. "Raise your foot to the height of that doorknob" is.

The tag point must, furthermore, be unequivocal: did the learner do it? Yes or no? If the answer is "Sort of" or "Maybe," it's not a tag point. Finally, and most crucially, the tag point must be something, however small, that the learner can actually do. If, after several tries, that person's foot doesn't reach the doorknob, for instance, that tells you it's time to break the behavior down further and start with a simpler and more achievable tag point: raise your foot to the height of a chair seat or a wastebasket, if the chair is too high.

Precise description of the tag point is in itself a learned skill. Coaches often think they are being precise; but they're not conveying the information the learner needs. In Theresa's gym, she takes me to watch some advanced students doing an exercise that includes running down a track at top speed. Two coaches are standing on the sides of the track yelling, "Run faster!" But the yelled words are bewildering because the gymnasts are already running as fast as they know how.

TAGteaching requires thinking up not only the right tag point but a way to express it vividly, so the students understand. One way to get more speed, Theresa says, is to pump the arms harder as you sprint. On each arm move, the fist should go forward as high as the runner's face and backward as far as the runner's rump. This action is observable, measurable, and specific. The students themselves name the tag point "cheek to cheek."

Try it yourself; I think what actually happens is that in moving the arms this far, the shoulders move more freely, rotating the torso, which releases the hips, too, and lengthens the stride. Like the tag point of straight knees before the flying dismount, this action changes not just the action of the arms but the movement of the whole body. TAGteachers call that a "value-added" tag point; it affects a good deal more than just the action tagged.

When you stick to "The tag point is . . ." in asking for new behavior, you eliminate a lot of potentially bullying language: "I want you to do . . . ," or, "You have to . . . ," or, "You must . . ." Commanding, demanding, and forcing responses through personal dominance is part of the culture of some sports; but it gets in the way of efficient learning. As with clicker-trained animals, deliberate use of intimidation almost certainly moves your learner off the SEEKING circuit and onto the conditioned fear path in the amygdala. You may get compliance, but learning slows way down.

Tag, Don't Nag

In coaching with the tag, one similarity to clicker training remains vital: ignore mistakes. This, of course, is hard for other coaches to accept. Ignore mistakes? How will the athletes learn anything if you don't tell them what they're doing wrong? Of course, in TAG, pointing out mistakes is not only useless—there is nothing to tag—but potentially harmful. Drawing attention to the mistake might activate those mirror neurons and actually strengthen the wrong movement. What can a coach do instead?

Errors are in fact useful information: they give you new tag points. You phrase each tag point in a pictorial way, something the student can visualize: "The tag point now is elbows next to ears." Then you fix mistakes one at a time, using these new tag points instead of correcting errors, so you keep your young learners happily in seeker mode.

Dance students often participate in big dance competitions. The judges' follow-up comments after each round can be extremely harsh and punitive. Beth Wheeler teaches her students to make use of the information (and defuse the pain) by turning each criticism into a new tag point for future practice.

TAGteach Outcomes

Very nice; but any coach would want to know, what's the result? Are you actually getting any improvement? Establishing TAGteaching in Beth Wheeler's dance school led to more wins in competition; more students being accepted by professional ballet troupes and schools; greater enrollment and longer student retention; more teachers with higher qualifications applying for jobs and less teacher turnover; and happier parents with fewer complaints. And, of course, more income. Click.

Tag Power

Why does it all work so well? Now, of course, thanks to neuroscientists, we know. The tag, properly used, is a conditioned reinforcer. Thus it travels on the old, direct path through the amygdala, bringing with it instant learning, long retention, and a sense of elation: a thrill. You can see that neurological activity in the general excitement when the tag comes out. You can see it in the focused attention, typical of the SEEK-

ING circuit in action, when a child is groping for the tag point. You can see it when, at the moment of the tag, the pupils dilate. The tag is a way to communicate directly with that part of the human mind that we can't reach well with words, that old, quick mind, rich in perceptions and awareness, that we share with other beings.

Teaching TAGteaching

Although clicker training grew rapidly, for a long time there were no standard guidelines. Clients and even the teachers themselves had no way to judge what was good practice and what wasn't. Charlatans and well-meaning but incompetent teachers proliferated.

TAG, however, is a much simpler and more evolved application. Once you get the hang of it, you can tag almost any physical skill, anywhere in the world. For example, a newly certified TAGteacher posts a video on the Web site showing a young Frenchwoman, visiting an American family, using tagging to teach the family's ten-year-old daughter how to pronounce the French *r* (with a gargle in the throat instead of a Spanish trill or an English *urrr* sound). Tagging the right sounds helps enormously in figuring out how to make those sounds again. The child learns in a few tries. Then the child grabs the clicker and TAGteaches her French guest how to pronounce the American *th* sound: *these, them,* and *those*, instead of *zeez, zem,* and *zose.*

Theresa and I are invited to Ireland, where Theresa trains a group of riding instructors to TAG their students, including adults with developmental deficits, while I am busy in another arena teaching the riding-school children to clicker-train the horses to do tricks. In Boston, I, who have never played tennis, teach a tennis coach to tag a player's backhand. In Iceland, Theresa TAGteaches a little boy with whom she does not have one word of language in common how to tie his shoes.

➤ **Watch the "Shoelace-tying" video in chapter 11 at www.reachingtheanimalmind.com.**

TAG Seminars and Certification

Aaron Clayton and I formed a new company with Theresa McKeon and her pioneering associates: TAGteach International LLC, or TTI for short. Working together, we develop a formal teaching and certification program and start offering two-day basic seminars around the United States and Europe. Once people understand the basics, what they are actually planning to use TAGteaching for is immaterial; it works for everything. TAGteaching is not attracting the sports coaches we anticipated, but we do get a huge range of other experts, including speech therapists, dancers, dog trainers, rock climbers, medical personnel (especially in rehabilitation and physical therapy), social workers, law enforcement professionals, and teachers and parents of special-needs children.

And the mix is valuable. Everyone is good at something, no one is good at everything. People learn from each other. In the two-day basic seminar each student is required to teach some special skill, through TAGteaching. I like to participate. So far I have learned a Pilates sit-up, a tricky maneuver in dog-agility competition called the front cross (with another student playing the dog), how to tie a necktie, how to kick a soccer ball with the side of my foot, and how to walk like Charlie Chaplin. See? You need to know those things. Besides, being tagged is so much fun.

Children without Words

Many people are signing up for TAGteaching seminars because they work with or live with people with developmental deficits, particularly autism. The most widely used method for teaching children with autism is called applied behavior analysis, a proven methodology. If teaching based on this kind of procedure is started early (the earlier the better) by an educated practitioner (often a state or nationally board-certified behavior analyst) and carried out often enough and long enough, learning definitely occurs, behavior improves, and ideally the child can then be mainstreamed into the regular school system.

By the time TAGteaching came along, I was already familiar with applied behavior analysis. It was carefully and extensively used in the New England school where I first consulted on autism. There is no doubt it is effective. Newcomers arrive with terrible behavior problems, and yet in a few weeks they are better, and in a few months they no longer need two full-time attendants or other initial precautions. The halls are serene, the classrooms calm. The children are not just cooperative, they are generally cheerful. Some children are successfully mainstreamed back into regular schools.

And yet, although applied behavior analysis is rooted in behavioral science, some standard protocols seemed counterproductive to me, such as alternating reinforcement with correction throughout a lesson; giving food repeatedly without linking that food to a particular action or behavior; using the same preplanned, written program over and over, though the child was making no progress, sometimes for years. I especially wondered at the failure to use conditioned reinforcers as markers.

Initially people objected to my tools, too. They said these children are sound-sensitive: they will be afraid of the clicker (never happens). They said you can't teach reading and writing and math with a clicker (turns out you can, but that's an application I'm not familiar with). They said a marker might work with "high-functioning" children—such as Timmy, who learned to tolerate a haircut—but not with truly low-functioning individuals. That turned out to be a misconception, too.

Why Click at All? Isn't the "Real" Reinforcer Better?

Neurologically speaking, no matter what you are using as your marker, there is an *exact* difference between learning with a primary reinforcer, such as food, and learning with a secondary reinforcer added in. Suppose you just give the organism something nice, which it can enjoy on the spot, every time it does what you like. That does make learning happen, but it's a kind of general learning. "This is a nice place, this is a good situation, maybe I should stay around and participate longer; more good stuff might come my way." (To me, this explains some of the differences we see between clicker-trained dogs and the pleasant but often passive dogs trained by the so-called lure-and-reward method.)

In contrast, a secondary reinforcer, such as the click, produces specific learning. If you want a specific behavior—press this lever, name this color, raise your right hand, come here now, look at me—then the conditioned reinforcer is the tool of choice.

It's not that using just a primary reinforcer such as food is "better" or that inserting the secondary reinforcer is "better." They are just different; they take different paths in the brain and produce different outcomes. One produces a general change of attitude about the whole environment. The other transmits accurate pieces of information. One helps people and animals to be more cheerful and well behaved. The other helps them learn specific skills and take the initiative to do so. It's not an either/or situation; both are good.

So Why Don't We Use More Clicks with People?

Holland wrote about the difference between teaching with primary and secondary reinforcers two decades ago. People, however, misinterpreted the findings to mean that the primary reinforcer taught a lot of stuff, and the secondary reinforcer just taught small bits of information. As a result, many psychologists, educators, and clinicians assumed that using the primary reinforcer was *much* better, and the secondary reinforcer was trivial, a curiosity, maybe useful only in the laboratory.

Even in science—maybe particularly in medical science—an inaccurate concept like this can cascade, spreading from one authoritative individual or journal article to many others, until it is universally accepted without further analysis. Perhaps that explained the widespread reliance I was seeing on using just primary reinforcers with children with autism: bits of cookies, sips of juice, jolly exclamations of "Good job!" The children are certainly getting the general picture and behaving well in a general way. How about specific skills? That comes much more slowly.

Clicking with Nola

Of my personal encounters with profoundly low-functioning children I think with the most joy of Nola. I'm walking back from lunch with the program manager, Myrna Libby. Myrna points out a student and a teacher walking in front of us. The student, a tall, husky girl of about fourteen, is leaning heavily on her caregiver, seriously burdening that young woman's efforts to escort her back to the classroom. "Look at Nola," Myrna says. "I don't know why she does that, she can walk perfectly normally."

I say, "Hmm."

"Want to try fixing it with the clicker?" Myrna asks.

Of course.

Myrna stops them and asks the teacher for a few of Nola's "preferred edibles," small pieces of Oreo cookies. We start off again, Myrna walking beside Nola, Nola leaning all over the poor teacher, and me following behind with the clicker. Nola raises her head to look at Myrna. I click; Myrna treats. Nola's head stays up. Click, treat. As we all continue walking down the hall, I click Nola for straightening her shoulders, then for taking a deep breath, and next for letting go of the teacher's arm.

Nola's stride lengthens. By the time we get to her classroom doorway, she is marching along like the athlete she was built to be, and her now unburdened caregiver is almost trotting to keep up. The next week Myrna tells me that Nola has not leaned on her caregivers since.

Nola is one of the children in the school who seem to understand some things they are told—she has some "receptive" language—but who have no spoken language. These children can sometimes learn the air, and click Nola for looking at it. I then move it left, right, backward, over my head, on the floor. I click each time when her eyes find it again. Myrna delivers the treats. Nola catches on immediately: six tries, six successes. Verbal praise may be just noise to her, but her amygdala knows a conditioned reinforcer when it hears one, and she's rapidly learned to look for the wastebasket.

Now, will she look for the table? I move the table about two feet to one side of its original position. Myrna gives the cue: "Take your plate to the table." Nola stands up, picks up her plate, and starts forward. The table is not right in front of her. Instead of just marching to the bookcase, she stops and looks around. Hey, there it is. She changes direction and carries her plate to the table in its new location. Click! That's worth a huge piece of Oreo.

We move the table to other parts of the room. Nola finds it every time. Furthermore, Nola thumps her plate down each time with vigor, almost with a flourish. Nola may lack many typical abilities, but Nola has *style.* I drive home that evening singing happily all the way. What a great way to communicate with someone who has been out of reach in so many ways.

Tagification

TAGteach International, or TTI, is now a consultant for several schools for autism as well as some state and regional educational systems and organizations. One of our clients, a group of schools in southern California, has folded TAGteaching into all of its programs, including using markers during applied behavior analysis sessions when appropriate.

That school has subsidized five of its staff members in seeking advanced certification, the level that will enable them to train and certify other TAGteaching personnel throughout the school. One step of the process is to carry out, record, and present an independent TAGteaching project. At our client's request, Theresa and I fly out to visit the school to assess the five candidates' final projects on-site.

The teachers have completed not just five independent projects but words in American Sign Language, but Nola has shown no abiliti that direction, either.

Myrna decides to see if, using the clicker, we can teach Nola so thing new. Despite years of instruction and effort, nobody has succeeded in getting Nola to carry her dirty dishes to the design counter in the cafeteria after meals. The absence of this simple skil great annoyance to her caregivers. Maybe we could teach her to do by shaping and reinforcement.

On my next visit we fetch Nola to a quiet study room. We sit N at a desk and move a small table to the middle of the room. Using clicker and bits of Oreo cookies, we shape the behavior of picking a plastic plate from her desk and carrying it to the table. We add a c "Take your plate to the table." Nola learns to do this just fine.

The following week Myrna again brings Nola into the room. she comes in, Nola moves her hand in the air. I pay no attention, Myrna gasps.

"She signed!" Myrna says with some astonishment, then expla her surprise to me. No one knew Nola could sign, but on coming ir this now-familiar room she clearly signed the word *play.* She has r only communicated, she has told us something I'm really glad to knc she's having fun!

Shaping is always fun . . . until you get stuck. Now we move the tal a few feet to the side and give the cue. Nola gets up, picks up the pla marches forward to the place where the table used to be, keeps wal ing, and sets the plate on a bookcase on the far wall. Three times.

At this point, people start getting aversive and scolding or, wi someone diagnosed as profoundly low-functioning, just give up. We you wouldn't give up so easily with a ferret or a fish; why with a persoı Have a little respect for the organism! On the next try I go out in froı of Nola to see if I can tell what's going on. Guess what. Nola's eyes aı focused straight ahead the whole time. Maybe she just hasn't learne the behavior of scanning around a room.

We consult; I will try clicking Nola for using her eyes to look arounc With Nola still sitting in her chair, I pick up a wastebasket, wave it iı over a dozen. All have been carried out with full research protocols and accurate data collection. All are slated for presentation at scientific conferences and some for publication; one has already been accepted as a master's thesis.

One of the candidates has used tagging to teach a child to mimic his teacher's motions. Some autistic children seem incapable of doing this, perhaps due to some deficiency in the mirror-neuron area. Can you teach mimicry as a skill? Clicker trainers can do it with dolphins and, though it takes quite a lot of training, with dogs. It's a great shortcut to developing more complex behavior. Why not do it with kids, too?

Some projects combine tagging, with its verbal cues and instructions, with basic shaping; when verbal instruction might not work, shaping is invaluable. Perhaps my favorite project in the day's presentations is a simple but ingenious example of shaping. Supervisor Rick Gutierrez presents us with a problem with an autistic three-year-old. We all have pet peeves, and the little boy's mother has this one: she wants the child to brush his teeth using toothpaste, but she doesn't want him to swallow the toothpaste, and she can't figure out how to stop him.

Speaking as a grandmother, if I wanted to teach a three-year-old to rinse his mouth and spit the toothpaste out, I might show him how I do it myself. Then he would try to do it himself, and so he would learn. But what if the child doesn't typically try to do what others do?

Rick Gutierrez uses the tagger to shape spitting on cue. First he finds a "spittable" object: the little boy's baby brother's freshly washed baby-bottle top. He stands the three-year-old on a stool, encourages him to lean over the sink, and tags him for holding the nipple part of the bottle top in his mouth. The reinforcer for each tag is a chance to push buttons on Rick's PalmPilot for ten seconds. Once this little boy can hold the bottle top in his mouth, the next tag point is to spit it into the sink. Soon he is doing that with enthusiasm, crowing for his turn on the PalmPilot.

The third tag point is to sip some plain water from a cup and spit that out. Given a cup of water, the three-year-old sips, then automatically swallows. He doesn't get his tag. Oops! His face clearly shows his understanding. No tag! Try again! He takes another sip, struggles visibly to organize his mouth to spit, and does so, right in the sink. Success! Cheers! After a few more tags, Rick sets him up with the whole little behavior chain: toothpaste on the brush, scrub teeth, sip, rinse, spit! Hurray! Happy kid, happy mom. Ten minutes. That project, like all the others we've seen today, more than meets our assessment requirements.

Rick supervises thirty in-home teachers, mostly in the Los Angeles area. I know L.A. has a lot of clicker-using dog trainers. I ask him, "Don't teachers run into parents who object to the clicker because it's for animals?"

"Sure," Rick says. "All the time. Here's what we tell them: All great scientific inventions, all the medicines we use, are tested first on animals. Wouldn't you *want* tagging to be worked out on animals before we use it on children?" Of course.

Clicker Training for TAGteachers

These teachers themselves are city dwellers and have next to no personal experience of animals; everything they know about operant principles and practices they have learned with human beings. That night over dinner, the school's founder, Joe Morrow, tells Theresa and me that the school has recently acquired an elderly Shetland pony to use as an educational experience for the children. We think Joe's newly approved advanced TAGteachers might enjoy shaping an animal. Joe agrees to have the pony brought to the school the next morning.

After lunch the next day we all go and meet the pony. I line up our teachers to share the job of shaping the pony to bump a target—a plastic toy—with its nose. One holds the lead line. One holds the target and does the clicking. A third teacher hand-feeds a spoonful of grain after each click. Every five clicks they rotate jobs until everyone has done each thing, by which time the pony is not only bumping the target but seems willing to follow it to China.

Theresa sees to it that the teachers also learn what the pony's fuzzy mane feels like; where the pony likes being touched (neck) and where it doesn't (ears); what its big, warm tongue feels like when it licks grain from your hand (*euww!*); and what the pony does when frightened by the noise of a passing truck (not much—it startles and throws its head up, but that is enough to frighten the people a little, too).

When we are through, they all race to the restrooms, anxious to get the horse smell and saliva off their hands. Rick, raised in East L.A., tells me that he has never been that close to any horse before. Our little shaping exercise has been enlightening for him: he is absolutely amazed that it worked! The fact that the pony can *learn,* just like the children, is, he says, "entirely awesome." Yes, Rick, I think so, too.

Tagging as Communication

Our contribution to the autism world as TAGteachers is not to "cure" the children, nor to say what specifics the child should be learning. The value of this methodology lies in its giving teachers and parents an additional way to communicate to the child and in allowing even a nonverbal child to communicate back. At an educational conference, one of the speakers, the mother of a fourteen-year-old autistic boy, tells me of a huge difference TAGteaching has made for her personally.

For years it had been impossible to run household errands unless her husband was home to take care of their son. She could not, for example, take this lively boy to the supermarket because he continually put things in the cart, took things out of the cart, put things in other people's carts, and rearranged the shelves. Now, however, with tagging (and a small supply of trail mix), she has shaped him to keep both hands on the handle of the shopping cart, all the way around the store; and he is happy to do it. She and her husband can each run household errands anytime; and they don't have to coordinate their schedules to make normal chores feasible. A small thing, but a huge difference in their daily life.

Flying on Tags

As far as I can see, every skill can be learned better with tagging than with the usual approach of verbal instruction mixed with correction. My son Mike Pryor spent some years training pilots for two international airlines. He brought the clicker into the cockpit and used TAG principles throughout. What he liked best about it was the effect on the students.

The training was far from fun for them. Some were already senior pilots who hated having to be recertified; some had language difficulties in an English-speaking school; many found the multiple demands of, say, instrument flying difficult. As Mike puts it, "With the tag, first, they actually learn, so that's good. Second, they can't help but enjoy it. It's that moment when you hear the click. It's like you won something. You get that great feeling: *I win!*"

What a good way to learn *any* new thing: with a sense of winning all the way.

Chapter 12

Intention

Natural Operant Conditioning

Gerry Martone was working for the U.S. Peace Corps when he ran into a particularly dangerous situation. Gerry was assigned to a country in Africa where the political situation was becoming highly unsettled. During a sudden and bloody uprising he and some other aid workers, inadvisedly walking through the capital city, are captured by a band of militants and hauled away in a truck.

This is not a good thing. No one is really in charge of these rebel soldiers, and there are no rules. Aid workers and other innocent bystanders in similar situations in other countries have been held for ransom, killed out of hand, or beaten and tortured and then killed for no known reason. The natural reaction of the hostages is anger and panic. Gerry's coworkers start crying, arguing that they are harmless noncombatants, and pleading for release. That natural response emphasizes their victim status. It also emphasizes the captor status of the bunch of guys in the front of the truck, who are already exhilarated, drunk, stoned, and a bit out of control.

Gerry takes a different tack. He thanks his captors whenever they do something that is, even in the smallest way, a comfort to the hostages. He thanks them for driving smoothly through a sharp turn. He thanks them when they pass the water jug to the back. He says a thank-you for their letting the captives sit down rather than keeping them standing. As they drive through ferocious scenes of looting, fires, and wreckage, he praises and thanks the militants for having picked them up in the first place, thus protecting both the aid workers and themselves from these dangerous conditions.

What happens? Instead of taking their captives away for malicious purposes, the renegade soldiers deliver them to the safe house of another aid worker on the outskirts of town. Then the soldiers post a guard around the house all night to keep the house safe from other armed militants. A change in the captives' own behavior led to a corresponding change in the other group's behavior, from that of predators to that of protectors.

Crying and pleading are emotional expressions of submissiveness. Bullying and aggression are emotional expressions of dominance. We share these feelings and these kinds of social displays not just with the primates but with lots of mammals and some birds. No wonder it feels natural; it is. No wonder stopping and thinking and then deliberately doing something else feels contrived, artificial, even morally wrong.

But using reinforcement isn't really about changing the behavior of others; it's about changing what you do yourself. And while on the surface that may seem artificial, changing your own behavior by intention is a fundamental act of survival in the natural world.

Intentional Behavior in the Natural World

Cues and reinforcers occur naturally in the environment, but an animal must often learn to change its behavior to make use of that information. Our pets are common examples of animals that haven't had that opportunity. A city dog let off leash in a pasture for the first time can be pretty amusing. The dog smells life all around, rabbits maybe, meadow mice certainly. Head down and tail wagging, it gallops in all directions, wild with excitement, following this scent and that, while every small mammal within fifty yards has long since dived into a safe hole somewhere.

What the dog should be doing is stalking. Stalking is a behavior with strong innate components easily recognizable in any species including us: a crouching pose, a lowered head, slow footfalls, fixed attention. But the knowledge of when to stalk doesn't spring up full-blown. If a coyote pup or bobcat kitten wants to catch its own food, and not just wait for Mom to bring it, at first it may rush after every sound or scent, like the dog in the pasture, without success. It has to learn to walk slowly and quietly enough to stir up the mice (or voles or garter snakes or grouse) so that, without actually panicking and fleeing, the prey moves just enough to make a rustle in the grass.

The rustle in the grass is a tertiary reinforcer, paying the hunter back for good stalking behavior, while also providing the cue—pounce here, now—for the behavior that brings success. These learning sequences abound in the lives of everything from fish to full professors. When clicker trainers or TAGteachers intentionally use a sound to mark a behavior, or when we respond to bad behavior from others by thinking carefully about what to reinforce, we are utilizing these natural laws by controlling what we do ourselves.

Human-Animal Cooperation

Our interactions with animals are often based on our intentions and their reactions; pretty one-sided. When, however, the human and the animal are each operating from a mix of innate behavior and intentional responses to cues given by the other, the outcome can be spectacular and the experience a colossal thrill. Upland game hunting with bird dogs is one example. Working cattle with a good cutting horse, steeplechasing, sheep herding: many people get hooked for a lifetime on these interlocking SEEKING-system experiences. I know a banker in Colorado who leads a secret life as a falconer. She gets up every morning at dawn, goes out for an hour or two before work, and deals with the town's overpopulation of starlings by flying a kestrel or sparrow hawk at them. The bird thinks it's a great plan, too. It could leave at any time and be a normal wild sparrow hawk, but it likes having such a reliable hunting partner.

Brazilian Dolphins

One day while traveling up the southern coast of Brazil I stumble across a spectacular example of human-animal cooperation, one that up to that time had been completely ignored by both the world media and the scientific community. The animals are wild bottlenose dolphins. The behavior is a cooperative fishery. I can see at first glance that the dolphins, not the humans, are in charge. What makes it particularly charming to me is that the success of the fishing depends entirely on the mutual exchange of cues.

Along the sandy shore of a narrow passage from the ocean into a big lagoon, men with throw nets are standing hip-deep in the water hoping to catch mullet, which come from the ocean into the brackish lagoon to breed. The water is muddy, and it's hard to see the fish, so even though the fish pass close by, the men don't always know when to throw the nets.

Bottlenose dolphins eat mullet, but the mullet are swift. Dolphins in the Black Sea and elsewhere drive mullet schools against a barrier, such as a rocky point, to confuse the fish and slow them down. Here in Laguna the legs of the waiting fishermen make a perfect barricade for disorganizing a group of mullet.

The dolphins of course have no trouble locating and herding a school of mullet even in completely opaque water. So, while thirty or forty men patiently wait in a line, a dolphin senses a school of mullet coming into the harbor, herds the school toward the line of men, ducks out at the last moment before the nets are cast, and then snaps up a confused fish or two that the nets have missed. The splash caused by the dolphin's evasive maneuver is the cue for the five or six nearest men to throw their nets. They might each catch twenty pounds or more of fish in a single cast.

This cooperative fishery takes place all day every day, almost year-round. A look in the town records shows that the fishing has been going on for more than a hundred years. Why I have read nothing about it? Because it looks too ordinary! This is not taking place in some remote jungle but in the middle of a busy industrial port town. The fishermen are not indigenous natives in parrot-feather headdresses but ordinary citizens in yellow raincoats and baseball caps, supporting their families and making the TV payments. Wholesale buyers take the fish away in refrigerated trucks as soon as they're caught. Spectators are watching on the beach. A little man is even selling sandwiches. A few marine mammal scientists may have stumbled across this sight by accident, as no doubt have many journalists; but they have all dismissed it as a tourist attraction, some local animal-training stunt, not worthy of serious attention.

In fact, the men don't train the dolphins at all. About thirty dolphins are involved, all (like the spotters in the tuna net) members of one interrelated group. The men know them individually by sight and by name, but they don't call them, they don't give them free fish, they don't make friends with them. They are careful not to do anything that might distract, disturb, or annoy the dolphins. They show respect.

The dolphins, on the other hand, are not necessarily respectful. One rainy afternoon when the fishing is slow, I watch a young male dolphin patrol the line for a while, then suddenly move a hundred yards up the beach. Gathering up their nets, all the men run through the water to the new location. When they are nicely settled in a line again, the dolphin moves back. They all pick up and run back to where they were. Don't tell me that wasn't fun for the dolphin. Typical bottlenose behavior; think of Josephine!

The success of this long-standing fishery is due to reinforcement. The primary reinforcer, for men and dolphins alike, is the fish themselves, but second- and third-level reinforcers abound, including the positioning of dolphins and men, the creaky noises the mullet make as they enter the inlet, and the dolphins' unusual splashing turn, which is the tertiary reinforcer or cue that conveys "Throw the net *now.*" This fishery arose and survives due to the willingness of both dolphins and humans to add, to their natural inclinations and reactions, some intentional behavior, such as waiting patiently in cold water for hours, that enables the other beings to do something new, too.

Trained Cooperators

One widespread general cooperative system is the use of dogs to help blind people get around. The guide dog concept arose largely from a military tradition. Punishment and deprivation were the principal tools, reinforcement was minimal, and the experience could be harsh indeed. I visited a guide dog training business once where tradition held that during the training, to eliminate future resistance, you had to choke the dog, no matter how hard it struggled, until it blacked out. It takes a tough dog to stand up to this kind of treatment. Well, the argument goes, it takes a tough dog to stand up to the challenges a guide dog will face in real life.

In this kind of situation we clicker trainers get pressure from the public to step in and help. But you can't dictate to people how they should be doing a job when they're already doing it successfully. Change has to come from the inside.

Michele Pouliot has been a senior guide dog trainer for years. She is now director for research and development at San Rafael Guide Dogs for the Blind in California and Oregon, one of the largest and most respected guide dog schools in the country. Michele uses clicker training with her own dogs and horses and is familiar with Kurland's training of Panda. She can see many ways in which clicker training might be useful for Guide Dogs for the Blind.

A first step is the introduction of food in the training. Customarily, guide dogs have never been given food outside of meals for fear they will start diving for every dropped hamburger wrapper on the street. The use of food makes an immediate difference in results. That opens people's minds up a little, among both trainers and administrators. Michele then introduces the clicker, but only for difficult training problems. San Rafael has been taking on some clients who are blind and in wheelchairs. The dogs can accept the wheelchair, but they just can't seem to understand that it's a bad thing to get one wheel on the curb and one off. Clicker training fixes that problem. Everyone begins to see that there might be even more potential here. The organization agrees, as an experiment, to train one "string" of dogs (thirty dogs of the same age being trained at the same time) completely by clicker training.

Two immediate and dramatic differences appear between this string and those that have gone before. First, the dogs are happy and confident, learning fast and visibly enjoying the work. Second, the success rate of dogs that make it through the training *and* through the first six months of service as a guide absolutely soars. A considerable investment of time and money goes into the training of each dog, so each dog that washes out is an expensive loss. In the prefood era about 35 percent of the dogs made it through (failures were "reassigned" to new careers, usually as pets). Reducing that drain would be a huge and obvious benefit.

Adding a primary reinforcer (food) had raised the success rate to more than 45 percent, with occasional classes reaching 65 percent, which San Rafael was justifiably proud of. Now, with the introduction of the clicker, up to 85 percent of some strings make it through the training and are successful on the job.

Another major benefit is that without a heavy regimen of compulsion-based training much more sensitive dogs can make it through the program. These softer-natured dogs are easier for blind people to handle, especially since nowadays many of the blind are quite elderly. Contrary to expectations, these sensitive dogs do not fold under street conditions.

Michele has an example. A task that even the toughest dog quails at is guiding a blind person down a crowded sidewalk, especially around Christmas. People don't even see the dog, so they brush right by, and one after another their shopping bags wallop the dog right in the face.

Now, however, because the learning is based on reinforcement, the dogs are remarkably confident. Getting buffeted by shopping bags or having some stranger step on a paw or a tail on a crowded bus is no big deal. The dogs that have been trained without compulsion are actually more resilient, rather than less, to mishaps on the job.

San Rafael hires psychologist and ClickerExpo faculty member Kathy Sdao as a training consultant. With her input the now clicker-savvy trainers solve a simple problem that every blind person faces:

walking into a waiting room or a coffee shop and finding a place to sit. The old way is always a bit embarrassing: you have to ask if someone would guide you to a vacant seat. Now you can just tell the dog, "Find a chair." The dog looks around for an empty chair, leads you to it, and lays its head on the seat. You ask, "Is this seat taken?" If someone says no, or if nobody answers, you can sit down.

Another skill guide dogs traditionally have difficulty with is finding buttons: crosswalk buttons, elevator buttons, doorbells. They're all in different places and look somewhat different. A clicker-savvy dog can generalize the basic concept of a push button and find any button, even if it's high off the ground or hidden by shrubbery. Furthermore, using clicker training themselves, blind people can teach their dogs these additional tools. Clicker games and clicker fun also brighten up life at home, for dog and owner, too, a lot more than drilling and leash corrections used to do.

Two more advances have recently been made at San Rafael: puppy raisers and their supervisors are being converted to clicker training, and—you saw this coming, didn't you?—TAGteaching has been instituted for training the blind clients. Meanwhile, in speeches and conference proceedings, Michele Pouliot is spreading the techniques of San Rafael's successful use of clicker training throughout the service-dog business worldwide.

Teaching Clicker Teachers

I never really liked the term *clicker training;* it's too specific. The usage arose in the early nineties on the first Internet clicker list and spread fast. It was not my doing; I actually campaigned for some other word or goo. For example, I thought maybe the German clicker trainers could come up with some nice combo word, like *schadenfreude* or *zeitgeist,* that might represent the real nature of this technology. But no, the Germans have stuck with the English name, clicker training. The French call it *entraînement au clicker.* In Norwegian it's *klikkertrening;* in Spanish, *adiestramiento con el clicker;* in Hungarian, *klikker képzés.*

In Japanese, it's just one word, *crikuru.* Like it or not, that's the name.

At ClickerExpo we faculty members know exactly what we mean and imply when we use the term, and so do most of our attendees. However, those who make their living as dog trainers and instructors are finding that's far from true in their communities. The term has enough cachet now so that their competition may be advertising themselves as clicker trainers in the yellow pages, though some are incompetent and others are charlatans, still bullying pet owners and putting choke chains on Chihuahuas.

We see the need for some kind of certification program to help our kind of trainers differentiate themselves from the competition. Our small company doesn't have the time or resources to develop an independent certification board, such as those used for medical specialties; but as an independent corporation KPCT can at least certify that a given person understands and can teach what *we* mean by clicker training the "Karen Pryor way." The next step is to develop an instructional program to prepare teachers for our certification. To do so, we set up a new organization, the Karen Pryor Academy (I am gradually getting inured to being a brand name).

After two years of hard work we have a certification curriculum consisting of six months of at-home online lessons and four two-day hands-on workshops that you must attend with your "practice" animal (usually a dog). We include some TAGteaching so students can learn to teach people as kindly and efficiently as they teach dogs. We add some business skills, from identifying your value proposition to using spreadsheets to project profitability. We know dog trainers are doing what they love; we want them to know how to earn a decent living while they do it.

Experienced clicker-training instructors, many of them ClickerExpo faculty members, sign up to teach the hands-on portion of the course at their own training facilities around the country. The course is rigorous but exciting, a SEEKING-circuit experience for teachers and students both (not to mention the dogs). We have an increasing number of Certified Training Partners across the United States and Canada, with an international program under way as well.

Specialized courses are in development, including one for zoo trainers and animal research laboratory workers. What I particularly like about the academy, besides its efficiency in spreading the technology, is that it doesn't depend on me or on any one person. With the systems, principles, and standards in place, other people can expand the programs and carry them onward. I get to watch and enjoy.

Teaching Tagging

Aren't we glad we worked all this out with animals first? Clicker training is much harder to teach and learn than TAGteaching for humans. The underlying principles are the same, but TAGteaching refines the information so it gets across much more quickly, and when you can use words instead of shaping and cuing, there really is less to learn. TAGteaching is useful for any application, which is a good thing, since we never know who will walk through the door next or what kind of teaching problem we will be called on to solve.

Amy Duz has been involved in the commercial fishing business since she was sixteen. Today she runs her own fishing-related business as a safety consultant. One of Amy's clients, Tim Meintz, operates a two-hundred-foot-long oceangoing trawler named *Seafisher.* The ship spends ten months of the year catching and processing fish in the Bering Sea and beyond. The work is demanding and hazardous. Accidents happen. Amy has recommended safety procedures and that helps; but communication is the big problem.

Seafisher carries a crew of fifty-two, mostly young, mostly male, mostly, like all fishermen, extremely independent. They come from the United States, Mexico, Central and South America, Cambodia, Vietnam, the Philippines, Japan, and Poland. Getting them trained to do things right is difficult, especially when no one understands exactly what anyone else is saying. Managers get frustrated when people don't do what they're told, and workers get frustrated when they're yelled at for no clear reason.

Traveling from Anchorage on an Alaska Airlines flight, Amy found a book someone left in the seat pocket in front of her: *Don't Shoot the Dog!* She read it and told Tim it could be the answer he was looking for. He asked Amy to train his managers to train the crew more effectively. Amy said, "Why not get help from the real expert?" They called my company, KPCT, got Aaron Clayton on the phone, and he put them in touch with Theresa McKeon, president of TAGteach.

TAGteach sounded good, but before committing any of their men to the program, Tim and Amy took the basic two-day seminar themselves. As Amy explained to me, "We wanted to make sure that this isn't some regular management-training deal run by suits. Our guys are wary around suits." (Suits are wary around fishermen, too, if that's any comfort. I've enjoyed some great moments in the past watching two or three tuna-boat captains accidentally terrify a roomful of bureaucrats just by the way they walk in.)

Well, the seminar was a lot of fun, and no suits were involved. Reassured, Tim and Amy signed up the *Seafisher* skipper and a bunch of crew managers for a customized TAGteaching seminar of their own, to take place at a dog-training facility near Seattle, owned by trainer Terry Ryan.

Terry feels that fishermen might want occasional backup reinforcers, so she goes to an Indian-run casino down the highway and buys tokens. During the seminar people earn tags and occasional tokens; on the second evening they all go to the casino and spend their tokens having fun.

Terry Ryan maintains a flock of hens so dog trainers can learn to shape behavior in an unfamiliar species. Now Terry provides a chicken-training lesson for the fishermen. Instead of teaching the chickens to peck, say, a red dot instead of the blue, Terry has them each clicker-train a chicken to peck pictures of a mackerel instead of a cod. When the weekend is over, all the *Seafisher* managers have earned basic TAGteach certification. They can be heard reminding each other of their new skills: "Don't yell, use tag language!" "He isn't getting it yet; break the behavior down!"

At the end of the fishing season Theresa has a feedback session with Tim, Amy, and the skipper of the *Seafisher*. How are things going? Everyone is truly using reinforcement and there is a lot less yelling. Clickers don't do you much good on a ship at sea—it's too noisy—but a word or a touch on the shoulder works fine. People get stickers on their hard hats identifying skills they've mastered, from gutting fish to running machinery. In the shipyard, where everyone is connected by radio, Tim is often heard reinforcing other people's interactions verbally—"Good thinking, guys"—from a distance.

However, the part of TAGteaching that proves most crucial for Cascade Fisheries managers is how to "break it down." When someone doesn't understand instructions, or some process isn't working, the answer is not to increase the pressure but to figure out how to divide the behavior into smaller elements and work on them one at a time.

For example, the manager says to a crewman, "Put the fish on the tray." But the guy is doing it *wrong,* every time. Why doesn't he *know* you're supposed to pack the fish head to tail so they lie flat and fit tight, not just heap them onto the tray any old way? The right way is so obvious, everyone takes it for granted; but this guy has no clue. Now, instead of getting frustrated, the manager stops to think. Well, he's not doing it, so break it down. Teach the little parts one at a time. "A head first, then a tail first, then a head first . . . now you've got it. That's right." Faced with a confused or resistant crew member, the managers now pause and say, "If I can train a chicken . . ."

Saving All Hands

TAGteaching gets everyone looking at problems in a new way. Unloading the blocks of frozen fish onto the dock is a problem. The blocks are heavy, the hold of the ship is kept extremely cold (minus twenty degrees), and the off-loading needs to go as fast as possible. The men throw the blocks from person to person to the conveyer belt, which then carries them off the ship. Blocks can be dropped. Injuries can happen. Perhaps they need to slow down.

The captain is concerned because this is no place to lose time; but he agrees they can try it. The men develop a cue for slowing the pace.

When the blocks come too fast, anyone feeling rushed can yell "Space," meaning, leave a gap between crates. Hearing that cue, people pause momentarily. One outcome is that the blocks are evenly separated on the conveyor belt, so off-loading becomes more systematic at the shore end. However, here's what really gets everyone's attention. Off-loading has been causing between ten and fifteen broken fingers a year, not to mention mashed, bruised, and sprained fingers that aren't actually broken. In the first year of using "Space" to control the timing, only one hand injury has occurred. Not only that, the off-loading actually goes faster than it used to.

The skipper's take is insightful. "This is good. It teaches everyone to think." Indeed it does. The guys are bright, that's not the problem; but now intention replaces mere reaction. It's true for animals and it's true for people: learning to interact this way makes you see things differently.

Cascade Fisheries contracts for more TAGteach training. This time the customized seminars will focus less on the clicker and its timing and more on how to work with yourself, so you no longer need to get mad and get everyone around you bummed out, too. Amy begins marketing TAG technology to her clients across the industry. It's a good time for expansion; TAGteach International has many certified instructors now. Furthermore, I tell Amy, I can guarantee that none of those seminar leaders, male or female, are Suits.

One Click at a Time

Operant teachers and trainers have now spread all over the world. Getting better. Seeing more. Sharing knowledge instead of hoarding it. Growing the technology. *Time* magazine technology writer Lev Grossman discussed a new phenomenon in the growth of ideas: "The idea that lots of people, potentially everybody, can be involved in the process of innovation is utterly transforming. . . . Two things make this possible, one obvious and one not. The obvious one is the Internet. The other one, the surprising one, is a curious phenomenon you could call intellectual altruism. It turns out that given the opportunity, people will donate their time and brainpower to make the world better."

This technology is a living example of that. People who learn it tend to transfer from their training experiences a host of skills and ideas that alter their personal lives and benefit many others. And we need that, planetwide. We are still leaving skill development in far too many areas to individual talent or lack of same, and to the inconsistencies of apprenticeship. School teaching is a particularly egregious example. Teachers learn protocols and subject matter and lots of theories, but skills such as handling students in the kindest and most efficient way, managing classrooms, and seeing that students actually learn are left up to individual teachers to discover on their own, or to learn from a mentor whose own skills may not be ideal. It's time to take this learner-friendly technology into the schoolroom; into medical schools; into rehabilitation and physical-therapy centers; into prisons; into the training of firemen and surgeons and musicians and football players; into every corner of society where compulsion and coercion often reign because people continue to assume that no effective alternative exists.

According to B. F. Skinner's daughter Julie Skinner Vargas, Skinner felt that his great discovery was that the postcedent, not the antecedent, governed behavior: not what happens first, but what happens afterward. That's the main point in this book: when we stop pushing at the front end of the string and instead attend to what happens as an outcome of our actions and those of others, we can not only accomplish marvels, we can commune on a whole new level with other minds.

I wrote years ago in *Don't Shoot the Dog!* that to me the most useful and wonderful aspect of reinforcement training is the window that the training opens into the learner's mind. I hope that this book has given you a feeling for what that's like. Even more, I hope you might feel curious enough to try this technology yourself, either with animals or with people.

In the back of this book, in a section called "Do it yourself," I've given four sets of step-by-step instructions for personal projects: one for cats, one for dogs, one for coaching, and one for you. If you want to explore further, look at the section called "Find out more!" You can also go to the Web site for this book, www.reachingtheanimalmind.com. There you'll find videos and photos of some of the stories I've told, downloadable articles, links to other important Web sites, schedules of upcoming clicker events, and a quick online source for clickers and training information.

Time writer Lev Grossman makes a prediction: "Until now the value of a piece of intellectual property has been defined by how few people possess it. In the future the value will be defined by how many people possess it." Exactly. That's what we clicker trainers and TAGteachers are doing together, and quite intentionally, too. Sharing the wealth. Changing the world. One click at a time.

Find Out More!

1: Reaching Minds

King Solomon's Ring. Konrad Lorenz. 1952. This deceptively simple account of Lorenz's animals and birds is a fine introduction to the science of ethology. With drawings by the author.

- "Comments on the 1950s applications and extensions of Skinner's operant psychology." Edward K. Morris. 2003. *The Behavior Analyst* 26:281–95.
- "When the President appointed me." Karen Pryor. 1995. *On Behavior*, chap. 15. See at www.reachingtheanimalmind.com.
- **Photos** in chapter 1 at www.reachingtheanimalmind.com.
  "Wolf Park" slide show
- **Videos** in chapter 1 at www.reachingtheanimalmind.com.
  "Clicker-trained Wolves at Wolf Park"
- **Links**
  Marine Mammal Commission, www.mmc.org
  The Skinner Foundation, www.BFSkinnerfoundation.org
  Wolf Park, Battle Ground, Indiana, www.wolfpark.org
  Sea Life Park, www.sealifepark.com

2: Shaping

Lads Before the Wind. Karen Pryor. New York: Harper & Row, 1975. Waltham, MA: Sunshine Books, 1994, 2000.

- "A day of great illumination: B. F. Skinner's discovery of shaping." Gail B. Peterson. 2004. *Journal of Experimental Analysis of Behavior* 82:317–28.

- "The red-footed booby colony (*Sula sula rubripes*) at Sea Life Park." Karen Pryor and Ingrid Kang. 1969. *International Zoo Yearbook.*

- "Sea Life Park and the Oceanic Institute." Karen Pryor. 1967. *Curator.* Vol. 3. New York: American Museum of Natural History.

- "The behavior and training of cetaceans in captivity." R. H. DeFran and Karen Pryor. 1980. In *Cetacean Behavior: Mechanisms and Functions,* ed. Louis Herman. New York: Wiley-Interscience.

- **Videos** in chapter 2 at www.reachingtheanimalmind.com.
  Shaping behavior in puppies, from *Clicker Puppy,* Joan Orr, 2007, DVD
  "Spotted and Spinner Dolphins"
  "False Killer Whale Double Jump"
  "Shaping Demonstration: Blowing Bubbles"
  "Spinner Dolphins Spinning"

- **Photos** in chapter 2 at www.reachingtheanimalmind.com.
  "Sea Life Park" slide show

- **Links**
  Sea Life Park, www.sealifepark.com

3: Communication

Don't Shoot the Dog! Rev. ed. Karen Pryor. 1999. New York: Bantam Books.

- "Why porpoise trainers are not dolphin lovers: Real and false communication in the operant setting." Karen Pryor. 1981. *Annals of the New York Academy of Science* 304:137–43.

- "Non-acoustic communication in small cetaceans: Glance, touch, position, gesture and bubbling." Karen Pryor. 1991.

In *Sensory Abilities of Cetaceans,* ed. J. A. Thomas and R. A. Kastelein. New York: Plenum Press.

- "Symphony conductors would make good porpoise trainers." Karen Pryor. 1976. *Psychology Today,* November. Cues and stimulus control in a human setting.

- **Photos** in chapter 3 at www.reachingtheanimalmind.com.
  "Cat High Five" slide show

- **Videos** in chapter 3 at www.reachingtheanimalmind.com.
  "Happy Ferret Dance" (The lightbulb moment)
  "Blue Bowl" (German Shepherd learns a new cue)
  "Agility Cat"

- **Links**

www.clickertraining.com. Karen Pryor's clicker-training main Web site, with clicker info and instructions. Monthly e-zine, store, huge library of clicker-related articles, training tips for dogs, cats, birds, horses, and more.

www.clickertraining.com/tv. Clicker-training video clips galore.

www.clickerexpo.com. Information on ClickerExpo clicker conferences held yearly in January and March at various locations in the United States.

www.learningaboutdogs.com. British clicker-training school, events, and publications.

www.canis.verlag. Norwegian clicker-training school, events, and publications.

www.karenpryoracademy.com. Karen Pryor's online and hands-on clicker-training instructional programs; multiple locations.

4: Feelings

- "Behavior and learning in whales and porpoises." Karen Pryor. 1974. *Die Naturwissenschaften* 6:412. See at www.reachingtheanimalmind.com.

- **Videos** in chapter 4 at www.reachingtheanimalmind.com.
  "Fainting Fish" (Training a fish to swim through a hoop)
  "Attila Szkukalek's Charlie Chaplin Routine with His Dog, Fly"

5: Creativity

A Guide Horse for Ann. Rosanna Hursey; photographs by Neil Soderstrom. 2005. Honesdale, PA: Boyds Mill Press.

- "The creative porpoise: training for novel behavior." Karen Pryor, Richard Haag, and Joseph O'Reilly. 1969. *Journal of the Experimental Analysis of Behavior* 12:653. See at www.reachingtheanimalmind.com.

- Hardwired vs. softwired in humans: Selections from *Nursing Your Baby.* Karen Pryor. 1963. New York: Harper & Row. Rev. ed. Karen Pryor and Gale Pryor. 2007. New York: HarperCollins. See at www.reachingtheanimalmind.com.

- **Videos** in chapter 5 at www.reachingtheanimalmind.com.
  "Creative Porpoise Experiment"
  "Gorilla Game"
  "Panda the Guide Horse in Action"

- **Photos** in chapter 5 at www.reachingtheanimalmind.com.
  "Peggy's Box Game" slide show

- **Links**
  Clicker training for horses: theclickercenter.com

6: Attachments

- *"Hydrodynamic performance of porpoises (Stenella attenuata)." Thomas G. Lang and Karen W. Pryor. 1967. Science 152:531–33.*

- “Social behavior and school structure in pelagic porpoises (*Stenella attenuata* and *S. longirostris*) during purse seining for tuna.” Karen Pryor and Ingrid Kang. July 1980. National Marine Fisheries Service Southwest Fisheries Center Administrative Report LJ-80-11C. See at www.reachingtheanimalmind.com.

- “School structure in spotted dolphins (*Stenella attenuata*) in the tuna purse seine fishery in the eastern tropical Pacific.” In *Dolphin Societies: Discoveries and Puzzles,* ed. Karen Pryor and K. S. Norris. 1991. Berkeley: University of California Press.

- **Photos** in chapter 6 at www.reachingtheanimalmind.com. “Tuna-Porpoise-at-Sea Research” slide show

7: Fear

Clicker Training for Your Horse. Alexandra Kurland. 1998. Waltham, MA: Sunshine Books.

- “Loading the problem loader: the effects of target training and shaping on trailer-loading behavior of horses.” Dawnery L. Ferguson and Jésus Rosales-Ruiz. 2001. *Journal of Applied Behavior Analysis* 34:409–24.

- “Reducing stress in northern bald ibis through training.” Elsa Mark. 2007. *ABMA Journal* 4:23–35.

- “The rhino likes violets.” Karen Pryor. 1981. *Psychology Today,* April.

- Changing the world, one click at a time: chaps. 10, 11, 12 in *Click to Win! Clicker Training for the Show Ring.* Karen Pryor. 2002. Waltham, MA: Sunshine Books. See at www.reachingtheanimalmind.com.

- Curing the cat-chasing dog: pp. 70–73 in *Clicker Training for Cats.* Karen Pryor. 2001. Waltham, MA: Sunshine Books.

➤ **Videos** in chapter 7 at www.reachingtheanimalmind.com.
"ClickerExpo"
"Feral Kitten"
"Touch the Goblin Horse"

➤ **Links**
The Animal Behavior Management Alliance. Zoo trainers. www.theabma.org.
ORCA, student organizaion at University of North Texas. orgs.unt.edu/orca/
International Association of Avian Trainers and Educators. www.IAATE.org
Department of Behavior Analysis, University of North Texas

8: Conversations

The Alex Studies: Cognitive and Communicative Abilities of Grey Parrots. Irene Maxine Pepperberg. 1999. Cambridge, MA: Harvard University Press.

Alex & Me: How a Scientist and a Parrot Discovered a Hidden World of Animal Intelligence. Irene Pepperberg. 2008. New York: Random House.

➤ "Reinforcement training as a method of interspecies communication." Karen Pryor. 1987. In *Dolphin Behavior and Cognition: A Comparative Approach*, ed. Ronald Schusterman, Jeanette A. Thomas, and F. G. Woods. New York: Erlbaum Associates.

➤ "If I could talk to the animals . . . reinforcement interactions as communication." Karen Pryor. 1992. President's Invited Scholar's Address, Association for Behavior Analysis annual conference, San Francisco. In *On Behavior*, pp. 353–63.

9: Questions

On Bullshit. Harry G. Frankfurt. 2005. Princeton, NJ: Princeton University Press. Dr. Frankfurt, Princeton emeritus professor of philosophy, provides us with a useful guide: "The bullshitter . . . is neither on the side of the true nor on the side of the false. His eye is not on the facts at all . . . except insofar as they may be pertinent to his interest in getting away with what he says. He does not care whether the things he says describe reality correctly. He just picks them out, or makes them up, to suit his purpose."

Coercion and Its Fallout. Rev. ed. Murray Sidman. 1989. Authors Cooperative. A classic text by a leading behavior analyst on the undesirable and largely unpredictable side effects of punishment. Available from www.behavior.org.

- "An Analysis of the Efficacy of Bridging Stimuli: Comparing the clicker to a verbal bridge." Lindsay Wood. 2007. Master's thesis, Hunter College, New York.
- "Clicker mad." Amy Sutherland. 2006. *Bark, the modern dog culture magazine.* November–December, pp. 42–45.
- "Wolves outperform dogs in following human social cues." Monique A. R. Udell, Nicole R. Dorey, and Clive D. L. Wynne. 2008. *Animal Behavior* 10:1016.
- "The poisoned cue." Karen Pryor. 2002. *Teaching Dogs* 1, no. 1 (August).
- "The Effects of Combining Positive and Negative Reinforcement during Training." Nicole A. Murray. 2007. Master's thesis. University of North Texas. See at Reachingthe animalmind.com.

10: Answers

Dictionary of Psychology. Ray Corsini. 1999. London: Taylor and Francis.

Affective Neuroscience: The Foundations of Human and Animal Emotions, chapter 8. Jaak Panksepp. 1998. Oxford University Press.

The Emotional Brain: The Mysterious Underpinnings of Emotional Life. Joseph LeDoux. 1996. New York: Simon & Schuster.

- "Amygdalar and prefrontal pathways to the lateral hypothalamus are activated by a learned cue that stimulates eating." Gorica D. Petrovich, Peter C. Holland, and Michela Gallagher. 2005. *Journal of Neuroscience* 25 (36): 8295–302.

- **Video** in chapter 10 at www.reachingtheanimalmind.com.
  "Laughing Rats"

11: People

The Power of Positive Parenting: A Wonderful Way to Raise Children. Rev. ed. Glenn I. Latham. 1994. North Logan, UT: P&T Ink.

What Shamu Taught Me about Life, Love, and Marriage: Lessons for People from Animals and Their Trainers. Amy Sutherland. 2008. New York: Random House.

Don't Shoot the Dog!: The New Art of Teaching and Training. Rev. ed. Karen Pryor. 1999. New York: Bantam Books.

- **Video** in chapter 11 at www.reachingtheanimalmind.com.
  "Handstand"
  "Chin-flick"
  "Coach Doing the Happy Ferret Dance"
  "High Jump"
  "Shoelace-tying"

- **Links**
  TAGteach International LLC, www.tagteach.com; www.tagteach.com/autism
  Cambridge Center for Behavioral Studies, www.behavior.org
  ABC School, Sacramento, California, www.abcreal.com

Association for Behavior Analysis International, www.abainternational.org

The New England Center for Children, www.necc.org

12: Intention

Happily, two books explain how to really teach a schoolroom, based on behavioral science. Both authors are good writers and leaders in the field with impeccable credentials. If you teach school, run a school, go to school, or send kids to school, get these books.

Behavior Analysis for Teachers. Julie S. Vargas. 2009. New York: Lawrence Erlbaum Associates. A groundbreaking textbook on the science of teaching.

The Teacher's Craft: The 10 Essential Skills of Effective Teaching. Paul Chance. 2006. Long Grove, IL: Waveland Press. A behavioral guide to using evidence-based best practices for teaching. If you are a schoolteacher, this book will make you proud of what you do.

- "A dolphin-human fishing cooperative in Brazil." Karen Pryor, Jon Lindbergh, Scott Lindbergh, and Raquel Milano. 1990. *Marine Mammal Science* 6:1.

- *Don't Shoot the Dog!: The New Art of Teaching and Training.* Rev. ed. Karen Pryor. 1999. Audio, 6 CD set, read by the author. At www.clickertraining.com/store.

- **Links**

  Karen Pryor Academy (online and hands-on instruction for trainers), www.karenpryoracademy.com

  Guide Dogs for the Blind, San Rafael, California, www.guidedogs.com

  TAGteach International LLC, www.tagteach.com and www.tagteach.com/autism

Glossary

Dear Reader,

This is my book, so this is my dictionary. I have attempted to define terms that pertain to the topics in this book as I now use them. If you want broader or more technical definitions for these behavioral terms or for others not in the glossary, I recommend the multidisciplinary masterwork *The Dictionary of Psychology* by Ray Corsini (Taylor and Francis, 1999).

Affect; state of affect The internal or emotional condition of an individual.

Aversive Any circumstance or event that causes pain, fear, or mental or emotional discomfort.

Behavior chain A group of behaviors that happen sequentially, linked by cues; the cue for each new behavior must occur during the previous behavior, thus reinforcing each behavior in the chain. Some behavior chains, such as starting a car, must occur in a specific sequence—you have to get in the car before you put the key in the ignition, etc.—but many can happen in random sequence, such as obstacles in a dog-agility competition.

Behaviors Specific describable actions.

Classical conditioning The association of an unconscious physical or physiological response with a conditioned stimulus. Example: Pavlov's dogs drool when they hear the bell that was previously paired with food. Sometimes called Pavlovian conditioning or respondent conditioning. See OPERANT CONDITIONING.

Command A verbal or gestural discriminative stimulus for a specific behavior, in which failure to respond correctly will be punished.

Compulsion A dog trainer's term for training focusing on compliance to commands and using punishment for errors.

Conditioned fear stimulus A conditioned punisher.

Conditioned punisher Any stimulus that has been paired with an aversive event and thus becomes in itself aversive enough to interrupt or stop behavior.

Conditioned reinforcer Any stimulus that has been paired with a primary reinforcer (something the animal needs or wants and will work to get).

Conditioned stimulus Any stimulus that has preceded a particular behavior or event sufficiently often to provoke awareness or response. See DISCRIMINATIVE STIMULUS.

Criterion (singular); **Criteria** (plural) During shaping, a single specific, describable, observable aspect of a behavior.

Cue A discriminative stimulus associated with a particular behavior that, if performed correctly, will lead to reinforcement.

Deprivation Reduction or removal of some desired condition or resource, intended either to punish misbehavior or to increase willingness to work for reinforcers.

Discriminative stimulus A conditioned stimulus that indicates an opportunity to perform a specific behavior in expectation of reinforcement or of avoiding an aversive.

Extinction The fading out of a learned behavior that no longer leads to reinforcement.

Extinction burst Escalation of a behavior that is undergoing extinction.

Extinction curve The graph of the rate of occurrence of a behavior undergoing extinction.

Extinction-induced aggression An inappropriate or excessive display of anger during extinction; for example, kicking the Coke machine after trying and failing several times to get a soda out of it.

Extinguishing Deliberately allowing a learned behavior to go unreinforced until it ceases to be offered.

Food deprivation Reducing food quantity for a time to make a research subject willing to work harder for a food reinforcer.

Marker; event marker Technically, any stimulus that's paired with food is called a secondary or conditioned reinforcer. Ogden Lindsley, one of Skinner's early graduate students and the founder of Precision Teaching, coined the term *event marker* for a secondary reinforcer that occurs simultaneously with a specific behavior and identifies it to the learner. Lindsley often told the story of using an event marker to teach his pet donkey to open a mailbox. Modern positive trainers tend to use just the word *marker* since one may be identifying an emotional state or a decision rather than a physical event.

Negative punishment Taking away something the organism wants or needs in order to stop or reduce some undesired behavior.

Negative reinforcement Taking away some aversive stimulus in order to increase a desired behavior. Most horse training is based on negative reinforcement, consisting of applying pressure or pain until the horse does the desired behavior, then "rewarding" the behavior by removing or easing up on the aversive. Negative reinforcement does not mean punishment, as it does increase behavior; but it *must* be preceded by aversives.

Operant conditioning Reinforcement of conscious behavior deliberately offered by the learner. Skinner coined the term to indicate that the learner is the "operator," deliberately giving a learned behavior so as to access reinforcers. See CLASSICAL CONDITIONING.

Pavlovian conditioning See CLASSICAL CONDITIONING.

Positive reinforcement training Under the acronym PRT, this is a preferred term for modern marker-based training in many zoos and laboratories.

Primary, secondary, and **tertiary reinforcers** Primary reinforcers are anything the animal needs and wants badly enough to work for them, from oxygen to tennis balls. Secondary reinforcers are conditioned stimuli that indicate that a primary reinforcer is on its way. Tertiary reinforcers indicate a behavior leading to secondary and primary reinforcers.

Punishment An aversive stimulus timed so as to stop or reduce a particular behavior.

Reinforcement The use of some desired outcome to influence behavior.

Reinforcer A specific item or event that increases the likelihood that a specific behavior will occur in the future. Both punishers and reinforcers are defined by their effect on future behavior. If you lavish a dog or a child with praise, but the behavior you are praising does not increase, then praise was not a reinforcer in that circumstance or with that organism. If you swat your learner for misbehaving but the misbehavior continues, then swatting was not an effective punisher but just a gratuitous aversive.

Reward A presumably desirable item or event delivered at a delayed interval after some desired action. Rewards are not necessarily reinforcing. They reflect the intentions of the giver, without necessarily being desired by the receiver or associated in any reinforcing way with the behavior being rewarded.

Secondary punisher An "anti-click" or "devil's click." A conditioned stimulus that signifies that an aversive is coming. Used to deter or interrupt behavior; if the behavior halts or changes, the aversive may be avoided. See NEGATIVE REINFORCER.

Secondary reinforcer See PRIMARY REINFORCER.

Shaping Building new behavior by selectively reinforcing variations in existing behavior, during the action rather than after completion, to increase or strengthen the behavior in a specific manner or direction. We used to think that *shaping* was the slang term for incrementally increasing behavior by selective reinforcement, and that the correct term was *successive approximation*, but that was not what Skinner meant at all when he coined the terms. See SUCCESSIVE APPROXIMATION.

Snell's window The locus of transparency visible directly overhead when diving under the surface of water. Snell's window is a function of the bending of light rays passing from one medium (air) to another (water). You can easily see Snell's window (and the surrounding opaque reflective water surface) for yourself by putting on a mask and going underwater in a swimming pool.

Successive approximation Increasing or altering a behavior incrementally by repeatedly changing the environment to amplify or extend the behavior. For example, increasing the weight of a load or the height of a jump by small increments to amplify the effort to pull a load or jump an obstacle.

Tertiary reinforcer A technical term for the cue, i.e., a discriminative stimulus, for an action that leads to reinforcement, never to punishment.

Traditional trainers; traditional training Trainers who focus on aversive methods to control and teach behavior. Also sometimes called compulsion-based training or force-training.

Trainer; modern trainer A trainer who uses marker-based, positive-reinforcement technology correctly, with both animals and humans.

Do It Yourself

Teach Your Cat to High-five

Before You Begin

These instructions assume that you have never clicked and treated any animal before, so they are designed to give you good skills from the start. You can then use the basic rules—how to click, how to treat, how to start a session, how to stop, how to strengthen the behavior by choosing what to click—for any behavior and any learner.

- Make sure the cat is a little hungry. Play this game just before the cat's mealtime. If you leave dry food out all the time, put it away for at least two hours before you start.
- Use a high-value treat—not commercial dried treats. Tuna fish is relished by all cats. Use small portions, pea-sized. It's handy to count out your treats first and put them on a saucer or a little plate; then you can offer the plate long enough for the cat to take one bite.

- Work alone, at least at the start, with no other dogs, cats, or human kibitzers present. The cat needs to concentrate and so do you. If there is no guaranteed quiet place in the house, take the cat into the bathroom and shut the door.

- Clicker training requires mechanical skills. You might feel rattled by trying to do different things with each hand at the same time. I recommend practicing first. Take the clicker and an empty saucer into the bathroom (without the cat) and practice clicking with one hand and immediately putting the plate down and taking the plate back, until it feels easy.

- Always keep your clicker hand still and out of sight, at your side or behind you. Always keep your treat hand motionless until the click has happened. Cats see movement well; if you don't keep your hands still, the cat may focus on your hands and ignore the click, which will spoil its chances of learning.

- Always treat after a click, even if you clicked by accident or at the wrong moment. That was your fault, not the cat's, so the cat does get paid.

- Oh, and shut up. Don't try to encourage the cat with cheers or praise; that just distracts it from the game.

- Keep a training log. After every session, write down where you started, where you stopped, how many treats you used, and any comments. This log is not just a practical help; you will find it reinforcing as you look back over your progress.

- Don't feel you have to train every day or for a certain length of time. This is for fun! The more little five-minute sessions you have, the better, but be easy on yourself. Animals remember well what they learn from the clicker. If you have three sessions a day, you'll accomplish six sessions in two days. If you have one session a month, you'll take six months to do the same training. Thanks to the power of the click, the cat will still learn.

The First Session

1. Get your clicker and open a can of tuna fish. Put ten pea-sized dots of tuna fish around the rim of a saucer. Sit down somewhere comfortable with the cat.

2. Hold the clicker behind your back, ready to click. While the cat is looking at you, click and put down the saucer. Wait, without talking or restless movement, while the cat sniffs the plate and licks up the first dot of tuna fish.

3. With your free hand, take the plate back immediately and put it next to you on a table or countertop. If the cat is bold enough to jump up after the plate, gently lift the cat to the floor, click when its paws touch the ground, and present the plate on the floor for one more treat. Message: floor is good, countertop doesn't work.

4. Watch the cat's right paw. Click the instant the paw moves, in any direction, for any reason. Put the plate down (or hold it out) for one treat only.

5. If the cat is sitting motionless and staring at you, lower a hand to lure it sidewise, then click when the weight shifts or the right paw lifts, no matter how slightly. Pull your hand back when you hear the click and present the plate for one treat. Put the plate far enough away so the cat has to get up to reach it.

6. As the cat eats its treat and you are taking the plate up, watch carefully and click that right paw as soon as it moves as the cat is turning back toward you. Put the plate down again for another treat.

7. Now put the plate back on the table and proceed from step 3, capturing spontaneous paw movements instead of trying to make them happen by tempting the cat to move again. Repeat until all the tuna dots are used up.

Starting and Ending Sessions

If the cat quits on you (walks away or turns its back and washes its face), don't panic. It's a good sign. It means the cat is starting to notice that something new is going on here and needs time to think it over. End the session, put the food in the refrigerator, and start another session in an hour or two, or the next day.

Always trust the cat, even if the cat wants to quit before you do. Three to five clicks is a *good* training session for a novice cat. If the cat is keen, prepare two treat plates and work longer.

Work fast; don't let dead time go by in which the cat can lose focus or, worse, feel disappointed or discouraged. It's better to stop the session early and pick it up again later than to pause in the middle of a session because you were distracted by, say, the phone or a visitor.

Next Sessions

1. Repeat as before, in the same place with the same setup. When the cat is deliberately lifting the paw, notice the difference between small moves and bigger moves. Click most moves but refrain from clicking any weak attempt. The cat will learn to try again, and try harder.

2. As soon as you have a clear lifting movement, click *during* the upward move of the paw. That will encourage a rapid increase in the height of the paw.

3. Click higher lifts until most tries are roughly shoulder height.

4. Now, as the paw goes up, quickly put your free hand, flat and open, under the paw as it starts to come down and click when the paw touches your hand. Then remove your hand and treat.

5. After two or three taps caused by interrupting the downward path of the paw with your hand, raise your hand a little. Keep the hand close to the paw; don't make the cat reach yet. Click

one or two taps at the new level. Repeat until your fingertips are at the height of the cat's shoulder. You want the cat to switch from just raising a paw to trying to tap your hand on purpose.

6. The offered hand now becomes a target for the paw lift. Present your hand in the right spot as soon as the cat has finished its previous treat. Don't click for random paw lifts anymore.
7. Now hold your hand slightly higher, so the cat must reach, and perhaps stand up, to tap your hand.
8. Rotate your hand to the side so it's horizontal, as you go on raising the height of the target.
9. Reinforce stronger swats, too, so the contact looks vigorous and intentional. If claws come out by accident—it is an automatic reaction sometimes—take your hand away and pause, no click, for a few seconds before offering the hand again.
10. Now rotate your hand so it's vertical, facing the cat in the traditional high-five gesture. This gesture, presenting the vertical palm, becomes the cue for the behavior. Keep a few treats handy (such as dry cat treats) and try it in other rooms and at other times of day. If you don't have a clicker handy, you can maintain the behavior in new circumstances by marking the behavior with a special word or a mouth click.
11. Teach the targeting hand gesture to other people, too, so the cat will tap its paw to anyone's raised palm. Amaze your friends and neighbors and the UPS man.
12. Congratulations. You are now a clicker trainer. Teach your cat to nose and then follow a target (a pencil or chopstick is good). Wave your wand and get the cat to jump on the couch, off the couch, onto the bookcase, from chair to chair, through hoops (embroidery hoops are good). Set up your own indoor cat Olympics.

Teach Your Dog to Hand-target

The first behavior you teach your dog with the clicker—the default behavior—is the one it will always remember best and go back to if it feels confused or anxious. Hand-targeting is a great first behavior because you can immediately use it for so many other things, including come, sit, down, get off the couch, get into the car, stay beside me, and much more. It's easy to train, and both you and the dog will love this new way of communicating.

Before You Begin

These instructions assume that you have never clicked and treated any animal before, so they are designed to give you good skills from the start. You can then use the same skills—how to click, how to treat, how to start a session, how to stop, how to strengthen the behavior by choosing what to click—for any behavior and any learner.

Use a high-value treat, not commercial dried treats. Hot dogs are relished by all dogs. Cut a hot dog lengthwise twice and then in twenty slices across. That makes about eighty one-calorie treats, which will keep well in the refrigerator. Pea-sized bits of chicken, beef, or other fresh-cooked meat work equally well. The point is not to feed the dog but to give it the experience of smelling and tasting and swallowing something utterly delicious.

Work alone, at least at the start, with no other dogs, cats, or human kibitzers present. The dog needs to concentrate and so do you. If there is no guaranteed quiet place in the house, take the dog into the bathroom and shut the door.

Clicker training requires mechanical skills. You might feel rattled by trying to do different things with each hand at the same time. I recommend practicing first. Take the clicker, a bowl of twenty treats, and an empty bowl into the bathroom (without the dog) and practice clicking with one hand and immediately moving one treat from the full bowl to the empty bowl with the other hand, until it feels easy.

Helpful Tips

Keep a training log. After every session, write down where you started, where you stopped, how many treats you used (if you bothered to count them out), and any comments. This log is not just a practical help; you will find it reinforcing as you look back over your progress.

Don't feel you have to train every day or for a certain length of time. This is for fun! The more little five-minute sessions you have, the faster you'll go, but be easy on yourself. Animals remember well what they learn from the clicker. If you have three sessions a day, you'll accomplish six sessions in two days. If you have one session a month, you'll take six months to do the same training. The dog will still learn.

The First Session

1. Take the dog, the clicker, and a bowl of thirty treats into a quiet place. The dog should be off leash and mildly hungry.

2. Sit down with the treat bowl in easy reach on a table or counter. Click and give the dog one treat. You may hand-feed or toss the treat on the floor. If you are fastidious and don't want to do either of those things, you may put the treat on a plate and just put the plate on the floor, but learn to do it quickly and smoothly so the dog doesn't have time to start begging for the food.

3. Now get your clicker ready. Open your free hand flat, with the fingers straight and together, and put it out an inch or two in front of the dog's nose. Click as the dog looks at your hand or sniffs it. *Remove* the free hand the *instant* you click and use it to deliver a treat. Repeat this sequence three times.

4. On the fourth try, present the hand a little to one side. Click for nosing or touching the hand in the new spot. Repeat three times.

5. Present the hand to the other side. When the dog is confidently nosing the hand on that side, try moving it downward a couple of inches, then upward. If at any time the dog stops trying to touch the hand, back up a couple of steps.

6. Present the hand in front of the dog but six inches away, so the dog has to reach for it. Repeat three times.

7. Present the hand farther away, so the dog has to move a step or two. If the dog doesn't move, get up and move a step or two yourself. Repeat three times.

8. Let's escalate. See if you can lead the dog a few steps with the flat hand. Click and treat. Try turning the dog in the opposite direction. Does he follow the hand? Fantastic! Click, give it the rest of the treats, and end the session.

Starting and Ending Sessions

Keep the training sessions to five minutes or so, at first. Counting out twenty or thirty treats ahead of time is a good way to manage the length of your sessions. You want to quit while both you and the dog are interested and excited, not when you are getting tired.

Work fast; don't let dead time go by in which the dog can lose focus or, worse, feel disappointed or discouraged. It's better to stop the session early and pick it up again later than to pause in the middle of a session because you were distracted by, say, the phone or a visitor.

If the dog turns away or seems to lose interest, don't panic. It's a good sign in a beginner. It can mean the dog is starting to notice that something new is going on here and needs time to think it over. End the session, put the food in the refrigerator, and start another session in an hour or two, or the next day. (In a clickerwise dog, its turning away or acting distracted by some other stimulus can be a sign that you are making a training error, usually by reinforcing too late or presenting confusing and inconsistent cues. End the session and think through your training procedures, preferably with a pencil and paper.)

Next Sessions

You have now taught the dog to target your hand. A flat hand presented swiftly at the end of a straight arm is already a cue, meaning "Come here, bump this, get a click and a treat." You don't have to use words to call attention to it; the presenting gesture will do that.

So now try some new games:

1. While you're watching TV, get a few treats—popcorn will do—and target the dog back and forth from one hand to the other during commercials, clicking for one touch, then only for the second touch, then only for the third of three touches. You can make a click sound with your tongue for convenience, since you are training with both hands. Can you fool the dog? Try targeting it onto its hind legs, or down in a bow, or up onto the couch and off again.
2. Walking the dog: bring a clicker and some dry treats in your pocket. When it is sniffing something near you, wait until it lifts its head, then speak its name just once. If it looks at you or toward you, present the hand target, let it bump, and click and treat. This will rapidly build a strong reaction to hearing its name, much stronger than if you just gave it a treat each time it turned to you. Now vary the circumstances when you speak its name and reinforce its attention with a hand target, perhaps by trying it when it has just noticed another dog in the distance or a squirrel.
3. Maybe you've seen people in the park trying to get their dog back with words by shouting at them: "Come here, boy. Dammit, I said come here!" Try using the dog's name, followed by presenting the hand target (followed by a click and treat on arrival) to call the dog from increasing distances indoors and out. This will rapidly become a fabulous long-distance rapid-response recall. Always click and treat on arrival.

4. If your dog is an escape artist, cue it to come to the hand target and make contact, but wait to click until you lay your hand on the collar. Click, take your hand away, and give the treat. Repeat, letting the dog go free a few times during the walk, before you have to put the leash on to go home. Don't make your recall always mean that the outdoor time is over.

5. Hand-targeting can be used to teach all kinds of moves, from "Wait at the door" to "Stay by me to greet visitors" to "Get off the couch" to "Stand still on the veterinarian's table even if you're getting poked." Teach your dog a formal "heel" position by hand-targeting. Pass the target over the animal's head, from front to back, to elicit a sit. Put the hand between the dog's front legs to elicit a down. Can you think up more? Share your creative solutions at www.reachingtheanimalmind.com/mytraining.

6. Find the car keys! Hold your car keys under your thumb, and hand-target the dog. Click for bumping or touching the hand with the keys in it. Close your fist, with the car keys hanging over the front, so the dog has to touch the keys instead of the hand. Move to floor level. When that works, leave the keys there and take your hand away. Now the keys are a new target.

   Move the keys a few inches left or right. Tell him: Find the keys. Put a small piece of paper over them. Put them behind a chair leg. He doesn't need to bring them, just to show you where they are. Now he will be sniffing for them, too, so can he find them under a pillow? Under the couch? On a chair seat? In your pocket or handbag? Down the hall? How about outdoors? Now teach him to find the TV remote.

Teach Your Coach to Tag You

Your coach may not be interested in TAGteaching. It doesn't matter; you can easily get almost any private coach to use the tagger according to your instructions. All coaches' clients are eccentric, and some of them ask for a lot weirder things than that.

These instructions are given as if for golf or tennis, but they can be adapted to absolutely anything physical you are trying to learn, from Pilates to speaking French. Try it.

1. Pick one part of the game, such as your swing. Your coach knows what you're doing wrong, and what he or she would like you to do instead. Give the coach the tagger and explain that you'd like to be clicked when you do something right.

2. Ask the coach to list all the things you are doing wrong (probably five or more). Ask the coach which is the *most* important one, the one that needs to be fixed first.

3. Starting with that move, ask the coach to instruct you, moving you physically if necessary, in the right position.

4. Try for the position several times. The coach should click you when you get it right. Move out of the position between clicks, so you can experience moving into it correctly each time. For example, if it's your stance, get your click, then move your feet away, then step back into the stance again for another click. If it is your grip, let go between clicks and take up the grip again each time. Shift your grip until you get the click. If the coach corrects or instructs verbally while you are trying, suggest that you'd like to have instructions before you try and listen only for the click (or no click) while you're actually trying.

5. Often, in sports, the tag point is part of a bigger move. For example, in a golf swing, the tag point might be the loca-

tion of your right elbow on the backswing. Incorporate this new position into a movement step by step. Practice by starting the swing slowly and stopping when you hear the click. Repeat three times or until you get it right every time. *Then* perform the whole swing, first slowly, then at normal speed, while the coach continues to tag the elbow as it passes through the right spot. *Then* actually hit a ball a few times with the new elbow position incorporated in the swing and the coach tagging it as it's happening.

6. Move on to the next tag point when you are secure in the one you've got.

7. Often in a sport, when we have learned the initial move incorrectly, we nevertheless compensate and manage to hit the ball pretty well anyway. There's a downside to compensating: you may never be as good as you could be, and the adjustment you make can become the cause of repetitive injuries such as tennis elbow. When you first learn a better way, you may lose your usual control of the ball for a little while. Never mind. Ignore where the ball goes until the new movement is established, and your control will come back by itself, with more force and less risk.

8. When you and the coach have fixed all five things that were wrong in the beginning, and maybe a few more things besides, call up a friend who regards you as a duffer and have a friendly game.

An Exercise for Grown-ups: Changing Your View

Here's an exercise anyone can try.

During the day, make a point of noticing something someone else is doing that you like. Someone at work, someone at home, some stranger even. It need not be something unusual. It could be something you already expect the person to do.

At the end of the day, find time to tell the person he or she did that thing right. Avoid the word *I*. "I liked the way you . . ." is all about you, not about the behavior. Just name the behavior. "It's good that you finished your homework." "You handled that phone call well." "The client report is done; that's great!" "The kitchen's all cleaned up, that's so nice." Then do it again the next day, for a different behavior.

With kids, try to find one or more things that were good during the day. Don't turn it into a big deal, just identify what the child did right. "Hey, you got down to dinner on time." "You fed the dog on your own." "You read to your sister, that was a good thing." Don't make things up at bedtime; really watch. What you are trying to train here is not the kids but your own observant eye.

This may feel weird. You may feel self-conscious. This tells you that you need practice at noticing and discussing things you like. (Do you have more experience at noticing and discussing things you don't like? That's true for most of us.)

Don't expect any particular response; this may be new for the other person, too, and may take some getting used to. Just keep it up. The change in the recipients of these observations will be rapid and obvious. The change in your own Snell's window on the universe will be more subtle and more profound.

Thanks

I'd like to thank my agent, Al Zuckerman, who took me on as both a client and a friend and has been a miracle worker from the start; my publisher, Susan Moldow, who had the perspicacity to see where this book concept might go; and my editor at Scribner, Beth Wareham, who saw me through a three-year, multidraft effort with warmth, kindness, humor, and brilliant intuition. Thanks also go to editor Whitney Frick.

Two other editors helped me immeasurably in the early stages of this work: my daughter, Gale Pryor, and my childhood friend and retired *Washington Post* editor William MacKaye. I'm supremely grateful also to my publicist, Heidi Richter, for her energy, imagination, and friendship, and to Web site designers Matt Kanaracus and Karen LeDuc, and Mark Irwin at KPCT.

The development of a technology—the application of a science to real-life uses—is organic, involving a lot of individuals and exploration and innovation. This process thrives on communication. I've been blessed with a wonderful assortment of trainers and thinkers with whom to trade and share new ideas, including the zoo and marine mammal communities, the ClickerExpo faculty, the Karen Pryor Academy faculty, students, and graduates, and the founders and developers of TAGteach. I'd especially like to thank my friends and scientific advisers Erich Klinghammer, Julie Skinner Vargas, Ernie Vargas, Jésus Rosales-Ruiz, and Murray Sidman.

Across the past ten years I have maintained challenging and enlightening running conversations on topics in this book with Barbara Boat, Aaron Clayton, Morton Egtvedt, Tia Guest, Cecilia Koste, Alexandra Kurland, Kay Laurence, Myrna Libby, Sherri Lippman, Lynn Loar, Theresa McKeon, Eva Mekler, Joe Morrow, Joan Orr, Emma Parsons, Irene Pepperberg, Michele Pouliot, Ken Ramirez, Michael Schulman, and Ingrid Shallenberger. I hope these conversations never stop. Thank you!

To my business partner, Aaron Clayton, thank you for building KPCT into such a wonderful outreach system, and for shouldering the workload while I worked on this book instead. The whole technology took off when you picked up the reins at KPCT; and it's a great partnership, besides!

Finally, profound thanks to my family, Ted, Carrie, Gwen, and Ellie Pryor; Mike, Eileen, Micaela, and Maile Pryor; Gale Pryor; Kolya Leabo; and Max, Wylie, and Nat Leabo. All of you were forced to put up with a mother, grandmother, colleague, and coworker who was inconveniently abstracted, unavailable, and often totally absent for weeks and months during the endless, horrible, exhausting writing of this book. Thanks, folks. I promise I won't do it again. At least not right away.

About the Author

Karen Pryor is a writer and a scientist with an international reputation in two fields, marine mammal biology and behavioral psychology. As cofounder and head dolphin trainer at Sea Life Park in Hawaii, she pioneered modern, force-free animal-training methods. She is the author of many scientific papers and popular articles and ten books, including *Don't Shoot the Dog!,* the classic bestselling text on positive reinforcement. She is a leading proponent of clicker training, a worldwide movement using new ways to communicate positively with pets and other animals. She is a founder and CEO of Sunshine Books Inc., KPCT (Karen Pryor Clicker Training), TAGteach International LLC, and their online divisions. Karen has two sons and a daughter and seven grandchildren. She lives in the Boston area with two clicker-trained dogs.